Portrait of India

By BRADFORD SMITH

J. B. LIPPINCOTT COMPANY
PHILADELPHIA AND NEW YORK

For our many friends in India
and especially for Gurdial, Sudhir and Arjan

Contents

Portrait of India

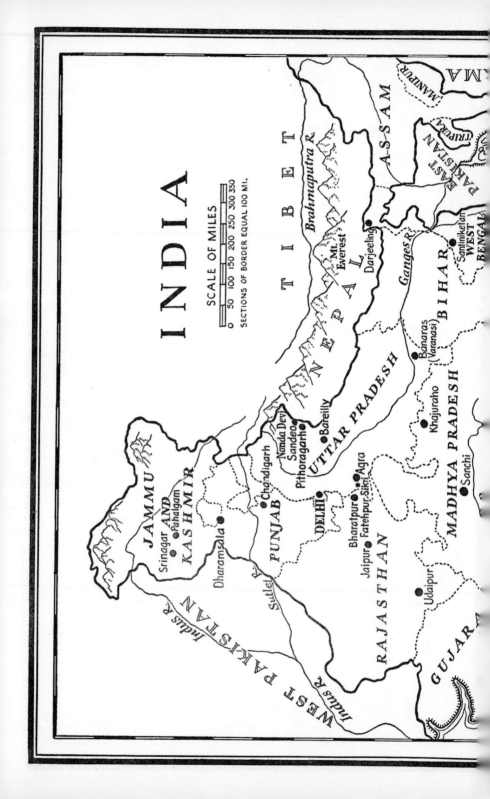

INDIA

SCALE OF MILES

0 50 100 150 200 250 300 350

SECTIONS OF BORDER EQUAL 100 MI.

TIBET

Brahmaputra R.

A S S A M

MANIPUR

EAST PAKISTAN

TRIPURA

BURMA

Mt. Everest

Darjeeling

Ganges R.

NEPAL

Santiniketan

WEST BENGAL

BIHAR

Banaras (Varanasi)

UTTAR PRADESH

Khajuraho

MADHYA PRADESH

Sanchi

Nanda Devi

Sandeo

Pithoragarh

Bareilly

JAMMU AND KASHMIR

Srinagar

Pahalgam

Chandigarh

Dharamsala

Sutlej R.

PUNJAB

DELHI

Bharatpur

Fatehpur Sikri

Agra

Jaipur

RAJASTHAN

Udaipur

GUJARAT

WEST PAKISTAN

Indus R.

ONE

On This Rock

Before the people were, the land was—a vast rock hanging like a pendant from the thousand peaks of the Himalayas, down into the Arabian Sea and the Indian Ocean.

Nearly everywhere in India rock thrusts itself above the dusty earth—huge slabs and juts of it, from Kashmir to Kerala, from Assam to Bombay. It forms the vast mountains in the north, rising nearly six miles above sea level. From their barren, snow-haloed tops, down their broad sides where the timber begins, to the watercourses clogged with great chunks of broken stone, the stern rock thrusts upward from unknown deeps.

Whether flying over Rajasthan, Andhra or Mysore, there is hardly a moment when you cannot look down and see some vast slab of rock thrusting itself up from the valley floor, or some mound of a hill which, from the lavish scatter of stone down its sides, must be one huge rock pile.

From the train window in Madhya Pradesh in mid-India you look out on mile after mile of fields so strewn with rock that nothing can be done with them. Bony cattle pick their slow way among the heaps, looking for a bit of grass the sun has not baked to a crisp against the oven-hot stones.

Bouncing along a road outside Bangalore, through countryside that looks good for farming, you come suddenly upon a great thrust of red rock rising slantwise out of the earth as if it had just now heaved itself above ground. The toilers in the field are so used to it they do

1

not see it any more, but the visitor cannot help feeling the rock that lies everywhere beneath the surface, making dwarfs of the men who scratch the brown crust above it as if to placate the vast animal who tolerates their presence.

Even Delhi is bisected by a stone ridge, one end anchored in the ancient city of Tughlakabad whose stone walls still rise with a forbidding sternness, the other protecting the University. Stray bits jut out in the garden of the American Embassy staff quarters, and the backbone of it runs from New to Old Delhi, where on its highest scarp stands the incongruous Victorian Gothic tower in memory of the British soldiers who fell in the uprising of 1857. Where trenches have been dug for water pipes, tons of rock have had to be taken out. Broken up into building sizes, they have been neatly piled, head-high, all over the Ridge. There is a shortage of brick in Delhi, but the piles continue to grow.

The Ridge rose directly behind our house in Old Delhi. When we tried to make a lawn out of a rocky triangle of ground, four men did nothing for four days but dig into the soil and pull out stones. When they were through, we had a pile of refuse big enough for two bullock carts.

At Tiruchirapalli (Tiruchi for short) in Madras a vast cone of rock rises with a sudden exuberance in the center of the city. Around its base cluster the bazaars. To climb it, you plod up hundreds of steps and past several temples cut into the solid mountain of stone, coming out at last on a bald dome of rock capped by a small temple from which you can see the whole countryside spread out like a map.

A little farther to the south the continental rock finally meets its only vanquisher—the waters of the Indian Ocean. At the southernmost tip of Cape Comorin bare ribs of rock expose themselves for the last time as they slant down into the sea, rising defiant once and again a little way out from shore before at last the triumph that had begun among the snows of the Himalayas sinks down defeated into the warm waters.

On the last thrust of available rock the people of India have raised a plain temple—rock, of course—as if to say:

"This is the stuff our land is made of; we too shall endure."

For thousands of years, all over India, men have cut laboriously at the rock, making temples of unimaginable vastness and intricacy, patiently carving thousands of caves out of the stern stuff, as if the rock being there compelled them to make their mark on it. To make only one of the Ellora caves, 3,000,000 cubic feet of solid rock had to be cut out. At Ajanta the caves are richly adorned. At Mahabalipuram near Madras they vary from primitive holes dug in the dome-like rocks to wonderfully intricate carvings on the rock faces or full-scale elephants released to life from the inchoate blocks of stone. At the Jain center on Mount Abu patience and consummate artistry have shaped columns and ceilings of ornate beauty.

One rocky item crops up again and again—in temples, by the road-side. It is the lingam—representation of the phallus. Sometimes discreetly geometric, sometimes recognizably human, varying in size but always large, it is India's sermon in stone. Women go and sit on it if they want babies they have been unable to produce. Wreaths and petals of flowers adorn it. Often it is blackened by libations of purified butter—ghee.

And what does it all mean?

Even out of the lifeless stone, Indians have managed to wring an evidence of their thirst for life. The vast temples of Konarak and Khajuraho are adorned with sculptures beyond counting which, in row after row and in amazing variety, plainly and exuberantly illustrate the act of love, of procreation.

Life pulses and throbs in India as nowhere else in the world. Walk into a railroad station and you can hardly make your way through the people squatting or lying about on the floors. Park you car in New Delhi, and before you can open the door, several youngsters are struggling for the privilege of doing it for you—and to get your nod as to which can be chaukidar—watchman—for the bit of bakhshish you will give when you return. Pull out into the highway, and you begin a fascinating game. Like a football player weaving his way down the field, you steer between and among bicycles, three-wheeled taxi motorcycles bearing from two to eight passengers, little two-wheeled horse carts with jingling harness, heavy deliberate oxcarts, and herds of water buffalo or solitary cows.

Beside the road a *basti*—slum—stretches its makeshift shacks of mud and straw to the curb. Its narrow alleys swarm with life. A woman with a baby riding on her hip comes to the single water tap. A horde of naked children pours out of an alley. A little girl detaches herself momentarily, squats, defecates, and runs to join the crowd again. Curled on a charpai (string bed) in the sun, a body lies completely wrapped in a gray rag. An obscenely fat pig roots through a pile of garbage already carefully picked over by human scavengers.

A field near the river is completely covered with laundry. Since early morning the *dhobis*—launderers—have been at work, sloshing the laundry about in tin tubs which must certainly have been the ones the first British brought out with them for their personal bathing. After beating it to death, they spread it on the withered grass to dry. The dust blows over it, bullocks wander through it, cows chew it, children play around the fringes. But no one drives them away. The *dhobis* are busy taking their morning naps while the sun does its work. Other *dhobis* meanwhile work in the silt-yellow river itself, whacking the clothing against the surface of the water, beating it with sticks, or as anyone will tell you, using the laundry to split stones. The wet smack of laundry on the rocks is one of the endearing sounds of life. At day's end the stuff is considered well cured and is gathered up and taken home.

Monkeys meanwhile drop down from the trees onto a nearby wall to see what is going on. There are fifty million of them in India, eating food the people need. But no one molests them any more than the cows—poor, hungry, bony beasts who wander aimlessly through the streets trying to find enough grass to keep alive. Some of them are strays. Others have a home to go to but are driven out during the day to find their own food where they can, even though it is against the law to let cows stray in the streets.

To put a stop to this a friend of ours, when he was Commissioner of Delhi, ordered his men to go out and squirt with red paint all the cows they could find. This is not so unusual in India, where people squirt each other with colored water during the Holi festival, and where on holidays they often decorate their beasts all over with painted geometric patterns, gild their horns, and hang garlands about their heads.

So the squirting campaign got under way, and by nightfall several thousand cows had been decorated. They went home as usual, but early next morning the Commissioner's men were watching at the gates of suspects. When a red cow sauntered out, they noted the address. Summonses went out. The first cow keeper came into court, and he was much aggrieved.

"You are charged with letting your cow stray in the streets," said the judge. "Do you plead guilty or not guilty?"

"My cow straying? Your honor, how can you say that?"

"The Commissioner's men sprayed all strays with red. Can you deny that your cow has been sprayed?"

"I do not deny it, your honor."

"Then I shall have to impose a fine. I shall make it light this time, but—"

"But your honor, I sprayed the cow myself. She is like one of our family. She is our mother. On every holiday we decorate her. That the cow is sprayed is true. That the cow is ours is true. But that the cow has been sprayed by the Commissioner's men—your honor, who can prove such a thing as that?"

The case was dismissed. A long line of accused passed before the judge, and each one had, by coincidence, just painted his cow, too.

Cows still wander the streets of Delhi. Life in an ancient land has a way of maintaining its own rhythms.

TWO

Dust, Heat and Marigolds

The plane whirred up to the apron, the motors roared and then died, and we were in Delhi. As my wife and I stepped out of the plane a blast of air like that from a steel furnace snatched our breath away.

Someone seemed to be waving at us. We gave a tentative wave in return—halfhearted enough so that it could be withdrawn without too much loss of face, vigorous enough (we hoped) to maintain the contact if it was for us.

The waver was an Indian of no particular age, rather stocky and with skin that looked as if it had been coppered by the sun, his curly hair parted in the middle. He was smiling as if he had known us for a long time and was welcoming us back. India suddenly did not seem strange to us at all. We must have lived here in some previous life—a perfectly ordinary idea in India as we were to discover.

"I bid you welcome," he said as we reached his side. He placed the palms of his hands together just under his chin, then stretched a hand to us, thus preserving the amenities of both cultures.

"How did you know who we were?" we asked, still wondering who he was.

"The office sent your pictures."

Then we knew it would be Arjan, the faithful office manager who kept things going at the Quaker International Center no matter what foreign directors like ourselves might come and go. His friendship was to sustain us, his wisdom to keep us from the grosser errors,

6

for nearly two years. We took a liking to each other immediately, and if we ever let him down unconsciously, he never failed as a support to us.

Now he led us skillfully through Customs, and out to a taxi for the long ride to Old Delhi.

The first thing that puzzled us about India was the vast amount of empty space. When we had thought of India, we had imagined a country crowded in every nook and cranny by its 438,000,000 people. Or, if we reflected that it was after all a big country, we were sure at least that the cities must be packed tight.

But the road from Palam Airport ran through miles of nearly empty country—acres of flat land lying idle, with here and there the remnant of an old wall or tomb, or a small new housing development. New Delhi itself, with its wide streets and garden walls and widely spaced bungalows (mostly of one story) half-hidden behind trees and hedges and half-drowned in their foliage, continued the surprise. Where were the crowds?

We drove past the Prime Minister's white-stuccoed house with its attendants in white and crimson, with great starched turbans; on past the plain residences of the members of Parliament, shaped like a child's building blocks, up to the vast presidential palace and down Rajpath—the splendidly wide, triple road bordered by vast lawns and leading from the main government buildings of two-colored sandstone down to India Gate and the stadium. Vast empty spaces with only a trickle of traffic. The buildings were splendid, the grounds and fountains impressive, but we felt vaguely cheated. This, India?

From Harding Bridge we ran past more government buildings, past the ruins of Kothlah Ferozshah, one of Delhi's many ancient cities, and through Delhi Gate into the old walled city.

Now we knew why New Delhi was empty. (This was an error of ignorance, of course, but as an impression it is accurate.) Everyone had come over here to Old Delhi. We tossed our heads from one side to the other, eager to see everything—the sidewalk merchants, the holy men in saffron robes, the bright saris of the women, the pink turbans wound about the heads of men who wore little else.

A cow ambled sedately down the middle of the road just ahead of us, leaving unmistakable evidence of her passage. From the sidewalk a half-naked girl of five or six dashed into the road, scooped up as much of the precious commodity as she could capture in two hands, and ran off into a little alley, a smile of pure joy on her face.

We detoured around a man who had stopped his bicycle in the middle of the busy intersection to make repairs. He paid no attention to the cars that whizzed past him or stopped with a squeal of brakes to avoid hitting him. He had a job to do, and he was doing it. Let others do the same.

We passed the Red Fort, its huge wall of red sandstone surmounted by umbrella-like towers. Shah Jahan had built it in such a way that he could look straight down Chandni Chauk (Street of Silver), whose shops full of silks and gold and jewels had once made it the most opulent street in the world.

Our limping taxi (most taxis limp in Delhi) carried us through the crowded shopping area at Kashmiri Gate and past the walls—still showing the cannon-ball wounds of 1857—to the Civil Lines. Once outside the wall, the streets grew wide again—tree bordered, with parkland stretching off towards the River Jumna.

Some fifteen miles from the airport our tired taxi rolled into the driveway of a bungalow of yellow stucco, and we were at home.

The American idea of a bungalow is a cozy little thing of wood with not more than four or five rooms. In Delhi, a bungalow is an impressive structure of brick or stone, usually covered with yellow stucco. Ours was of two stories, with wide verandas sprouting rows of big columns. Bougainvillea climbed the walls, bursting into flame as it mounted to the roof. Hundreds of potted flowers stood on the broad entrance steps. Generous lawns surrounded the house, and a hedge of banana trees flanked the brick wall separating us from the road.

We had little time to adjust our ideas to this new concept of a bungalow because, as we entered, a row of people waited in the big hall to receive us. Arjan introduced them all—gardener, laundryman, bearer, cook, night watchman, sweeper. Each one put a wreath of marigolds about our necks and welcomed us either in Hindi* or in English.

Freighted with flowers and somewhat dazed, we took a quick look at the living room. From its twenty-foot-high ceiling two gangly pipes hung down. At the end of each a pair of broad fan blades whished through the air. Every room in the house had its ceiling fan—an item far more important than piped hot water, of which we had none. As large as three rooms, this main room would have made a cozy little theater or a restaurant. We began to revise our ideas about space and crowding in India. But a few days later, when we had a chance to see some of the mud huts in the slums, we had to do some revising again.

In any case our spacious bungalow was none too large for the work we had come to do. A Quaker Center is a somewhat unusual place—having no ax to grind, limited by no rigid program or platform and making no effort to proselytize, under no political thumb, sensitive to people, thinking beyond national confines, and working toward the international mind and world of the future. The Delhi Center, one of a dozen throughout the world, was supported by both British and American Friends. Although hospitable to all religions—at our weekly Meeting for Worship we had more Hindus than Christians —the Center was not a religious institution. We welcomed visitors from all parts of the world, arranged seminars and parties for international student groups, invited government and university people to meet with distinguished leaders like Arnold Toynbee or Jayaprakash Narayan, presented Indian music, Japanese flower arrangement, world folk dance—in short, did whatever we thought likely to enhance international understanding. Since we often served tea to a hundred and more, or dinner to twenty-five, the staff and the big rooms were essential.

* The form of Hindi spoken around Delhi is actually Hindustani, a mixture of Hindi and Urdu, but since independence and the growing Sanskritization of the country under nationalist pressures, everyone calls it Hindi.

Although Marion and I had plenty of work to do here at the Center—it was to be our working place as well as our home from 1959 to 1961—we were eager to get out and see for ourselves what India really was like. Habitual walkers, we prowled much of Delhi during the next two years, and never tired of it.

That very evening we slipped out after dinner to see what we could discover. Music was pouring out of a tent across the street at the end of our garden. A crowd was gathering. Vendors squatted behind their little stands of foodstuffs—nuts, sweets, and cool drinks —with a flickering candle or a lantern to attract customers, though it could hardly illuminate their wares.

As we approached the tent, the curtains parted, and under one glaring 200-watt bulb a pair of ornately dressed actors strutted forth in front of a gaudily painted backdrop and began to declaim. When they tired of declamation, they sang. When they tired of singing, they declaimed. Or postured. Unable to guess what it was all about, we wandered away.

We nearly stepped on something lying on the sidewalk. It moved; it was a man, wrapped in rags and, apparently, in sleep. Gradually we came to know that living in India is like living in one vast common bedroom. Often, when I had driven someone to an early plane, I would come back through Delhi just as it was growing light. At the underpass near the post office, where the whole sidewalk had been covered with sleeping forms, the rags would be stirring and bodies rising still swathed in them like some horrible medieval picture of the Last Judgment. A man would cast off his rag of a blanket and stand naked but for a thin pair of shorts. Standing at a public water tap he would splash himself with water which in winter would be ice-cold.

Indians, we learned, excel in the art of preserving modesty while performing their most intimate acts in full view. When a man wants to urinate, he does so wherever he happens to be. Whether he is wearing dhoti or trousers, he manages, by squatting, to arrange matters so that there is no exposure. Women are expected to contain themselves until dark, but in the slum areas they take a full bath at an outdoor tap without loss of modesty. The sari is the invention of a culture which believes in modesty but not in privacy.

When a child is ready to nurse, its mother feeds it wherever she happens to be, but without exposing herself. Squatting is as natural as sleep to Indians, so there is no need of a chair for comfort. Indians squat to eat, read a paper, defecate, smoke or—even more commonly—just squat. Sometimes a whole queue of people will squat to wait for a bus. I have seen a mother squatting to nurse her baby, and making good use of the time to comb and pick the lice out of the child's hair.

Despite the modesty, there is no feeling about nudity. I saw a man walking stark naked down one of Delhi's main streets. No one paid any attention to him. Why should they? He wasn't behaving strangely or doing anything to attract attention to himself. And several times I have seen an equally naked woman prowling the bazaars that surround Delhi's great mosque, Jama Masjid. No one turned to look at her. No one sent for the police, and no one, so far as I know, offered her any covering. If she wanted to go about as nature had made her, that was her business. There is a whole religious sect, the Jains, one branch of which traditionally favored nudity. For practical purposes most Jains have given up the idea, but in their monasteries they are still said to go naked.

On that first evening walk we learned that the charm of India consisted in the pulsing, pushing variety of its life, every detail of which was lived in public. And that the throb of this immense vitality had a poignancy almost desperate, because want pressed so close. The stalls in the bazaars might be piled high with everything good—toasted cashews, oranges, sticky yellow confectionery dripping with ghee—but of those who passed by, many had never tasted these luxuries. New Delhi was wide and spacious, but on the sidewalks in Old Delhi whole families would bed down. The thousands upon thousands in the little makeshift shacks were not much better off.

When a poor household is ready to eat, someone in the family brings a little brazier out to the sidewalk to start the fire, feeding it carefully until the dried cow dung kindles. Every evening at supper time a layer of yellow-white smoke hangs over parts of Delhi where the dung fires are most numerous, and the acrid smell becomes so familiar that one learns to be homesick for it.

A kind of gaiety commands the crowds which pass slowly by the open stalls. Lit by the blue-white light of acetylene lanterns, the piles of food, the tables full of brilliant saris, the piles of books make the night seem like a holiday, and the crowds make every night in a bazaar like the last shopping days before Christmas.

More fascinating than the shops that stay in one place are the vendors who carry their goods about with them, often on their heads. When stopped by a customer, they squat, lower the tray to the ground, and sell a few coppers' worth of food. A higher order of merchant carries a collapsible stand to set his tray on, while a really prosperous capitalist pushes a huge cart piled with great pyramids of fruit or nuts or sweets, crowned with a handsome acetylene light.

Most fascinating of all these vendors is the "pan" merchant. He usually squats on the sidewalk, his little cabinet in front of him, a potful of leaves immersed in water at his side. Pan is a peculiar delicacy to which most Indians are as addicted as Americans to coffee or Coca-Cola. There are many kinds of pan, and the little cabinet is full of drawers to hold the various spices. If you step up to the vendor and order a typical pan, he will take a leaf from the pot, smear it with white paste (lime) and brown (cutch), then put in a few cardamom seeds, a piece of silver foil, and rolling it up, spear it in place with a clove.

Yes, silver. Pure silver. Silver beaten as fine as the thinnest paper is a common decoration on candies and confections. Most Indians believe firmly that it is good for the health. Thus thousands of dollars' worth of silver goes down the drain every year. Oh, yes—gold is good for the health, too.

You pop the whole edifice into your mouth, chew first in a mood of cautious evaluation, then firmly and with pleasure. The chewer exudes a spicy odor and, when he has finished, the inside of his mouth looks like a raw wound. Considered good for the health. Some men chew twenty or more in a day.

Other merchants, more humble, squat in the dust with a few bits of leather in front of them, ready to repair a shoe. Here is a fellow with a pan of dirty water and a row of tools carefully laid out in front of him. He fixes bicycles and tires. Or here is a man who has split one coconut into six or eight pieces. It is his whole stock in trade. If he sells it—if he goes back and gets another and another— then what? Can he keep himself alive?

Or the scavenger who comes trudging down the street with a few scraps of paper in a basket, looking for more. Suppose he fills his basket, how much will he get for it?

Next, a sidewalk barber. While my wife looked at saris I watched him work.

An ancient customer had squatted in front of him, removing his shirt so that he was naked to the waist. The barber, taking his tools from a little metal box as he needed them, quickly snipped off all his hair except the little lock at the crown which all Hindus keep. Then he ran his clippers over the head until it was egg-smooth. Next the nostrils, eyebrows and ears were trimmed. (Many Indians have hairy ears.) He got a complete shave—well, nearly complete. It included his face, chest and underarms. Then the barber cut his toenails for him, and finally rubbed something oily into his scalp. The old fellow quickly rubbed his own hands in it and then spread the stuff over his face, neck, shoulders, chest, underarms. Both men had squatted all through the performance, yet they rose without any signs of stiffness. Maybe it was the oil.

The smell of cooking oil—like doughnuts frying—lured us farther down the street. An old man stood behind several big brass pots that boiled and bubbled over a makeshift stove of loose brick. Mixing a dough which seemed to be made of cornmeal, he shaped it into thick cakes which he dropped into the oil. When the cakes were done, he lifted them out with a decrepit ladle and tossed them into a battered and greasy cabinet.

Four boys, their ages ranging from about three to eight, came wandering down the middle of the street. The oldest had some sort of drapery which covered him from shoulder to heels. The next boy wore shorts, the next a shirt with tails long enough to cover his maleness, and the smallest a brief shirt which covered little or nothing. Suddenly he squatted in the middle of the road, his little bottom scraping the dust. From somewhere or other the older boy produced pieces of a squashlike vegetable which they all began to eat. If the food dropped to the ground, they picked it up with grimy fingers and popped it into their mouths.

Grime, dust and dirt are recognized as inalienable elements of life—an attitude no doubt far more sensible than ours. We try—ineffectually—to banish dirt. India learns to live with it. People lie in the dust to sleep whenever they tire. Children play in it, birds scratch in it, horses roll in it, women dry their laundry in it, and everyone walks barefoot in it. The dust of Delhi is a rich compost. All sorts of animals wander the streets. People relieve themselves almost as readily as animals. Then all this rich organic product dries in the hot sun and mixes with what is already there. When the street cleaner comes, he—or she—carefully sweeps the dust out of the gutter and places it with care on the sidewalk so that it may blow where it listeth. He doesn't carry it away. Why should he? It would soon be back. If he should by some miracle succeed in getting rid of it, he would be unemployed. Better to kick it around with negligent industry, knowing it will come back—the good friendly dust which gives a bare living to so many sweepers.

The dust they live in, the dirt they eat, the dung they plaster onto their walls until it is dry enough for burning—all this gives the common people an intimacy with earth, a belonging to the whole creation, which illustrates their faith in the unity of all life and existence. We fight our environment, try to change and shape it beyond recognition. They accept it, merge into it, become one with it. There is a wonderful tolerance towards many things—misfortune, life in all its forms, corruption, illness, death.

It was not a long walk, that first evening, but we had begun to know and to love India.

THREE

Brooms and Banks

We awoke next morning to the sound of someone breaking up coal in the kitchen beneath us, and to the smell of smoke, then of bacon, and the slapping of a dust rag as Ashok the bearer rearranged some of the dust in the living room.

It was a new experience for us, having a houseful of servants who would be taking care of our needs while we still slept. (Well, not entirely new, since we had lived for five years in Japan long before, with a Chinese cook-boy and a Japanese baby's maid.) I stared up at the gently circling fan, and out the window to the great trees nodding in a gentle wind, then at the somewhat battered furniture in the room. The house was full of rather ancient furniture which gave it an easy, homelike air. Yet the big rooms seemed to demand regal appointments. The two qualities never got together, and so we lived in a shoddy magnificence quite the reverse of the neat simplicity of our Vermont home.

As I walked down the broad stairs and glanced from the balcony at the big room below, Mali (the gardener) came gliding in on silent bare feet with a vase of fresh flowers in each hand. He wore a khaki-colored dhoti (a roll-your-own kind of pantaloon) and a shirt with long tails hanging down. A spiral of pink turban circled his head. His fierce big moustache hid a small face which lighted from within in a wonderful childlike smile when he saw me. Every morning he renewed the ten or fifteen bouquets with which he adorned our rooms.

Then he went out to work among his flowers or vegetables, and often in midmorning he would come and find us wherever we were to show us a trayful of cauliflower or radishes or carrots—freshly scrubbed and gleaming—that he had just picked. And his face would be shining, too, with an unhidden joy. I think I have never seen anything shine like his vegetables and his face.

Ashok, the bearer, was tall, young and handsome. Only he of all the household staff spoke English. It gave him an opportunity he was not slow to manipulate, for he had a quick pride and a love of drama in everyday life. It was fun during our first days to watch the devices and maneuvers he could think up to see how gullible his new mistress was and what he could get away with. His respect for her grew as he discovered that she knew how to be friendly but firm, and that she was not going to be satisfied with shoddy work. He also came to know that when his wife or baby was sick, she could be counted on to drive them to the doctor day or night, get the necessary medicines, and see that special food was available. Yet the sparring never quite came to an end. He was a man who always had to pull on the rope to see how far it would stretch.

So, as we came into the dining room that first morning, he stood waiting behind her chair, tall and proud of his position and of knowing how to fill it well, bowing—"Good morning, madam; good morning, sir," and pushing in her chair at just the right moment.

Out in the kitchen old Dev Prakash worked his miracles over a small coal fire. How he managed to make toast, coffee, bacon and eggs on the one small burner we never discovered. Of course he had extra burners he could use when he needed them, and an ancient kerosene stove with a small portable oven in which he managed to produce tender pastries and great firm tea cakes. We stepped into the kitchen after breakfast to greet him. He was small, with skin like old wrinkled leather, and he was squatting on the floor with a heap of fresh vegetables in front of him. Although he had tables, he did most of his work on the floor.

Out in the living room Mohanji, our sweeper, was squatting, too.

"Namaste," we said, placing our palms together at our chests in a gesture which had already become as natural to us as it was beautiful.

He responded from where he squatted, then went on with his work—washing the terrazzo floor with a wet rag. Mohanji squatted most of the day—first in the house while he did all the floors, then outside while he swept the big verandas and the whole yard. All of this he did with a handleless broom. Mrs. Bunker, the American ambassador's wife, had tried to popularize our kind of broom. Touched by this everlasting squatting of all the sweepers of India, she had caused a number of brooms to be made and put on sale. Mr. Nehru approved the idea. The Delhi Corporation decreed that sweepers would use brooms with handles. We brought one home and presented it to Mohanji. Tall and thin as a beanpole, he actually stood up to receive it, though he never quite stood up— from a lifetime of squatting, his back had an unerasable bend. His smile was wonderful to see. We had visions of helping Mrs. Bunker to raise the sweepers of India to their feet.

Mohanji reverently carried the broom to his closet under the stairs. Then he picked up his handleless broom, squatted and went to work. He never touched our broom again. And when we left India, the street cleaners of Delhi were still using brooms without handles.

What shocked us more than this persistence of custom and tradition was the way everyone in India threw things on the floor for the sweeper to pick up. Visitors would grind their cigarettes into our floor, or drop their empty cigarette packs on it. Ashok brushed the crumbs from the table to the floor. By the end of the day Arjan's office looked as if a sudden wind had blown through it, leaving scraps of paper, pencil shavings and old newspapers all over the place. If by accident anything had fallen into the scrap basket, Mohanji dumped it out on the floor anyway. Squatting there, he picked over every scrap, flattened out the paper, and carried home all the bits. Weeks of patient scavenging would bring in a few extra coppers to help clothe his six children.

Everyone seemed to take it for granted that someone would pick up after him. Sometimes we wondered who did the picking up for

Mohanji. Was it his wife? But then who picked up for her? The oldest child? And so on down the line? Was this, perhaps, why there was always a new child coming?

Custom and tradition are a tightly woven web. To the outsider it may seem easy to remove a faulty thread. But the weaver knows that the cloth would be ruined.

We had a check to cash, so we thought we would stop in at the nearby bank during our lunch hour. Arjan had been doing everything for us, and we thought we would surprise him by doing this for ourselves.

We walked confidently up the drive and into the main entrance of a self-important building that announced itself as the Bharat National Bank. The doorman aimed at us a barrage of Hindi which halted but did not enlighten us. We waved our check at him. Smiling at us then, as one smiles at a child who proposes to become an elephant or fly to the moon, he pointed to the door we had just come in.

"Isn't this a bank?" we asked, in the only language we had handy.

As usual in Delhi there was someone within earshot who spoke English and who quickly came to our aid.

"This is the office of the national headquarters," he said. "Perhaps you wished to open an account at our branch next door?"

We did.

Approaching the branch was not as simple as we had thought. Although there had been no riots or major public disturbances since 1948, a high barbed-wire fence separated the branch from the august offices of the national headquarters. We had to walk all the way down the main drive at some loss of personal dignity, out into the road, down the road, and back into the compound by another gate, passing within three feet of where we had just been.

The branch was a lowlier building with two small alleys for the public and a large inner space where a room full of clerks worked or idled. We stood in a row of patient customers, awaiting our turn at one of the windows. Some ten minutes later—not a long time to wait in India—we reached the window and handed our check through the grille. The clerk let it lie there and went off to talk with someone at a desk behind him. When he came back, he said:

"You wish to deposit this?"

"No," I said with the dignity that befits a man of property, "we want to cash it."

"You have an account here?"

"No. But we can identify ourselves. Here is my passport."

He took the passport, studied each page carefully, and handed it back.

"To cash a check, it is necessary to have an account," he said.

We consulted briefly. "All right," I said, "we shall open an account."

Check and passport came back through the bars. "To open an account it is necessary to see the manager." He waved in the direction of a cubicle near the door. We entered, squeezed by a huge desk which took up most of the space, and sat on a bench while the manager talked to an ancient lady capitalist with a gold ring in her nose, and feet drawn up beneath her on the chair. It looked like a lengthy conference, but after a while he broke it off, asked what we wanted, and gave us a handful of papers to fill out.

Five or ten minutes after we had filled them out, he was ready to look at them.

"Where is the money you wish to deposit?" he asked.

We showed him our check.

He smiled patiently. "There must also be cash," he said. "We do not open an account with a check only."

"Why not?" we had the impudence to ask.

"It might be returned to us—no funds."

"This happens to be a check on the Government of the United States."

He thought about that. "They might not accept your endorsement."

I opened my passport and handed it to him.

He thought about that. "The check might be intended for another Bradford Smith."

"I'll give you the name of someone to phone at the Embassy if you like."

"Our rules call for a cash deposit," he said.

I rose, trembling a little. "I'm sorry to have bothered you," I said, and dropped the forms back on his desk.

"One minute," he said. "I will call the district supervisor." He called the district supervisor. They talked for some time in Hindi. Then he hung up and beamed at us. "The district supervisor says we may make a special exception for you," he said.

We now went back to the teller's window and stood in line again. Ten minutes later we had delivered up our papers and received a counter—a piece of metal with a number on it. We backed out of the way and waited to see what would happen next.

Nothing.

The teller had simply placed our check and papers on a desk behind him and turned to the next customer. They lay there having their noon siesta for some five minutes, after which the teller examined them with devoted attention, made entries in a couple of big ledgers, and called a messenger who carried the check to a desk hardly twelve feet distant. The presiding officer at this desk glanced at the check and dropped it onto the desk to lie there for another nap. When it had ripened sufficiently, he examined it on both sides, made some more entries, and called for a messenger. After they had exchanged news and views for a few minutes, the messenger carried the check to another desk where the signature was compared with that on the card I had just made out. It had a good rest there before the messenger got around to carting it a full fifteen feet to the cashier.

This august person, locked into a wire cage with his bags and packages of money, let the check lie again until a dozen others had come to rest on top of it. He then called our number and shoved a bulky bankbook through the cage.

"We want to draw a hundred rupees now," I said.

But he had already finished with us. As from a great distance his voice reached us: "The check must clear first. Come back in about a week."

We never went back. When we needed money, we let Arjan get it for us.

FOUR

In Hot Water

Every evening before dinner Mohanji heated the water for our bath. The heater was an oversized bucket with a cylindrical core in its center, in which he made a charcoal fire. In about an hour this device could cook up enough water for one good bath or two totally inadequate ones, so we usually took turns going first. Our tub—placed in a bathroom big enough to have served the average family as a living room—had old-fashioned claw feet and drained onto the concrete floor. Usually the water found a hole in the corner, but occasionally, when things went wrong, it flooded the whole room.

We saw an advertisement in the paper for an electric hot-water heater. With two years ahead of us, and a long succession of people who would no doubt follow us in the job, we thought the investment worthwhile.

We drove down through Kashmiri Gate, through the cows and bicycles and handcarts to Faiz Bazaar. We walked into the shop—a dark, windowless place completely filled with crates, boxes, sagging shelves negligently piled with odds and ends, and two desks in the middle of the confusion so piled with papers, old letter files and miscellaneous debris that the man in charge had to stand up to see over it and could locate the telephone when it rang only by marking where the sound came from.

Behind all this, in a storage room even more cluttered, half a dozen shiny white water heaters lay around on the floor. They looked

22

good, and the price was reasonable. We asked to have plumber and electrician come out and estimate installation charges. They came. We were satisfied and telephoned back to order the heater.

"You kindly come pay us for it and take it away."

"I have to pay for it before it's installed?"

"Yes, please."

"No delivery?"

"You have a car, isn't it?"

Unanswerable argument. I went to get the heater, and wrote out a check for it. They wanted the installation money, too, but at that I balked.

I took the heater home, discovered that the vent pipe had been put in crooked, took it back and got another. I hurried back, because the plumber had promised to start work.

Towards noon a little man appeared on a bicycle, bringing four bolts and a few tools rolled up in a cloth. His job was to make four holes in the brick wall, and cement bolts into them that would hold the heater—that and nothing more. Not for him the making of other holes where pipes would go.

Then the electrician came. Two days ago the electrician had come to measure, but this was a different man—the first was "out of station." He hadn't brought enough wire, so he said he would have to go and return. He made good on the first half of the promise, which was better than the plumbers, who didn't appear at all.

But two days later they all descended on us—a task force of eight plumbers and electricians who gathered in the guest bedroom next to ours where the heater was going. They squatted in a circle, considering the work to be done and menacing the unsullied walls with threatening gestures.

Then, suddenly, they began. Two men got up and began knocking the walls down with hammers and chisels while the others watched. Then two men went downstairs and brought up several lengths of pipe. Barefooted, they held it with prehensile toes while they cut or threaded with their hands. Another pair went off to install wire from heater to meter. The fourth couple mostly squatted. When they got tired of that and wanted to work, there was always someone willing to relieve them. India, with its millions of underemployed, has perfected the art of featherbedding without the featherbed. A man needs very little equipment; he is quite happy to squat or lie on the bare ground. One can hardly object to loafing practiced with such Spartan devotion.

Where there is a surplus of manpower, spreading out work to as many as possible becomes a necessity. Hence the two-man shovel, the greatest invention for letting two men do the work of one since featherbedding was invented. The device consists of an ordinary shovel to which a rope is attached. One man grasps the shovel in the usual manner and thrusts it into the ground. That completes his duty. The other man, standing out in front, now pulls on the rope. This lifts the shovel out of the ground and scatters the dirt somewhere else. Number one pulls the shovel back into position and they go round again.

While our heater was being installed upstairs, another drama was taking place down below. In order to have the heater, we had to install an extra electric meter. The negotiations had begun some time ago in hopes of some day having an air conditioner, and while we had been rallying our forces for the installation of the heater, Arjan had been pursuing the negotiations with his usual flair for diplomacy and maneuver. When the permit had finally been issued, he had taken it to the man whose job it was to issue the meter.

"There is none available," he was told.

This was a signal for a bribe. But Arjan went to a friend who happened to be an official of higher status. He phoned the first fellow and told him where the meters were, in what godown and how many. He ordered him to issue the meter, then phone back that he had done so.

Arjan had now arrived with the meter and with seven men to do the job. Since they usually seemed to come in pairs, no doubt the eighth was out of station—a phrase which seemed to cover business journeys, attendance at funerals, and just plain soldiering. The seventh made up for his absence by loafing twice as hard. While the other six swarmed about the veranda, he never did a thing. But when they had finished, he lingered behind and held out his hand for a tip.

Arjan grasped it, though handshaking is not usual in India.

"Thank you, friend, and good-by," he said.

We now had our meter and our heater. We dashed upstairs to try it. Nothing happened. The electricians, we discovered, had left a loose connection. We repaired that, then waited for the water to warm. It heated beautifully. Only, when we turned on the tap in our tub, it merely dribbled. The plumbers had so managed things that turning on the water somehow cut off the pressure. It continued to dribble for two years, and still dribbles. Work that is done so thoroughly stays done.

Another feature of workmanship is the fraternal way in which one man prepares the way for another. The carpenter smashes up the brickwork, so you have to get a mason. The mason messes up the wall so you have to get the whitewasher. The plumber slathers cement around after the rest of them have finished, and you have to call the whitewasher back.

To discourage pigeons from nesting in our deep and no doubt comfortable clerestory window holes, we called in a pair of carpenters. When we needed workmen, Arjan sent Mohanji to the bazaar where workmen sat waiting to be called. So we never got the same workman twice. This was probably a good arrangement, since we never had one we wanted back.

When the carpenters came, we explained our simple requirement —a wooden frame to be built so that it would fit snugly inside the hole and thus be flush with the wall of the building. A few minutes later we came out to find that they were attempting to nail a frame against the brick wall—outside the window hole. I tried to illustrate the principle by holding a couple of sticks against the nearest window. This only confused them. They thought I had changed my mind and wanted *that* window fixed. (It already had a screen.) So I climbed the rickety bamboo ladder and demonstrated again. Success.

We got an unexpected and additional lesson in craftsmanship a few days later when Om Chander, a friendly gentleman who called often at our place, came to see us. Om, like many Indians, dressed as if clothes were an afterthought—floppy white pajama trousers, shirt with long tails hanging down to the knee, buttoned at the neck but with no tie, and underwear hanging out at the wrists.

Om brought with him a couple of rather nervous but nicely dressed young men whom he introduced as brilliant young engineers.

"They have invented an instantaneous hot-water heater which they wish to demonstrate to you," he said.

"I'd be glad to see it, but you know we have just installed a hot-water heater."

"Oh, not to buy," he said; "just to see. You have a meeting here this afternoon, at tea time perhaps?"

He was well informed. It was true that a group would soon be coming for tea and a discussion.

"We can demonstrate it for them, too," he generously offered.

I tried without hurting his feelings to convey the notion that a meeting to which we had invited guests for an international discussion was not a good place for a commercial demonstration.

"Then we shall demonstrate it for you alone," he said, steering his brilliant young engineers to the bearer's pantry where they were at the moment a little less than welcome. "It will take only a minute," he promised. "Instantaneous."

One of the brilliant young engineers now produced the wonder gadget—a nickel-plated cylinder about a foot long and three inches in diameter with a little quarter-inch pipe sticking out at one end and at the other a cold-water fitting which would fit no faucet I ever saw.

Would we supply them with a length of rubber hose? We had none.

"Then we shall go and return with the complete apparatus," said Om Chander. I reminded him that we were about to have a meeting, but he assured me that it would not inconvenience him in the least.

The complete apparatus, which arrived twenty minutes later, consisted of a short length of red rubber hose and two pieces of string. The brilliant young engineers tied the hose to our faucet. They tied the other end to their brilliant young invention. They tied a ground wire from gadget to faucet. At this point our guests were beginning to arrive. I told the brilliant young engineers I would have to leave and would be busy for about two hours.

During our meeting I began to be aware of a continuous scurrying on the porch, just outside the open window; then clicking sounds. The electric lights flickered, dimmed and went out. Arjan, always calm, quiet and in control, slipped out to the veranda and told the engineers they would have to stop playing with the electric current until the meeting was over. The lights stuttered and came on again.

When I went to meet them at last, Om Chander was patiently waiting in the pantry.

"We will come back another time and give a full demonstration," he said.

Seems the gadget blew a fuse every time they plugged it in. Instantaneous.

They never came back.

Not long after, I was meeting someone at Palam Airport when a Russian Aeroflot jet wheezed in, its landing parachute flopping, symbol of the modern age. It taxied in, swung around with a roar on the apron, and whistled to a stop. About sixty men looking like Lilliputians gathered around the wheels like ants on a limb and began pushing and shouting. Nothing happened. They kept at it. At last the huge ship began to move just perceptibly, then gathered speed, and was finally shoved to the spot where they wanted it.

India in the jet age! Yet this is how India has got to push herself along. Out of the labor of her millions must come the energy to produce the goods they need. But for the eighty per cent—350,000,-000 people—living in villages, neither the jet age nor the industrial revolution has arrived.

How do they live? What are their hopes, their prospects?

FIVE

Village

Our friend, Swami Viswananda, came for us in a Jeep.

He wore the saffron robes of the Hindu who has dedicated himself to a life of celibacy and service—plain cotton homespun draped somewhat in the manner of a Roman toga. His curly black beard seemed to muffle a voice already soft and gentle. The Jeep and the Swami—this was the sort of thing we soon became accustomed to—the sturdy vehicle of a rich and ancient culture hitched with incongruous effectiveness to a motive force that was modern and streamlined.

We were about to have our first look at an Indian village.

As soon as you arrive in Delhi, people start telling you that of course the real India is in the villages where some eighty per cent of the people live. The argument whether to emphasize village or industrial development is one that quickly comes out in any conversation about India. Like any either-or argument it is of course spurious, since India must develop both industry and agriculture. She must rapidly expand industry in order to supply jobs and goods for the rapidly growing population. She must greatly increase agricultural productivity in order to feed her own people and avoid importing food, thus by the drain on foreign exchange further slowing industrial development.

The argument continues because Gandhi believed that the best course to development was to encourage self-sufficiency in the villager —to show him how to grow his own food, make his own sweetening,

29

cooking oil, pottery, cloth and other needs. Since most of India's agriculture is based on the yearly monsoon, farmers are left with periods of the year when they have little to do. Gandhi wanted them to spin and weave, at least to clothe themselves, and then to make more for the market if they could. So the government of India still subsidizes the production of khadi—homespun—although farmers themselves prefer the stronger and cheaper machine-loomed cloth. It is said that the subsidy is entirely eaten up in administrative expense so that the farmer gets nothing out of it anyway—only the meagerest of wages. The production of high-quality handloom products by professional weavers is another matter.

These things were in our minds as we set out with Swamiji over the flat, dusty plateau that surrounds Delhi, traveling along the Grand Trunk road which for thousands of years has borne the historic traffic of those who yearned to possess India—Aryans, Persians, Turks, Greeks, Moguls. Even Alexander the Great led his troops all this distance, so magnetic was the name of India. The British when they came used another route, yet it was they who of all the invaders came closest to imposing a uniform administration upon the subcontinent, thus paving the way for their own withdrawal and India's independence.

So, along the road that had seen mighty conquerors like Tamerlane and Aurangzeb perched in a silken tent atop a lumbering elephant with their incredible array of brightly uniformed guards, flashing spears, and files of sneering camels, we drove in our Jeep, making a less considerable dust but far better time.

"Oh, the water buffalo!"

There they were, a whole herd of them, in a "tank" beside the road. To stop for such an everyday scene must have been a bore for Swamiji, but he pulled to the side with his accustomed grace.

A "tank" in India is what we would call a pond. Many—perhaps most of them—are artificial, having been built centuries ago to catch precious water. Some of them still show enough masonry here and there to prove their human origin, but most of them look like ordinary holes in the ground, filled with water so laden with earth that it seems to need a shovel rather than a bucket.

Every tank has its water buffalo. We walked down to the edge
of this one to get a look at them—huge, placid beasts with black or
dark brown hides. Most of them were up to their nostrils in the
water, the big horns curving upward as if to keep them from disappearing entirely.

Since the buffalo spend hours at a time in the tanks and relieve
themselves there, they produce a rich compost for the other activities the tank supports. In one corner a flock of naked children
jumped and splashed, while nearby several women were doing their
laundry by the time-honored method of beating it against a rock.
The Indian method of laundering is far from nonviolent. The piece
of clothing is dunked, shaped into a long narrow piece three or four
feet long, and then used like an ax—raised high above the head and
brought down with full force on the unoffending rock. The wet
smack of laundry on the rocks is one of the endearing sounds of life.
But the result seems to be one of universal telltale gray.

We watched the buffalo, the children, the washers. We saw a
woman with two great brass pots balanced gracefully on her head,
one above the other, come to the tank, squat, remove and fill them,
replace them and walk away again. What a wonderful unconscious
demonstration of skill and grace! Yet no one in India would give
it a second look or a second thought.

We never failed to be fascinated by the dexterity—or would it
be "capitity"?—of the Indian head. Where masons are at work,
women serve as hod carriers. Only they use no hod. They squat beside a pile of bricks, adjust a ring of cloth on their heads, and picking
up two bricks at a time, load themselves with as many as ten bricks,
and so loaded they will even climb a ladder.

But men are equally "capitous." Whether it be a small package
or a roomful of furniture, the head is the proper place for it. It is a
common sight to see a man walk down the middle of the street
with a bed on his head. Since Indian charpais are simple wooden
frames laced with string, this makes the act easier, yet it is somewhat surprising to see this Biblical injunction being followed every
day.

So, as we watched all the activity around the tank we failed to see the old lady until she was right in front of us. She wore a faded red sari and her face had the leathered look of people who labor in the hot sun. Although as foreigners we must have been interesting to her, she addressed herself to Swamiji as soon as she had made the gesture of greeting to us all.

"She asks whether we would like to come and have tea with her," Swamiji told us.

We looked at the tank water, at the woman still in sight as she walked with her pots toward the mud houses, and at the buffalo.

"Perhaps we ought to be getting on?" we said. Swamiji agreed.

But the woman had more on her mind. She talked quite earnestly for some time. Even though we knew no Hindi, we could see that something was troubling her. Swamiji in his saffron robe was obviously a wise man, and a holy one, who could answer her need. In India there is no separating wisdom and holiness. God is a daily presence, manifest in all things but most in the man who, by giving his life to the service of man and God, comes closest to the divine. So it was a rare opportunity for this village woman to talk with Swamiji.

He told us afterward what she had said.

"Guruji—teacher—there has been much trouble lately. There was all this matter of the panchayat [village committee] elections, and there have been several murders, and our road here from the north is the one where the conquerors have always come. There is this talk of new trouble in the north. Is it true that a new raj [ruler] is coming?"

"There is nothing to fear, grandmother," he told her. "We have our own strong government now in Delhi. Chacha [Mr. Nehru] is in charge of things, and you know Bapu [Gandhi] approved of him. Do your work, and encourage your grandchildren to study, and remember God, and all will be well."

After saying our farewells and glancing at the scene which could not have changed much in three thousand years, we turned to climb into the Jeep. And there across the road rose the tall, sleek towers of a powerful radio station which no doubt sends out the latest news every hour, including that from the China border. Yet across the road lived a village without radio or newspaper. The old woman had to wait for a wise man to come along so that she could ask him what went on in the world.

When we reached the village where Swamiji worked, the Jeep was ringed about with children so quickly that we could hardly get out. For us they had shy smiles and greetings, but they swarmed about him like bees on a stalk of blooms freshly burst.

We had stopped in the center of the village. The pump was here —a hand pump mounted on a big wafer of cement—a great improvement over the open well from which the women had drawn their water with rope and bucket. This marked the village at once as progressive. The school nearby was a tent with its sides rolled up. The youngsters sat cross-legged in the dust, the teacher at a rough wooden table, with a blackboard on an easel behind him.

Swamiji led us first to a whitewashed building with one large, bare room, its brick walls covered with charts in livid colors which showed how to bathe, how to brush your teeth, which vegetables to raise for a well-balanced diet, what handicrafts were available to villagers.

"The villagers built this themselves," Swamiji said. "They are very proud of it."

As we stood in the middle of the floor, a pair of sparrows scolded and chased each other overhead, darting in and out of a window hole near the ceiling. No one—well, hardly anyone—excludes birds from his home. There is a clubhouse in Delhi where the birds chatter and flutter in such numbers that they drown out any speaker who tries to compete with them. Yet no one thinks of dispossessing them.

Of more interest than the birds, however, was a Gandhian spinning wheel sitting forlorn in the middle of the floor—a primitive object made mostly of wood. When we indicated an interest in it, Swamiji sent a child to fetch a woman who would run it for us. She seated herself on the floor in front of it, placed one bare foot on a sort of projecting leg, picked up a wad of cotton in one hand, and with the other turned a crank. As if by magic, the thread seemed to pull itself out of the cotton, drawn onto the spindle by the motion of the wheel.

"Now let them see the modern one," said Swamiji, his eyes shining. This was a more mechnical-looking gadget, many of its parts machined out of metal, which could spin four threads at once.

"How much can a woman make at this work?" we asked.

"If she works two or three hours a day she will easily earn four annas," Swamiji assured us. That is five cents.

We walked out into the hot sun now for a circuit of the village. From the main road, smaller alleys branched off. We took one of these.

"We would like to see an average household," we told Swamiji.

Ever obliging, Swamiji led us to a little one-storied mud house not very different from our own Indian adobe houses in the Southwest. The wall facing its little yard was covered with dung cakes. The women of the household shape them by hand, then smack them against the wall with a firm pressure which leaves the hand mark plainly visible. They stay there until they are dry enough to burn. There is no other fuel available, they say, yet vast quantities of wood are consumed in burning the dead. It would be better to put the dung on the fields, but this is the sort of hard choice India is faced with at every turn.

"The rest of the world has an economy based on steel," Mr. Nehru once said. "But ours is a cow-dung economy." Cow dung indeed has many uses. Mixed with mud, it makes a firmer floor. Mixed with water, it can be used for cleansing. Holy men put it in their hair, and in olden days it was taken as a medicine.

A couple of naked children played in the walled yard as we approached. The woman of the household was scouring a pot with sand, but she stood up when she saw us, drawing her sari up over her head—a feminine gesture equivalent to removing an apron when company appears. A golden nose ornament disfigured her face, but this sort of decoration is highly favored. About her ankles wound coils of heavy silver jewelry.

After greetings, we stepped over the mud threshold to have a look inside. It was hard to see because there were no windows in the two rooms, one behind the other. There was not much to see, anyway. Windowless to keep out the hot sun and for safety, the house like those of the poor everywhere in India was used mostly for storage and for bad weather. Even in the north the daylight hours are mostly hot and dry. So just about everything is done outdoors.

The women bring their mortars out into the courtyard to grind their spices, and their little braziers to cook on. There they will squat to nurse their babies, to chat with a neighbor. In the cool of evening the family will bring out its charpais and, unless the night is very cold, will sleep there.

So what we saw inside was two dark, small and gloomy cubicles with a few garish chromos of the gods on one wall, a couple of huge storage jars for grain, and a few bits of household equipment—mortar, shallow pans for frying or toasting chapatti (unleavened bread), some village-made pottery and two shapely brass vessels for carrying water. Since the inner walls, like the outer, were of unpainted mud, the effect was more like a cave than a building.

The woman came and poured water into two glasses—she apparently did not have a third—and offered it to us on a tray. We never entered a home without being offered water, tea, fruit or whatever the house afforded.

We looked at the water, then at each other, wondering: pump or tank? For freshly arrived foreigners, water held a number of threats. Should we offend the woman, or our stomachs?

We took the water, thanked her, and tried to sip without swallowing.

As we left the house, I saw the family plow in the yard—an instrument of ancient design, but at least with a steel edge. In some parts of India farmers still refuse to use metal in tilling; they look upon it as desecration thus to tear the body of Mother Earth.

Followed by our troop of dark-eyed, friendly children, we toured the village with Swamiji.

First, the potter. He, too, was working in his courtyard, his wheel of heavy stone mounted so that it spun just above the ground while he squatted at his work. By thrusting a spindle into a hole in the stone he could work his wheel up to a good speed. We watched him shape a few small vessels in a clay which, as we could see from finished pieces nearby, turned a handsome terra-cotta red when it dried.

Next, the oil merchant. A good deal of India's cooking is done with vegetable oil. Moreover, every self-respecting person anoints his head with oil daily. We heard the crunching of the press as soon as we entered the yard. Through an open doorway we looked into a windowless room just large enough to leave space for a bullock to trudge endlessly around a crude-looking mortar like the hollow trunk of a tree. A heavy pole stood up in it, another led crosswise to the bullock and was fastened to him with a harness. As he came around we saw that he was blindfolded.

We passed a field where several men and women were threshing grain. Women came with sheaves which they threw onto straw mats laid around a pole. A pair of oxen plodded round and round, trampling the grain until it was loosened from the husk. Nearby a man stood on a box, holding a shallow basketware scoop on his shoulder and letting the grain fall slowly in the gentle breeze. The chaff blew away, the grain fell onto a mat. His glistening body, his arms, his face, even his eyebrows were matted with chaff.

As we left the field we saw a Persian water wheel scooping water from a small reservoir and splashing it from small buckets into the next field. It must have belonged to a man rich by village standards, for a camel was turning it. We walked over to see him, for camels have always fascinated me. They leer down upon all mankind with a knowing and scornful glance which is healthily corrective. That perfect twist of the big lip, and from such an elevation, always serves to remind me how truly small I am. I do not worry about the camel getting through the eye of a needle; what concerns me is the battering my ego gets through the camel's eye. I can think of lots of people who ought to be under the constant scrutiny of camels.

From this habitually humbling experience we moved back to the center of the village. An old man in the long, loose-fitting shirt known as a *kurta* came toward us. His head was wrapped in a great coil of cloth. The turban is no mere decoration. It witnesses to the Indian conviction that the head, as the noblest part of the body and the home of the spirit, deserves respect. Indians wash their heads, anoint them, wrap them carefully at the least sign of cold, cover them completely when sleeping.

This old man, like the others we were to meet, had a magnificent beak of a nose undergirded by a white moustache. I rarely saw a grizzled head or beard. Indians seem to go from handsome jet-black hair to snowy white.

He came to invite us to the men's meeting room where a few of the fathers were smoking a pipe and talking over village affairs. Of course we accepted.

The meeting place was a sort of veranda open on three sides. Built at the top of a small knoll, it overlooked the well where at least one or two women were always drawing water. It also overlooked a few shops, the dingy little post office, and the home of a "wealthy" man who had apparently made good in the city but preferred to keep his home in his native village. His house had an elaborately stuccoed façade, with a balcony and plaster bas-reliefs, the whole painted in glaring colors—red, yellow, purple, blue.

India loves bright colors and mixes them together in ways we find shocking—orange and purple, green and blue—the whole palette together. Saris are often startling in color; temples and homes, too, are crowded with chromos of the gods, the colors of which blare louder than trumpets. No wonder Indians think our cities drab.

As we entered the room, half a dozen men rose and gave us the sign of greeting. They were all old—retired, apparently, from field work. And they all owned big, aristocratic, architectural noses. The people of this part of India, thanks to the historic incursions from the Middle East, look more akin to Turk, Persian and Arab than to anyone else. This Middle Eastern aspect of their features was at first a constant surprise.

Swamiji introduced us.

"Your country is old in independence and we are very young, so judge us gently," said the oldest of the men, a patriarch whose flowing beard was his only clothing down to the waist.

"But yours is an old culture, so we have come to learn of you," said my wife.

An immense hookah pipe, its water bowl of brass, stood on the trodden dirt floor. One of the fathers pulled it towards him, made a tube with his fingers so that his lips would not touch the mouthpiece, and drew in a couple of puffs. Then he pushed the pipe to the next man. Eventually it came to me. No smoker, I had to reach a quick decision. To explain a refusal, I decided, would be more difficult than an outward compliance. Yet when I had finished my meager puffs and passed it on to Swamiji, he merely set it in front of the next man. His saffron robe, no doubt, made explanations unnecessary.

Thanks to his effortless, unobtrusive interpreting, we were able to carry on a conversation of sorts.

"Are these fathers members of the panchayat?" we asked.

All of them were.

The panchayat is India's ancient village government—a council of elders or at any rate of recognized leaders somewhat like the selectmen of a New England village, who decide and act on all matters of general concern. During British rule the panchayats lost their importance since a centralized administration tended to make decisions from the top. After independence, the new central government's drive to improve village life through a Community Development plan, with villages gathered into blocks and officers sent out to encourage better agriculture, sanitation, schooling and home economy, again tended to put authority at the top. Villagers began to think that government would do everything for them.

To reverse this trend, some states such as Rajasthan and Punjab had begun to encourage the villages to elect responsible panchayats. A panchayat *samiti* (assembly) would then be responsible for a whole block of about a hundred villages. We had heard that there was difficulty in working out the relationship between the *pradhan*— the officer who spoke for the elected *samiti*, and the *vikas adhikari*, formerly known as the block development officer, who had previously been the chief officer in the block. Now the *pradhan* was supposed to act as a channel for the voice of the people and see that their wishes got translated into development plans. A power contest thus seemed inevitable.

Had the panchayat in this village, we asked, formulated its own development plan?

"We are thinking about it."

"What are some of your thoughts?"

"We are waiting to see what the panchayat *samiti* will recommend."

"What sort of thing does your village need?"

"We are thinking that we should have a better Ramlila celebration this year. The village next to us is smaller, but its parade is finer."

"How about water? If you had more water, could you grow more crops?"

"The people already have enough work to do. Perhaps they do not wish to raise more crops. Unfortunately, we are lazy."

I was pretty sure we were speaking to landowners, and that what they might have said was this: Those who must rent land from us are not going to raise any more on it, because the share they get does not make the effort worthwhile. So why should we spend money on improvements?

In the Punjab, where this village lay, remission of land revenues was being offered to villages which would choose their panchayats unanimously and without party strife. For the fighting of panchayat elections along party lines had led to outbreaks of violence and diverted attention away from the great need—to revive in the villages a sense of initiative and local control.

Swamiji and the Gandhian group he represented had come to work in this and neighboring villages to help restore the local initiative Gandhi had preached, and to help revive the ancient crafts and skills which, Gandhi believed, would lead to self-sufficiency. But here too a basic conflict underlay the apparent cooperation between Community Development and the Gandhian and *bhoodan* (land gift) philosophy. *Bhoodan* as taught by Vinoba Bhave also emphasized village self-sufficiency, but on a base of land redistribution to the poor which would overcome the great handicap of a landless, debt-ridden people who had little incentive to work harder when most of the fruits would go to landowner or moneylender. We shall take a closer look at *bhoodan* within a few pages.

Both the government's Community Development plan and the Gandhian philosophy aimed at an improvement in the lot of villagers whose average income was about sixty dollars a year. Community Development officers, after directing things from the top down, had come to the conclusion that they must generate local initiative, and to this extent they had swung around to Gandhi's view. But Gandhi had emphasized the simple, timeless village life with its hand crafts, its use of things that could be locally made, its self-sufficiency not only as a means but as an end. There was a strong strain of the ascetic in Gandhi, as in India (more of this later). Anyone looking at the by-products of industrialization—cheap advertising, meretricious consumer goods, and atomic wars—is bound to sympathize with Gandhi's feeling that if this is what industrialization brings, India can do without it.

But—another of those dilemmas in which India seems to specialize —the onrush of new citizens at the rate of eight million a year (and rising) leaves no choice. India must industrialize or starve. (Gandhians heatedly dispute this, but everyone else is convinced they are wrong.) In 1959 India had to import a quarter of a billion dollars' worth of food grains. Efforts to raise productivity of the land—Japanese farmers produce three times as much per acre as Indians—even if successful would not meet the need, and as yet there has been little rise in productivity. Another dilemma—if India could use the dung of its 200,000,000 cattle as fertilizer, productivity would rise. But most of India burns the dung to do its cooking. Artificial fertilizers are coming into use, but the supply is far short of the demand. Here, again, it is the well-to-do rather than the poor farmer who can afford modern methods and reap the benefits, and thus —as seems to happen everywhere, including the United States— plans to aid farmers tend to aid those who need help least.

At this point the Gandhian argument seems to make sense, because it is aimed at the poorest farmer. Yet, if India followed a course of village self-sufficiency without industrial development, many villagers would starve. The Gandhians deny this. "For every new mouth there are two new hands," they say. Yes, but India is already full of hands that are idle for months every year. It was to keep these hands busy that Gandhi and his followers developed the various crafts—hand weaving, pottery, oil pressing, soap, paper, sugar and mat making. They have even developed an ingenious device which will convert dung to cooking gas, leaving the organic matter to be used as fertilizer. But for one reason or another—mostly cost and custom—it has found little use.

The craft approach has not provided the answer. Other things have been tried, and tried simultaneously. Restrictions on land ownership and efforts to redistribute farm land, farm cooperatives for working the land, purchasing supplies, getting credit and marketing the product, education, irrigation, flood and erosion control, improvement of livestock and culling out the millions of useless animals who denude the land—all are being tried to the limits of India's capacity and against the dead weight of custom.

The nub of the argument between Gandhian and industrializer is this: whether the effort and capital being poured into industrial development is or is not benefiting the villagers. Gandhians argue that where villagers are drawn into industry, they are more damaged than helped—their traditional ties broken, the family often divided, the workers condemned to urban slums. They do not oppose small industries, operating in villages and small towns where family life will not be disrupted. But they think the result would have been better if village problems had been attacked directly rather than through the building of a great national industrial base. Leaders like Jayaprakash Narayan stand for decentralization, for encouraging local initiative, responsibility and control. In a way, their attitude is like that suspicion of bigness in government or business that has run through American life.

The argument is likely to continue, because Gandhian thought is deeply rooted in Indian culture, while industrialization is a foreign thing. Government, while paying lip service to Gandhi—and purse service, too, in the form of subsidies to his beloved handicrafts—has had to industrialize not only to keep pace with its rising population but to keep pace with the world in which as the most populous democracy it rightly wishes to play a leading role.

The men we sat with, the village we could see from our elevated veranda, were inextricably involved in these great issues and decisions. How much of this, we wondered, did these old men feel? We asked a few more questions, but the responses were cautious, hedged by custom and habit and centuries of putting up with what life brought. In the West, man changes his environment to suit his needs. In the East, he changes himself to conform with the environment. It may take another generation or two to modify that deeply etched habit. Gandhi, in this respect, was essentially of the East. Either way offers a road to survival, and who can say which is better in the long run for man?

So long as the two ways took parallel paths, they could both exist. But now that they have merged, a necessitous logic is bound to replace the rutted dirt road with the wide paved highway.

Yet for the moment, as we sat with these turbaned, strong-beaked old men, we felt their past flow through us, too. We felt the years of toil that had knotted the muscles in their darkened arms and legs. We felt ourselves walled in by the village—its toil, its round of festivals, its weddings and funerals, its gossip and backbiting, its belief in ghosts and miracles, its strange notions of health and illness, its hazy image of the rest of the world.

Swamiji glanced at us, stirred, and rose. We followed, thanking our hosts with one of our few Hindi words—*"Shukriya."*

In the market place a group of women awaited us. This much modernity and Gandhiism at least had come to the village, that women were not to be shoved any longer into the background. They greeted Swamiji, then us. Would they like to sing something for us? Swamiji asked. They would.

The song, a simple phrase of four notes which they repeated over and again, would have gone on all day, but at last Swamiji raised a gentle hand to indicate that there had been enough.

"Perhaps you will sing for them?" he inquired.

The only thing we could think of was Auld Lang Syne, which probably sounded as monotonous to them as their music had to us. At least it came to a quick and definite end, after which Swamiji led us around several corners to a house in a row of houses—a one-room apartment, actually, with a veranda in front. Here we were to have lunch. A waterpot stood at the veranda's edge. Swamiji poured water onto our outstretched hands from a lota—a small brass pot.

A woman of middle age came to the door to greet us. We slipped off our shoes and stepped in. The floor had been decorated with a graceful but peculiar repeated pattern—like a rake with a heel attached. Beside it ran a softly curving line ending every few feet in a pattern of leaves, then starting again.

"This is a festal day for the goddess Kali," Swamiji told us. "The pattern represents her footsteps."

On the far wall of the windowless room half a dozen cheap lithographs of the gods were pasted up in a haphazard way. Boxes and suitcases formed a sort of shrine, and on the floor in front of them was another beautiful geometric pattern, done in colored powders. Every Indian woman knows how to do this graceful work. In some parts of India the entire housefront is decorated in these charming patterns. How could a people with such artistry in them accept the lurid prints, or put up with a room as cluttered as this one, piled with all the household goods?

We kept running into this contrast everywhere—beauty and ugliness intermixed without any feeling for the incongruity. Government offices with bare, grimy walls, university lecture halls with windows that had apparently never been washed, homes where the rooms had the barren, scattered look of a place long abandoned. We wondered at first whether poverty was the explanation, but decided otherwise, for a little spit and polish would usually have conquered the difficulty. A lack of concern for the material world? No, for Indian women are very conscious of their own appearance. We concluded that it was simply a lack of awarenes of the total effect. Decorate the floor, and the rest is not seen. Put the gods on the wall and who will notice that the wall is streaked or cobwebbed?

So we entered and sat on the floor in front of a feast. The feast had already begun, in fact, for two or three thousand flies were dining on half a dozen platters heaped with food. Our smiling hostess dispersed a few with a symbolic wave; the rest paid no attention for they had not finished their meal. We would have been willing to wait for them, but Swamiji began to help us from the mounds of rice and highly spiced and curried vegetables—some very hot, but all of them cold. I especially liked the tamarind.

We tried to eat like Swamiji, picking up the food with the fingers of our right hand. In theory the left is never used, because with this hand one cleanses himself at stool. Indians do not use paper, but wipe themselves with a finger dipped in water. We soon discovered, however, that the left hand was used in breaking off a piece of the delicious unleavened bread called chapatti. This piece was then used to scoop up some of the more liquid food, the package being conveyed to the mouth with the right hand.

Indians use their fingers with the utmost grace. They say food tastes better this way, and we are willing to agree. But this was our first trial. Fortunately we were sitting on the floor. I found that the space between my knees was exactly placed to catch all that got lost between my fingers and my lips. I did not worry about this, because I knew the flies would be back. They had not, in fact, gone very far. Our smiling hostess kept waving at them as if to say, "If you must go, come back again soon."

For dessert we had a delicious pudding made of rice, milk and coconut boiled together, topped off with candy made by boiling milk until it becomes solid, somewhat like fudge. This, of course, was covered with silver. Though parched, we left the water untouched.

After washing again on the veranda—we did not follow Swamiji in washing out our mouths, though knowing Indians regard this lapse as slovenly—we said good-by to our hostess and headed for the Jeep. The crowd of naked and half-naked children soon caught up, surrounding us with their curiosity and their shy friendliness. We waved back at them through a cloud of dust as we drove away.

SIX

Vinoba

The more we tried to learn about village life and the problems of the farmer, the more we heard about Vinoba Bhave, the acknowledged saint who was walking over India demanding land from those who owned it for those who had none. As the political leadership of India had gone from Gandhi to Nehru, so the spiritual leadership had gone to Vinoba.

Vinoba, born in 1895 to a Brahman family, made a vow of celibacy at the age of ten, burned up his papers and left college at nineteen, and, longing to be at one with God, went to the holy city of Benares in search of Him. Offended by the filth and sanctimoniousness he found there, he was drawn to Gandhi and became the leader of several Gandhian ashrams (places of retirement, reflection, and the pursuit of a simple religious life) in succession. Teacher, worker for village improvement, he was often jailed during the struggle for independence. Completely in tune with Gandhi's teaching of a life based on nonviolence and love, he became at Gandhi's death, the leader of the *Sarvodaya* movement of selfless service. *Sarvodaya* was a word Gandhi coined in 1908 when he was translating John Ruskin's book, *Unto This Last,* which had made a great impression on him. The title of the book came from the parable in which Jesus taught that God cares for all "unto this last."

So the message of a nineteenth-century philosopher, inspired by a parable of Jesus, brought a vision to a Hindu who was looking for a way to reinvigorate his people with a message the simple could

45

understand, but with a challenge that would stir them. *Sarvodaya* is a stirring example of the way East and West can and do meet. In the teachings of Jesus, Gandhi found a reinforcement and reapplication of the power of love and peace which were also in the Hindu tradition.

Gandhi's *sarvodaya* embodied the idea of regeneration in the individual and in society. An individual attains *sarvodaya* when he has schooled and trained his body to vigorous health, when his heart is pure and loving, his intellect clear and penetrating, and his spirit extended to include the whole world within itself. A society has attained *sarvodaya* when every individual has reached the summit of his capabilities. Such a society is a body in which all of its members function harmoniously with all the rest.

Vinoba believes with Gandhi that such a social order can be built—that men can be awakened by love. Love, truth and nonviolence are his basic principles.

"The rich are fallen long since and the poor have not risen at all," he says. "Both need to be lifted up."

No closet philosopher, Vinoba undertook the task himself. In India saints still walk the earth, still speak to humble men in their villages, still seek ways to bring God's rule to earth. To a Christian, Vinoba's ways and words are strikingly like those of Jesus.

In 1951 Vinoba was traveling on foot in an area where Communist guerrillas had been actively trying to establish a foothold from which they could expand their influence as Communists had done in China. Police action seemed ineffective. Vinoba had preached that love and truth were stronger than force and police; now he had a chance to prove it.

The government offered to send along a police escort, but this was against Vinoba's principles. With a few of his fellow workers he went on foot from village to village, speaking to the people about *sarvodaya*, the life based upon love and truth and nonviolence.

One evening when he had finished his talk, an old untouchable got up at the back of the audience, put his palms together under his chin and said:

"It is very fine, Acharyaji, what you tell us. But what are we land-less ones to do? The rich have thousands of acres, but we have not even a bit of land. Therefore, sir, we want land for ourselves."

Vinoba, not knowing how to answer him, said: "How much land do you want?"

The old man began to confer with the friends who sat near him. Vinoba waited patiently. At last the old man arose, placed his palms together again, and said: "Sir, we want eighty acres."

Vinoba turned to the audience. "You have heard what this old man has said. Is there anyone among you who is prepared to meet his demand?"

Not knowing what he would do next, Vinoba waited in silence.

Then a man rose in the darkness. "Sir," he said, "I have five hundred acres of land. We are six brothers. I am head of the family, and on behalf of my brothers and myself I am prepared to give a hundred acres for these landless people."

And this was the beginning of *bhoodan,* the land gift movement.

After nine years of walking and talking throughout India, Vinoba has acquired four and a half million acres. Compared to the fifty million acres he wants, this may seem a small amount. Yet it is a miracle, really. Never mind if half the land is of little use for farm-ing, or divided up into bits and patches, or involved in legal disputes. To have collected it at all is a miracle.

Marion and I wanted to meet the saint who had done this thing. It was not often that he came near Delhi, and he avoided the city completely, but when we learned that he would be within fifty miles of us we got up one morning before dawn and drove to Panipat where he was expected. Not knowing exactly where to look for him, we wondered how to proceed.

"Don't worry," our Indian friends had told us. "Just go, and you will find him.'"

Vinoba had found advance planning too limiting. Now he made his schedule only four days ahead, going to those villages which most wanted him. To locate him at all took a certain amount of know-how.

When a close associate of his, an Englishman, wrote to ask where he could meet Vinoba, the reply came back: "Come to India and ask what state I am in. Go to the state and ask what district I am in. Go to the district, and they will tell you where I am walking. Come there and you will find me."

Our trek was not quite so lengthy. We merely drove up the Grand Trunk road. Outside Panipat we saw some half-finished buildings where hurried preparations seemed to be going on. The people there were wearing khadi, a hopeful sign. Those who wear khadi are mostly Gandhian workers of one sort or another and members of the Congress Party.

Yes, Vinobaji was on his way here to speak, to rest, to spend the day.

We left our car and started down the road to meet him. His usual custom was to rise at four, and after prayers to walk to the next place he had agreed to visit. Usually he walked twelve to fifteen miles a day, at the rate of four miles an hour.

Within about a mile we saw a crowd of people coming towards us. At their head we could see, when we drew closer, an elderly man with a sparse gray beard, heavy-rimmed glasses, a cap of green cloth with a visor which shaded his eyes, a bedroll of bright blue across his shoulders, and under this a long shirt and dhoti of home-spun, with a pair of sneakers on his feet.

He answered our silent Indian-style greeting with a brief bow, and the crowd moved on. We fell in, walking quickly to keep up with Vinoba's spry gait. Arriving at the meeting place, we walked up a path that had just been lined with whitewashed brick, past a beautifully executed basketwork pavilion covering a gaily painted pot into which donors could put their handful of grain. The path led to a newly finished meeting hall where another pot hand-painted in bright colors stood on each side of the door Vinoba would enter. We were permitted to enter with him.

The bare room had been partly laid with thin red carpet of the sort that is habitually placed on the ground whenever crowds are expected to sit on it, or when a shamiana—a sort of tent—is put up for some ceremony or other. For Vinoba there was a slightly better carpet, a low table covered with a piece of handwoven material, and a bolster to lean against. He greeted us briefly, then began to receive a succession of callers who bowed their noses to the floor, touched his feet—the deepest mark of respect (exceeded only by putting your head under a great man's foot, a difficult maneuver)—and then usually grasped his calf, then his knee. One man came forward with a handful of marigold petals, dropped a few on Vinoba's head, and handed him the rest—which Vinoba doled out piece by piece to those within reach.

Perhaps the marigold maneuver was designed to have Vinoba's eyes fix upon those present, for it is believed that a man's glance is the only thing passed on from one reincarnation to the next; that one can tell a true holy man by the look in his eyes, and that a direct glance conveys great benefit.

Vinoba then went out onto a small platform that had been set up in front of the veranda, where several hundred people awaited him. He was now enshrouded in a sort of sheet which covered everything but his face. He sat on the platform, crossing his legs in front of him, and waited until every motion was stilled, every whisper silenced. Then he spoke, but in a voice so small that it seemed unlikely the crowd could hear him. We wondered what would happen in the evening, when thousands would come. Yet they had not come primarily to hear him, but to see him, to be in his presence, to receive his darshan—a word which literally means vision or revelation, but which also seems to imply a kind of charism which is transferred from the great one to the viewer. Indians will go a long way and endure the discomfort of huge crowds only to receive the darshan of a Nehru, an Eisenhower, or any man who has a reputation for wisdom or holiness.

Having walked thirteen miles in a little over three hours that morning, Vinoba now retired for a brief rest, having told us we might come back at eleven, bringing written questions with us if we wished.

We returned to the hall when we heard chanting. Vinoba then read from the sacred Indian books and from the Bible—he quotes from it daily, especially the words and works of Jesus—and then there was more chanting.

When the prayer meeting ended, we moved forward, sitting on the floor as close to him as possible, for we had discovered that his speaking voice was very faint. Vinoba has long been in frail health, suffers from ulcers, and eats nothing much but curds and honey.

Close up, Vinoba is not an impressive-looking man. Rather short and slight, he has a beard and moustache which cover much of his face, giving him a look rather like that of the well-known picture of Chaucer. On the left cheek where the beard leaves off is a peculiar scar or wrinkle where two creases cross at right angles. He takes off his heavy glasses to read, and then he looks much younger. His complexion is fair, and though the moustache is white, the lock of hair which strays out from the piece of white khadi wrapped around his head like a cowl is only slightly grizzled.

I did not feel that he had a penetrating gaze, or that he looked into my soul, or that there was anything particularly spiritual about his face. He struck me as a quiet, unassuming, gentle person, a little old and tired, yet driven by his sense of mission. Yet the young women who attended to him looked on him with adoration at every move, every word.

He had a quiet sense of humor. "There's too much lecturing around here," he said at one point, and then, referring to a recent *Sarvodaya* meeting at Sevagram (the famous Gandhian headquarters) which he had purposely stayed away from and which had gone off well: "It seems I have succeeded in making a zero of myself." He is friendly without being warm, spiritual in thought without shedding any radiance around him, intellectual without being brilliant, thoughtful without being very original.

This was one of the things we kept running up against—that commonplaces and truisms are taken for wisdom and depth. Perhaps we have refined ourselves too much; no doubt it is a corrective to live in a culture which embraces the great commonplaces, the sublime truths without ever growing tired of them. It is this thirst for *the truth*, the oneness in diversity, the good that resides in evil, the everlasting, changing yet unchanging, eternal yet ephemeral reality that captures the mind of India. And Vinoba speaks to this need.

Yet even on Indian terms, which make large allowances for a holy man, he is not on the surface impressive. He does not speak with the volubility and ease which almost every educated Indian commands and which never failed to impress, fascinate, and sometimes over-whelm us. He does not have that radiant charm which comes nat-urally to many of his countrymen—the quick warmth, the bright eye, the welling up of an ego both childlike in its openness and mature in its confidence and spiritual overtone.

In a country that is full of charming and colorful and intelligent and vital people, he is actually conspicuous for his quietness and lack of brilliance. Perhaps his uniqueness resides, in part, in this. Many a holy man is clearly colorful and often conspicuous, with his saffron robes or meager loincloth, his hair and beard matted with dung, his forehead covered with yellow paint, his eyes wild yet com-manding. Vinoba, by contrast, seems a plain, well-intentioned old man.

Yet he is a master of the great commonplace, a genius at interpret-ing basic, fundamental truths in a way that carries them directly into the hearts of a people who are still largely illiterate but deeply nurtured in a rich culture. The things Vinoba teaches are not Hindu or Christian but universal. He presents them with absolute sincerity and simplicity. For a man in his sixties to walk all over India asking gifts of land for the poor—that act in itself is so simple, so humble as to be profound. India, as if in penance for its talkativeness, its big promises, its big hopes and its big despairs, knows how to value a man who ignoring all the forces of the world and asking nothing for himself appeals for a life of renunciation and simplicity. Perhaps not too many will follow, but they understand the call and they honor the man.

He was kind enough to offer to answer any questions we wanted to put to him, but preferred that we write them down. We had done this, and he had the paper in his hands as we sat beside him on the floor.

We had recently visited Kashmir, and we had asked what he thought were the prospects of a settlement there.

"Kashmir is now bordered by China, Russia and America," he began. We pricked up our ears at this. Russia, of course, is separated by a sliver of Afghanistan. In swift parenthesis he added that America's military aid to Pakistan effectually put the United States into the Kashmir picture. A political analyst would have put the matter in a more complicated way; Vinoba with his gift for simplicity went to the heart of the matter.

"So Kashmir is in the arena of world politics. When the time is ripe, some solution which will allow both India and Pakistan to share interests there will be right. The agreement over water rights is already bringing the two countries closer together."

What were the chances, we asked, for world peace and disarmament?

"The atomic bomb has had the advantage of making war impossible. Khrushchev and Eisenhower appear to be sincere in their desire to bring about peace, though this is difficult in the world of power politics. If the present opportunity [April 1960] is lost, another will not come in a decade."

How successful was *gramdan*—his idea of a whole village sharing its land and labor so as to produce a sufficiency for all?

"Most of the small villages are in aboriginal areas where the people are as yet too backward to seize the idea, but perhaps in time they will."

This was a frank appraisal from a man who was trying to create a social revolution through love, truth and nonviolence.

Nearly everyone in India feels that Vinoba has conceived of a society that conforms to what is best in Indian life, philosophy, aspiration and culture. At the root of Vinoba's vision is dharma, the moral law or man's relationship to God. Gandhi had taught satyagraha—a way of life based on the force of truth, love and nonviolence. For him, and for Vinoba, this means a social and economic structure where there are no privileged classes and where voluntary association and local control largely replace government.

After Gandhiji's death in 1948 the *Sarvodaya* movement, set in motion to find ways of carrying out his ideals, gave birth to the Sarvodaya Samaj (Society for the Progress of All) and the Sarva Seva Sangh (Society of the Service of Truth).

When Vinoba, the spiritual leader of this movement, received the first gift of land in 1951, a new pathway to the achievement of satyagraha seemed to open up, calling for a revival of dharma in every village in the country. The values issuing from the Upanishads, making clear man's relation to God and to His creation, had found a fresh voice and a new channel. *Bhoodan* was the new revelation of God's purpose and man's opportunity. Gandhian workers took up the program with enthusiasm.

But then Vinoba had a new revelation—*gramdan*, a whole village where land ownership would be merged and all would work together. Trying to achieve *gramdan*, the workers got bogged down in areas where the response was strongest, and as a result the momentum of revolutionary change towards a *sarvodaya* society all over the country slackened.

Vinoba's revelations continued. *Gramdan* was followed by *shanti sena*—the peace army which would ultimately recruit one worker for every five thousand people in India and which would in time replace the courts and the police.

Then came *sarvodaya paatra*, another of those inspirations which translate an ideal into a humble but dramatically attractive symbolic act, like Gandhi's marching to the sea to make salt in defiance of the British salt tax. *Sarvodaya paatra* was a way for the humblest family to support the work of the *shanti sena*. Each day the smallest child in the family would take a handful of grain from the family bin and place it in a jar. Periodically, the grain would be collected. Unfortunately, the grain collected varies greatly in quality, different kinds of grain get mixed together, and the collection requires a lot of time.

For city people, Vinoba found another way—*sampattidan*. (The root *dan*, by the way, means gift. From this Sanskrit root we get such words as "donation.") Householders would contribute one-sixth of the amount of their family expenses to further the work of creating the new society. There followed also *buddhidan* and *jivandan*—the dedication of intellect or of one's life to the service of truth and nonviolence.

All these were to be integrated into one united thrust towards the new society, towards the achievement of satyagraha. Vinoba's purpose is no less than to build a new nonviolent society. The voluntary gift of a handful of grain is a kind of assent superior to voting—a sharing, an act which will bring closer the "kingdom of kindness" Vinoba envisions.

But the visions came too fast to be implemented. Vinoba lacks Gandhi's genius for organization; in fact he does not believe in it. Living in a manner that is entirely responsive to the spirit, he feels that God is working through him and that he is a symbol of a new spirit that is on the rise throughout the world. He is unattached to results, in the manner of the ancient Hindu tradition.

"What I say and do today I may not do tomorrow," he says. "I have no concern at all about the practical results of the movement. I feel joy as I witness the response of the spirit, and my purpose is to become more responsive to God, to become absorbed within and dependent upon God."

It is a prompting deeply embedded in Hindu culture. It is both the strength and weakness of the movement, for it is a chime which sets something vibrating in every Indian heart. But it has not led to a strong organization.

Everyone looks to Vinoba for leadership, but this is contrary to his desire. He wants people to take responsibility upon themselves. The heart of his message is in the voluntary nature of all that he asks. Men are to begin by self-renewal. Villages are to take upon themselves the responsibility for cooperation. The new nonviolent society can come only from the roots. If renewal happens to individuals, to villages, then a stateless society, and one in which property will exist for the benefit of all, will emerge.

The situation within the *bhoodan* movement resembles that of the government of India. The leader of each is so strong a personality, so dynamic, that his very presence seems to inhibit others from taking responsibility. As one of Vinoba's greatest admirers and close assistants said to me, "Without Vinoba the movement might be bettered. What Vinoba wants to convey is not rigidity or a pattern to be slavishly followed. Rather, he wants to arouse a new responsibility for the common good. But, ironically, his own presence prevents this."

Perhaps. But perhaps, for reasons which will soon be explained, there is something in the Indian personality which demands a strong leader, demands surrender of the will to him, demands that some higher authority make the decisions. If Vinoba went, there would have to be another leader.

Meanwhile, Vinoba talks of finding an area inhabited by a million people where his ideal of a society based on love and cooperation rather than force and conflict could be tried—where the people would agree to live without courts and police and the government would agree to the experiment. At least one city has already shown itself ready to support a hundred *shanti senaks* (peace workers), thanks to the organizing ability of one dedicated physician.

Although Vinoba walks chiefly in the villages, for that is where the majority of Indians live, he wants to carry his program to the cities too. He visited Indore in 1960 with the hope of establishing thirty-five full-time workers there, supported by ten thousand households making the daily gift of a handful of grain. His program for Indore included, in addition to payment of the workers' salaries in grains, a truce among political parties leading to a united program of civic welfare, reordering life so as to do away with exploitation, removing educational institutions from government control, and encouraging business people to contribute one-sixth of their family expenses to the movement.

To what extent has Vinoba succeeded with his mission and his vision?

Some of the *gramdan* villages are inspiring demonstrations of his practical idealism; others are coasting along on the help his movement gives them, or have lapsed into the old ways. Some of the redistributed land is being fruitfully operated, but much of it remains idle, legally entangled or useless. It can hardly be said that *bhoodan* has measurably increased India's food production.

On the material level, then, the results can be read either way, according to the bias of the viewer. But Vinoba's program is something more than material. If it were not, it would not be Indian.

Vinoba is the conscience of India, the voice of what Indians would like to be but cannot quite bring themselves to. He expresses one side of the ambivalent attitude towards the West—the side that regards industrialization and the power state as evils to be avoided. Yet India would like to find a place in the world commensurate with its size and historic importance. The nation does not quite know whether to capture greatness by outdoing the West in dams and steel and agricultural production, or whether to be true to deeply felt ideals of religious truth, renunciation, simplicity, self-denial, non-violence—reducing material requirements to a minimum and making the village the center of all.

No doubt Vinoba idealizes the village. Such a village as he wants never existed in India or anywhere else. Nor is it likely that Vinoba can bring about the stateless society, based on love and nonviolence, that he dreams of. It seems as if he is fighting a battle against human nature which he cannot possibly win and which he knows he cannot win. Perhaps he will be content if, by calling men to their spiritual natures and duties, he can at least moderate the shattering impact of industrialization and urbanization upon family and village patterns.

Like St. Paul, Vinoba says: "Be ye not conformed to the world, but be transformed in your minds." Like all the great religious teachers, he asks men to transform themselves so that society may be transformed. Meanwhile the government of India has taken a different route. It proposes, with steel mills and dams and fertilizer factories, to create improved economic conditions which will in time work their changes upon men.

Which is right?

One of India's most prestigious political personalities has cast his vote in favor of Vinoba.

SEVEN

"J. P."

Mention the letters "J. P." anywhere in India, and anyone will know whom you are talking about. It is one of the paradoxes of India that renunciation is almost a guarantee of esteem. Jayaprakash Narayan by renouncing party politics has become one of India's most potent political figures, and after Mr. Nehru would be the most popular choice for Prime Minister. Mild rather than energetic in manner, he combines friendliness with a dignity that is inborn rather than consciously aloof. There is something immediately familiar about the squarish line of cheek and jowl, the scholarly looking bifocals, the piece of handsome homespun thrown around his shoulders, but perhaps most of all the voice with its traces of eight years spent in the United States. There is no sign in him of the egotist. He does not monopolize conversations. He does not push himself or his ideas. He seems to be trying to understand the complications of modern life and to find answers which will be satisfying to the mind and spirit.

Tall, fair-skinned, with even features that seem more European than Indian, J. P., with his mild manner and thoughtful speech, seems more like a college professor than a political leader. Or he might be the director of a community service or even the minister of an intellectual congregation—Unitarian, for example.

Yet he is none of these. Though not widely known abroad, he is the political leader of the *Sarvodaya* movement, the successor to Gandhi on the political side as Vinoba is on the spiritual. For al-

57

though Mr. Nehru nominally enjoys that position, he has moved in a direction which Gandhiji probably would not have approved. The New India of Nehru is far from Gandhi's Hind Swaraj (Indian self-rule). Gandhi's dream was of a rural, self-governing, decentralized society. The New India with its five-year plans and industrialization, based on technology and rationality, is basically at odds with the moral society Gandhi envisioned—based upon self-restraint in all things, rooted in the village, and in the conviction that a higher kind of life would emerge from renunciation than from the proliferation of goods, desires, services, and cities on the Western pattern.

J. P. speaks for those who feel that the New India has somehow gone astray and failed to become the free country of Gandhi's dream —faithful to the old virtues and culture, exerting by example a moral influence on the whole world.

So when J. P. with his quiet but persistent voice raises the cry for a return to Gandhian standards, he is like a preacher exhorting his flock to return to the old-time religion. His faith in village virtues is naturally flattering to the majority. His criticism of parliamentary democracy pleases most of those who are disenchanted with an independence which has brought its share of inefficiency, bribery, nepotism and corruption.

Who is this man who quietly demands a complete renovation of the body politic, and what are his basic ideas?

Jayaprakash Narayan, born in 1902 in Bihar, came to the United States as a student in the twenties. For eight years he struggled to get an education while working as a waiter, factory hand and common laborer. Impressed by the apparent collapse of capitalism in the depression, he turned Communist.

"I believed that if the environment was changed," he said, "the individual would change because the individual was a product of his environment. Therefore I thought that once capitalism and feudalism were abolished, and the private profit eliminated from life, everything would be all right."

When he saw what happened under communism, however, his views changed. He turned to socialism, helped found the Socialist

Party, then became head of the Labor Department of the Indian National Congress. Finally, in 1957, he resigned from the Socialist Party, announcing that he regarded party politics as unsuited to India's needs.

"The kind of democracy we won was not the kind pictured by many of us while fighting for freedom," he explained. "The people must play a more intimate and continuous part in democracy. To vote every five years is not enough."

Again: "Parliamentary democracy and panchayat democracy are like oil and water—they will not mix." "The Indian soil and climate is unsuitable for this kind of Western democracy." The people of India, he says, feel as if they have been left out of the governmental process.

"The boat of the party system has many holes in it and is, therefore, sinking. If you remain on it, you will also sink with it." He fears that caste and language divisions in India are in danger of destroying democracy.

What, then, is his proposal?

Ultimately, he would like to see that complete regeneration of society that Gandhi and Vinoba Bhave have dreamed of. He wants to replace parliamentary democracy with panchayat democracy. This would take the form of a five-tier government based on the village and rising to the national level, but with power and initiative at the local level.

J. P. admits that the villages are currently stagnant, full of class differences, feuds, civil conflicts, poverty and usury. Political parties, he feels, only intensify these frictions, so he would abolish them. Instead, he would ask that the voters, rather than the parties, choose the candidates. In a constituency of 60,000 voters, sixty groups of a thousand each would select delegates to a nominating convention which would choose the candidate.

Panchayat raj, moreover, would assure that the chosen representatives of the people actually look after the welfare of the village. The village council would, in turn, elect a representative to the regional council, but the focus of action and of political power would be in the village. Taxes, instead of being drained off to be expended by the central government, would remain largely at the local level and be spent on things the village really needs.

"Political government must be accompanied by economic self-government," says J. P. "Economic development must be in terms of the people and the well-being of the people. A small machine can be as efficient as a big machine." He believes that sixty per cent of industry should be under the control of the districts, twenty-five per cent under the control of state governments, and only fifteen per cent in the hands of the central government. For, as Gandhi said, powers should become less as you go up, greater as you go down. He would also like to see voluntary associations playing a greater role.

Speaking in a quiet voice, his head reflectively lowered, Jayaprakash might be discussing a change in the weather instead of a change in Indian politics which if it occurred would amount to a revolution. Though he speaks well in public, his private conversation is often hesitant, tentative, almost brooding. It gives one the feeling of a mind at work—weighing and balancing great issues, modest in the assay of its own competence, but firmly seated on moral principles. J. P. is more a moralist than a politician, in fact, which is one reason for his strength in a country which—however short it may fall in practice—respects morals above politics. (In this way, too, Indians are remarkably like Americans.)

How practical are his proposals?

Academic critics, government officials and politicians have all joined in condemning J. P.'s ideas. "Incoherent," "obsessed with ancient and outmoded village institutions," they say. Dr. Gyan Chand, a leading economist, says that central organization is essential for the development of the country. "The ancient village institutions were suited to their days," he argued in a Delhi seminar where half a dozen critics joined to shoot their barbs at J. P., "but they need to be reorganized rather than revived in their old form. The defects of parliamentary democracy cannot be removed merely by introducing indirect elections."

Max Lerner argued that J. P. misunderstood the nature of the party system. The unanimity and lack of conflict J. P. desired is neither possible nor desirable in a democracy where different interests are bound to pull in different directions. Parties play an important role in crystallizing, organizing and harmonizing these differences. "Mr. Narayan is obsessed with the cult of the golden age," he said— a golden age which never was.

M. K. Haldar, Professor of Philosophy at Delhi College, said real village life did not match J. P.'s picture and only a dictator could operate the system he was recommending.

Gunnar Myrdal felt that J. P. had avoided the real problems of poverty and inequality, while the Director of the Indian Institute of Public Administration, V. K. N. Menon, claimed that J. P.'s indirect elections would result in manipulation by party bosses and keep able candidates out. "I totally disagree with Mr. Narayan's views," he said.

But India does not seem to agree with these experts. It looks to J. P. for the spiritual leadership in political things that it found in Gandhi and in the holy men of its long tradition. J. P. in his musings about India's future seems to be more concerned with people than with politics, with community than with economics, with human satisfaction than with industrial production. And India likes it that way.

Looking at the huge problems we have created with our industrialization, our overproduction, our overcrowded cities, at divorce and delinquency and militarism, J. P. wants none of this for India.

"There must be something wrong in the foundation, in the very springs of civilization," he says, "that in the course of a lifetime there should be two world wars."

J. P. wants to evolve a system which, based on the village life, will be cooperative rather than competitive, voluntary rather than enforced, equable rather than with wide discrepancies of income.

"Mahatma Gandhi insisted that while there has to be a social revolution, the starting point of that revolution must be man himself," he says. "It is only through a human revolution that we can have a social revolution that is meaningful. The *bhoodan-gramdan* movement is an example of this double revolution." And he goes on to explain:

"The village community in an assembly decides what is to be done with the land—whether it should be farmed collectively as a single unit, or whether it should be reallocated on some just basis among the members of the community who are prepared to farm the land. The whole decision as to what should be done is in the hands of this small village community. This is an economic revolution of the most fundamental nature."

Self-help through voluntary association is the heart of J. P.'s plan. He has experimented with it in Bihar, his home state, and talked about it throughout India.

"We have been thinking how in the fields of industry, commerce and the professions we can go forward: from sharing of incomes to a new kind of industrial property, a new kind of industrial organization where there is human fellowship and where, instead of impersonal rules and laws, human relationships bind and run the organization and govern its life."

Jayaprakash, perhaps more than any other Indian leader, sees that democracy is not acquired by setting up ballot boxes and a parliament. The lesson has been given again and again in Asia, the Middle East and South America. These marks of democratic government are a mockery unless the spirit of voluntarism enters into the people.

J. P. is groping for ways to achieve this. Quite rightly, he is looking for sturdy Indian roots. His success would have worldwide consequences. For, if he finds ways to infuse the spirit of democracy into the village, he may provide a model for the whole developing world. And if he does this, he will achieve a high place in history whether or not he becomes India's next Prime Minister.

EIGHT

Caste, Kin, Community

Is the Indian village waiting to blossom out into the flower of democratic self-rule? What is village life really like?

The most important social influence, although it has been abolished by the constitution, is still caste. Every detail of village life is influenced by it. Whether in village or city, most Indians are uneasy with a stranger until they know his caste. Everyone has a position in the caste structure which determines whom he can eat with, sit with, allow in his house, touch, or marry. While caste has been breaking down under city and industrial conditions, in the villages where everyone knows everyone else it is as strong as ever. If anyone should attempt to ignore the rules, he would be brought before the council of his subcaste and disciplined according to the offense. Caste, in a way, is a subgovernment which controls the behavior of its members. It holds its own courts and metes out punishment to those who break its unwritten laws. These punishments can be very serious— even to a complete boycott of the offender or expelling him from the caste.

A potter was said to have beaten a cow which had strayed into his yard. When he beat her, she panicked, leaped over a wall and injured herself so seriously that she later died. To kill a cow is in some ways more serious than to kill a child.

"Would you kill your mother?" an Indian will ask if you inquire about his strong aversion to cow slaughter. The cow is so strongly accepted as a symbol of motherhood that it seems to have become mentally identified with the real mother.

So this was a very serious charge against the potter. When he denied it, a council convened and went out with him to the main temple. There two tabs were placed in a pot, one marked "sin," the other "merit." The pot was offered to a small child, who drew out the lot that confirmed his guilt.

In former times the culprit would have been expelled from the village and forced to live for several weeks in a lean-to in the fields. No one would eat or speak with him. Then he would have had to go 150 miles to a holy city to bathe, return for purificatory rites and give a feast to his subcaste mates. In this case he spent only a day on the edge of the village before going for his purifying bath, but he still had to pay a stiff fine and feast his subcaste mates.

Fear of pollution underlies the whole Hindu concept of life. Each caste is more or less pure, and all of a man's social relations are affected by the amount of ritual purity he possesses. The higher are defiled by the lower. There is no escape, except possibly through death and rebirth.

Some castes are vegetarian; some eat one kind of meat and some another. Vegetarians are generally (not always) higher on the scale, and consider themselves contaminated if a meat-eater should draw water from their well. The rules as to who can accept what kind of food from whom are extremely complicated. Members of so-called superior castes will not eat food which has been cooked or touched by those rated as inferior. They will not even sit with such people outdoors while eating.

The origin of caste is usually explained in this way. Out of Brahma, the creator, came the four original castes—Brahman from his head, Kshatriya from his arms, Vaisya from his thighs and Sudra from his feet. This accounts for the priest, the warrior, the merchant and the worker. (Farmers are usually regarded of good caste, but there are countless variations of the caste pattern.)

Then how did all the other castes develop?

One myth has it that a powerful Brahman seeking vengeance

against the Kshatriyas for the murder of his father, vowed to kill all he met. To escape, the Kshatriyas hid their weapons and took up various occupations. When the vengeful son arrived and said, "Are you a Kshatriya?" the answer would be, "Look, I am pressing oil; how can I be a warrior?" or "Did you ever see a Kshatriya make pots?" or "What—a Kshatriya herd goats?"

In this way the many occupational castes developed—barbers, tailors, tobacco-curers, weavers, basket makers, blacksmiths. Occupation is not only a matter of tradition—it is also a religious obligation and a thing determined by karma—destiny.

Even a small village may have as many as thirty castes. Since caste determines occupation, a village must have a number of castes in order to function. The higher castes cannot perform the function of the lower or of the outcastes, for they would be contaminated by the nature of the work. The tanner is defiled by his contact with dead animals, the sweeper by his contact with human feces, while even the barber is soiled by handling the hair and nail parings of others. A preoccupation with cleanliness (or with filth, depending on how you view it) runs through Hindu life. Any soilure can be debasing; hence, in part, the drive to get into white-collar jobs. Indians are impressed by the willingness of Americans to dirty their hands, to pick up a suitcase, to change a tire. In India there is always someone around to do these things, and you lower or even defile yourself by doing them.

To speak of caste, however, is only the beginning, for everyone belongs also to a subcaste which may originally have had some regional or ethnic origin. Each caste has many subcastes, though in a given village a caste may be represented by only one of its subcastes, or at most two or three. To draw up a census of all the castes and subcastes in India and their interrelations and positions on the ladder would be a vast undertaking. It is clear, at any rate, that within the village it is a man's caste which determines his relations to others, while his subcaste is more important in his relations with nearby villages. The reason for this is simple enough. There may be only one family of a given subcaste in a village.

Members of the subcaste gather from nearby villages for social and ritual occasions, and their inter-village council handles such matters as breaking the rules against interdining, or eating forbidden food, or having sexual relations with forbidden castes, or marrying within a forbidden degree of kinship, or killing a forbidden animal. Subcastes are further divided into clans, but this, as well as the various degrees of exogamy and endogamy permitted, is too specialized to be looked at here.

Relationships are even further complicated by the pretty custom of ritual kinship. On a certain evening in midsummer a group of young people come to the house of a teacher. Each makes a tilak mark on the teacher's forehead. (The tilak is the spot of colored powder or paint.) He does the same to them, and blows three times in the ear of each. The candidates return to him the following morning, when he whispers a sacred verse into the left ear of each youth, who then gives him a coconut and a small cash gift. The teacher then pours water into the cupped hands of each candidate, who lets it fall to the ground. These young people who have heard Ram's name together are now brothers and sisters. Each year the connection is remembered when the "sister" ties a *rakhi*, or thread of protection, about her "brother's" wrist. (Real brothers and sisters do this, too.) If two unrelated men become friends, they may similarly become brothers to each other's wives.

In the life of the village, then, caste, subcaste, clan, and kinship whether by blood, marriage or symbolic association are vitally important. The village headmen of the panchayat handle matters of more general concern, including disputes between members of different castes. If quarrels get out of hand, however, the police may be brought in from outside.

Quarreling, in fact, seems to be the principal source of diversion, aside from weddings, funerals and the yearly round of festivals.

"There is a great tradition for argument," says S. C. Dube, a careful student of village life, "which can easily drift into becoming a noisy quarrel or altercation. Tempers rise easily, and abuse may be showered volubly by both sides; but differences are patched up as easily, and it is not uncommon to see two people walking together as great friends although on the previous day they may have quarreled bitterly on some trifling issue. . . . People are hypercritical and very sensitive. This leads to a perpetual attitude of fault-finding. . . . Possessiveness and love of domination characterize most of the thoughts, ambitions and actions of the people,"* Dube concludes.

Village fights often arise out of caste conflicts. If the member of a lower caste wears an ornament which is supposed to be reserved for a higher, or rides on a horse to his wedding, a fight may break out. Lower castes also may seek to upgrade themselves by taking on the food and marriage tabus of the Brahman.

Although caste seems to have originated in part as a way of preserving the peace and allowing people of very different habits to live side by side through a system of social isolation, in these days when liberal democracy is on the rise and people are throwing over the old restraints, it makes trouble.

Function and race were both involved in the creation of caste. The Sanskrit word for caste (varna) means color. The Aryans who entered India seem to have brought along a class system. The Dravidian society which they came to dominate had a system based on occupations, while the pre-Dravidians still operated on a tribal system. When these three cultures met, all kinds of potential conflicts were present. There were obvious racial differences. Matrilinear and patrilinear family structures confronted each other. An aura of magic clung to the crafts and guilds. Primitive ideas about the power of food to transmit its qualities to the eater, an elaborate set of food and behavioral tabus, belief in reincarnation—all these things were factors encouraging the formation of castes as a way of permitting men both to live apart and side by side at the same time.

The system has, after all, worked for centuries. Village life has gone its way with very little change as dynasties and conquerors have come and gone. The villager lives pretty much within the village circle. With subcaste members in nearby villages he will also have close contact, and he may have occasional visits to or from

* S. C. Dube, *Indian Village*, London, 1954, pp. 181 and 234.

a more distant village where he got his wife. He may now and then visit a market town. He may be aware of the capital city so far as its laws and programs touch him.

Many villagers still do not know the names of Mahatma Gandhi and Jawaharlal Nehru. Their effective universe is bounded by the visual horizon.

Villages under the Community Development plan do have contact with government through the *gram sevaks* or village workers. Because they must attend to all details of the program—agriculture, health, social service, village industries and community relations—they tend to get drawn away from the important tasks and to fritter away their time on settling differences and attending to personal demands. The real need is for a program concentrated on increasing food production by controlling soil erosion and providing irrigation, fertilizer, better seed, credit, and teaching the right methods of farming.

The Japanese Ambassador to India told me that a team of plain-dirt Japanese farmers had come to India to demonstrate the Japanese methods of rice cultivation which result in the highest yield in the world. The method calls for absolute precision in timing and manipulation—in tilling, flooding, seed selection, culture of seedlings, transplanting, fertilizing, weeding, insect control, draining. When word of this new method began to spread, a delegation of farmers from the Bombay area traveled a thousand miles at their own cost to invite the Japanese team to come and show them how to do it.

But as yet there are few villages which have this sort of initiative. Too often, if they need a well or a school or a program against erosion, they will wait to see whether government will do it for them. Recognizing this, government is now trying to encourage initiative through panchayat raj, and is to this extent in agreement with J. P.'s thesis.

I asked a foreign agricultural student, just returned from several weeks of living in a village, what life was like there. He himself came from a poor country, but he was still shaken by his experience.

"It was awful," he kept saying, like a man still gripped in the trauma of an accident or disaster. "When I got there the monsoon was just beginning. I had to live in a little mud hut with a family that didn't have enough room for itself. The rain came pouring through the roof of rusty tin and thatch. We had a cow and a calf living in the same small room with us. Dirt floor, nothing but a corner for the man and wife and two kids to sleep in. It was a young couple or there would have been more kids. No furniture, of course. Hardly any food in the house. Sometimes all we got for a meal was a few chiles boiled in water. Rain water ran into the well and polluted it. We four students fell sick one after the other—the Indians the same as me.

"The land has worn so thin you can see the sand seeping up through the thin layer of topsoil. The farmer was scratching it with a worn-out wooden plough. Of course a good plough wouldn't have made any difference. That land will never grow anything, but he keeps on trying. What else can he do? Well, of course he ought to grow grass crops and plough them under until he gets some soil back. But he can't—he only owns this little bit of overworked ground.

"Another solution would be cooperative farming. But the villagers are terribly suspicious of each other. And they are ignorant—they wouldn't know how to keep the proper records. And of course the resources they have are so meager, it would be a gamble. It would probably end in a terrible fight."

"Hasn't the government done something to help them?" I asked.

"They've had visits from *sarvodaya* workers and government people who promised to come back and help them. But they never do. So they don't think much of the government, and they are suspicious of all outsiders. Can you blame them? Meanwhile they're getting babies like mad. I don't see any way out. It's awful—really awful."

This village was only twenty-five miles from Poona and one of India's best schools of agriculture. What then is it like in the remote villages?

"The trouble," said a very sympathetic American observer who is spending millions for an American foundation on this and other rural problems, "is that the Indian villager has no conception of a life above the level of bare subsistence. Nothing in his experience teaches him to plan for it. If he has enough to survive on, he isn't interested in a second crop."

"Not so," countered an Indian sociologist. "The whole trouble is land ownership. Most of our small farmers are renters. They know they will only get thirty per cent of the crop, so why should they break their backs over it? Put the same man on his own land, and he will do well."

But many of those on their own land have plots too tiny or too worn out to manage properly.

We spent several days at a village in Orissa where the American Friends Service Committee had set up a pilot project before the government had got its own vast Community Development program under way. Barpali Village Service was an all-purpose program of village renewal—agriculture, sanitation, health, education, cottage industries, cooperatives. There is no doubt that it has raised the level of village life in many ways, chiefly by the ever-present example of irrigated fields green with healthy crops, weavers once again producing their traditional and beautiful fabrics, healthy babies and safe deliveries, good drinking water.

In Barpali as elsewhere the emphasis has fallen rather heavily on sanitation. After years of experimenting, Barpali produced an inexpensive and ingenious type of well, formed by rings of cement and fitted with a simple old-fashioned hand pump.

One day we went out on a tour of wells. The first one we stopped at was right in the sizable village of Barpali itself. In India, a well is always surrounded by women who have come to draw water. But no one drew water here. Nearby, a woman stood with a baby straddling her left hip while he nursed. In South India women often wear the sari without the brief blouse which is worn in the north, so the natural demands of the baby can be met with ease.

"What's happened to the well?" our guide asked her.

She nodded her head sidewise in that charming and characteristic gesture which can mean anything from "Who knows?" to "You may think what you like; it's all right with me."

"The handle has gone," she said.

Just then the headman of the subcaste which had installed this well came down to greet us. It turned out that the well had been repaired by the Barpali mechanics, who had removed the handle until their fee was paid.

"Where are your people getting their water?" our guide asked.

The headman pointed across the road to where a row of women were walking back from a tank in which buffalo napped, the big brass waterpots balanced on their heads.

"My wife prefers the tank water anyway," said the headman. "She says this well water has no taste."

We visited several smaller satellite villages, welcomed by crowds of grinning children who ran after the Jeep yelling a friendly greeting. About half the pumps we saw were out of commission.

Well, then, how about the latrines?

Here again Barpali had pioneered a very simple item which could be cast in concrete in one mold, set over a pit, and flushed with a small can of water which also provided a water seal. We had used it and found it perfectly satisfactory once we got used to squatting.

The traditional village method is to step out into the fields. Every morning when we woke and looked out our window at Barpali we saw the women going to the fields, each with her little lota, or brass pot, of water for cleansing purposes. Would the Barpali latrine replace this ancient custom?

In one of the small villages we stopped at the home of a village worker who had been trained at Barpali and was actively promoting its program. I glanced inside the little roofless enclosure where his latrine was—roofless because the idea of going to stool in a covered place does not appeal to village people. The latrine had obviously not been used for months, if ever.

When we got back, I looked at a latrine next door to the place where we were staying. It was not in use either. I stopped inquiring about village latrines.

We drove out to see a big irrigation pump that was drawing water

from a new canal and delivering it to the Village Service demonstration fields. The area had turned a lush green, while everything
around it was a brown desert.

"Let's go look at our other pump," said our guide. "It's on loan
to a fellow who's got more gumption than most of them. It's awful
hard to sell new ideas to people here."

We drove from the hard-topped road into bullock-cart tracks,
dipped down to ford a nearly dry stream bed, and came out on the
edge of a canal. The pump was there, but obviously it hadn't been
used for weeks. The work had begun but been abandoned. No crops
would grow there that year. It turned out later that the owner had
got wind of a project that promised to make him more money. He,
of course, was not an average villager, but something of an operator.
Our guide was too saddened or too upset to make any comment, but
we knew how he felt. For eight years the Village Service had been
waiting for this irrigation water and for a chance to see it raise living
standards for the people.

Yet we did see in other places encouraging signs of good agriculture, healthy crops and modestly prosperous looking farms.

Of equal interest was the work of the weavers, organized into
a cooperative to revive their craft and find an outlet for their product.
The Barpali weavers practice a precise and difficult art—that of tie-
dyeing. They predye their thread—by tying off, binding and waxing
—in such a way that when the thread is woven, the splotches of
color turn into beautiful patterns of elephants, fish or geometric
figures, all in brilliant colors.

We visited several of the weaver families. Ranged around the small
open courtyard inside the house, every member of the family old
enough to be helpful was doing something. Several looms, set up
under roofs but open to the court, were brilliant with the dyed
threads. The weavers sat on the earthen floor, their feet in a pit with
the treadles. They threw the shuttle back and forth by hand with incredibly swift motions, then slapped the thread into place before
throwing it back again. Two brothers, their parents, their wives and
several children worked together—skeining, tying, dyeing, setting up

and weaving. They did only two patterns—this was their inherited skill. Each family had its own lore, its own inherited pattern or two. Their product was now finding a market in the United States, and the weaving families who had once been nearly driven out of business by competing machine cloth were now making a modest living.

Barpali is only one of many village projects supported by overseas agencies interested in seeing India's great experiment succeed. Gandhian agencies are doing a similar work. In Madurai (South India) I talked to a *sarvodaya* leader who works in the area where of 300 villages under development about 83 are *gramdan*. An American with thirty-five years of devoted service behind him, he is that rare and precious person who can be critical without losing his idealism. One hundred development workers and 200 teachers in basic education schools are trying to lift village standards.

"There has been a great change in the villages," he asserted. "Irrigation water is upgrading agriculture, so people now have money to go to town, and there is now a bus to take them. We're beginning to get electricity to pump our irrigation water and run small industries. And banks—they're willing to take the women's jewelry for loans. That's a lot better than the moneylender with his interest at twenty-five per cent and more.

"Through basic education—Gandhi's system of training village people for the kind of life they are going to live—we're making good progress. Young men are learning trades they could never have got in the old way. The younger men are beginning to get elected to the panchayat, and that is good. They have none of this resistance to new ideas and scientific farming. We're putting animal manure back on the land, and in time we hope to use human fertilizer.

"Some of our *gramdans* have been formed from large land gifts so that they are cooperative from the start. But of course when we give land to a man without anything, we have to give him bullocks and a plough too. It takes money."

"Is *gramdan* working in your area?"

"Definitely yes. Definitely. India is mostly villages, you know—over half a million of them, with more than four-fifths of India's people. The future depends on village development along Gandhian, cooperative lines. There's no other way. Each village has got to be self-sufficient, or nearly so. Of course you've got to have some heavy industry. But to take care of the underemployment, we've got to find work that can be done in the villages."

Underemployment is one of India's major problems. Of the supposedly gainfully employed labor force, 14 per cent work for an hour a day or less, and even counting six hours as a full day, 46 per cent or 64 millions out of the total labor force of 138.8 millions is severely underemployed. The average income of the farm laborer is $21 a year. But 68 million farm laborers live on less than $19 a year. This rural underemployment or overpopulation is the greatest challenge to rapid economic growth. And it is getting worse.

Between 1950 and 1956 the average number of jobless days went from 90 to 128. The daily wage dropped from a miserable twenty-three cents to nineteen. The annual household income dropped $2.10 while expenses jumped $32, leaving a gap of $36 a year between income and expense, so that there was a steep rise in indebtedness.

The first six years under a national plan, meant to upgrade farm labor, brought an increase in landlessness and unemployment, a loss of wages and heavier debt.

One way out—the Gandhian way—is to work for greater village self-sufficiency. Although village industries are inefficient and require large amounts of labor, the Gandhians argue that since labor is the one great surplus, it should be used. You cannot move eighty per cent of the population or any considerable part of it out of the villages. Therefore work must be found in the villages. Since 1953 the All-India Khadi and Village Industries Board had been fostering this sort of work. More than a million and a quarter people are spinning, with another 150,000 weaving and dyeing. Although this is not a large number for a country the size of India, it has tripled in the space of five years. More important than any statistic is the chance given to the idle to use their talents creatively.

While Gandhians, the Khadi Board and the village workers in the Community Development program are urging villagers to take up these hand crafts, there are others who think it all a waste of time. The Khadi Board has only succeeded in spending a pile of money on administration without putting a cent in the farmer's pocket, they say, meanwhile piling up such surpluses of unwanted cloth that the khadi shops keep dropping the price—already low— in one special sale after another. Only by a quick build-up of modern industry with the help of large amounts of foreign capital can India reach the take-off point.

The argument never comes to an end. Related to it is the argument over the Community Development program. Late in 1959 a United Nations Evaluation Mission hailed it as "one of the major experiments of the twentieth century, the results of which are of world-wide interest"—"an effort of unprecedented magnitude to establish a progressive system of agriculture in a land of impoverished soil and a more democratic social structure in a hierarchical (caste) society." It found evidence of progress in such items as the tendency of farmers in Community Development blocks to spend less on weddings and more on improving their lands. Demand for irrigation water, for better seeds and fertilizers was growing, and the fatalistic attitude toward disease was disappearing. They recommended less expenditure on roads and buildings and more on programs that would increase productivity. They also suggested that more of the land revenue be returned to the panchayats for local investment, and they counseled the use of agricultural task forces in areas where an intensive program would increase productivity. (The Ford Foundation has since underwritten such a program.)

Six months later the Indian government's own Progress Evaluation Organization found grave defects in Community Development.

"One gathers the impression of an inadequately co-ordinated endeavor, governmental rather than popular in character, and sustained more by hope than achievement," it said.

Improved agricultural practices were spreading very slowly due to shortage of supplies and lack of irrigation. The lack of good drinking water and latrines was still serious, and combined with inadequate medical aid was a continued drain on health. Men were taking craft training only in order to collect the stipend; they often had no intention of following the craft. More than half of the youth groups and women's clubs had lapsed or died, and the community centers were headed in the same direction. The people looked on the Community Development program not as their own but as something imposed from outside. Worse still, they showed little interest in the activity of their own panchayat which was working in their behalf.

So the argument goes. Meanwhile population is increasing at such a rate that by 1971 it will easily be half a billion. It is currently increasing by eight millions a year. By 1966, as things are going, India will need 28 million tons of foodgrains beyond what it can produce. "No conceivable program of imports or rationing could meet a crisis of this magnitude," declares a Ford Foundation Agricultural Team.

We were driving around a traffic circle in New Delhi when I had to put on the brakes to avoid hitting a man squatting in the middle of the pavement. He was clearly a dairy farmer, for beside him stood a bicycle with the familiar narrow-necked milk can holding about two gallons. Every day hundreds of these men cycle ten or fifteen miles into Delhi and back again with their meager supply—two cans balanced on their handlebars.

The man in front of us had apparently had a minor accident, for one of his cans sat beside him in the road. As we drove by we saw what had happened. He had tipped over, spilling some of his precious milk. But by good fortune the milk had fallen into one of Delhi's numerous potholes. He was carefully scooping the milk out of the hole with his hands, and putting it back in the can.

Now we understood why all our milk had to be boiled. (The government has started a "scheme" of pasteurized milk in Delhi, but the demand far exceeds the supply.) And we also understood a little better the precariousness of life, when a farmer will risk his life in the middle of a busy street to save a few handfuls of milk.

The poverty of village life is balanced for the visitor by its sudden and unexpected aesthetic thrills—the women in bright saris walking up a village lane with the graceful brass pots, one on top of another, on their heads; the patient toy-like donkeys; the naked children, their eyes darkened with lampblack and oil around the lids; the creased faces of the old men, wrapped in their dhotis and turbans; the mother giving her heavy breast to the child balanced on her hip; the cooking pots drying upside down on a string bed in the court-yard; the Persian wheel turning as the bullocks made their slow round.

Yet life in the village is precarious and often grim. The graceful scene of women drawing water at the well may be marred by a leper or a cripple in the background. (Cripples seem to be numerous in India.) There is no privacy but often privation, not too much of con-tentment and rather too much contention, superstition that passes for religion, and religion that divides instead of uniting.

But the villages are being stirred up as never before. However slowly, they are changing, and they cannot turn back.

High up in the Himalayas, close to the Nepal border and not far from Tibet, we visited a country fair sponsored by the Community Development program. Here the people, though often dark of skin, had the unmistakable stamp of an Oriental origin. Hundreds of them trudged past the little booths exhibiting the best produce of field and household, then settled down in front of a stage for a program of songs and skits. The women wore huge rings in their noses and the color of their tight bodices and long skirts was even brighter than in the plains.

But in spite of the nose ornaments, the dark skins and the great sweep of snowy mountains beyond the ridge, I felt at home. At home as in Vermont, where we also gather together what our lands have produced, and have a fair, and watch our children perform on the platform, and measure ourselves and the community we are part of. I am more at home in Vermont for having known the villages of Kashmir, the Himalayas, Orissa, Punjab and the South. Never again can I enter into the life of my own town without having beside me the men and women of village India.

NINE

To Kill a Cow

In India you are literally never in a place where you cannot see or hear some form of animal life. Even as you sit in the bathroom, a lizard will be scurrying across the wall or freezing into an antediluvian immobility while he measures your potency as a menace. Just outside the window the doves will be cooing in the trees or tramping around on the metal awnings that shade the windows from a scorching midday sun.

The strange catlike call of the peacock comes piercingly from the ridge, or, if it is night, the eerie high siren whine and cry of the jackals as they prowl in slinking packs through the streets, complaining to each other over the lean pickings. Where so many human scavengers have worked, there is not much left for jackals.

Step outdoors, and the birds are whirling and circling endlessly overhead. Kites, mynahs, pretty small doves with rainbow necks and a call like a telegraph message, buzzards in huge treetop nests, sparrows—ah yes, the sparrows.

A pair of them looking for a place to set up housekeeping decided that the metal mailbox on our front veranda was ideal. He carried her over the threshold and they began to arrange the furniture. Every time we went to get mail—which is three times a day in Delhi, whose postal efficiency puts us to shame—we also received a delivery of dried grass and old string. We removed it. We kept removing it. Whether it was this discouragement, or the fact that they kept getting our mail I don't know, but after days of maintaining their claw-hold on our box, they disappeared.

78

A few days later, as we were having lunch, we became aware of activity overhead when a few bits of grass and feather floated down into the butter. Directly over the middle of the table hung the ceiling fan. A metal cup designed to fit against the ceiling had been so installed that it was wide open at the top and made a perfect nest for a pair of honeymooning sparrows. The cup is always installed that way. Never have I seen one placed flush to the ceiling. Indians truly believe that all life is one, so why not leave those ceiling cups, which would otherwise be empty and useless, for the use of our feathered friends? They might, after all, be your grandparents. And in some future life you might be coming back and needing to occupy the property yourself.

A good many homes come equipped with birds in the ceiling fan. A friend of ours had been so occupied by sparrows that when we visited him the house seemed more theirs than his. Sparrows were nesting in his shelves, flitting peaceably in and out amongst the cups and saucers, perching on chair backs, and chirping so incessantly that our conversation was like that of two men shouting across a river.

"I wanted to get rid of them," he yelled with a smile of utter acceptance, "but my wife and daughter won't let me."

Who speaks for man? Man. Who speaks for sparrows? Women.

The plight of our sparrows was after all the plight of India—lebensraum. Squatters build in the very streets. Life is so abundant, it must cling to however precarious a perch.

One day shortly after the monsoon had begun, we drove towards New Delhi on the Ring Road—a double highway which cuts around the heavy traffic of the old city. Suddenly we found our way completely blocked. Overnight a group of squatters, driven out of low ground by the rains, had moved their makeshift huts up onto the road. Traffic had to divert itself to the one side which the squatters had considerately left available.

Our experience with the sparrows was amusing; that with another bird, unknown to America, was shattering.

As spring came on with its hot days and cool nights a horrible creature began tuning up before daylight in a tree just outside our window. His song was not quite as musical as the screech of a boiler factory whistle, but nearly so. My first impulse was to get up and slay him, either by showers of Irish confetti or, if necessary, by cutting the tree down. (I know you can't kill a bird that way, but that's the way my mind works when I'm half asleep, and I can't help it.) I never grew quite conscious enough to get up and get out at that time of day, but we began to make inquiries about the bird.

"Oh," said Arjan with that wonderful smile of his that embraced all of life, "you mean the coil" (that's what it sounded like—it is actually koel). "We are very fond of him; he wakes us up in the morning."

"Is that anything to be fond of him for?" I asked.

Arjan, like most Indians, is an early riser. Even in winter he rises in the dark around five o'clock, takes his bath under a freezing cold stream of water, and then goes off to buy the family milk at a place where, presumably, it has not first been run through holes in the pavement. Most milk, he told us, is watered. That is why many households get their milk from a vendor who walks the factory right up to the door and draws the liquid from the spigots in the house-wife's presence and into her own pot.

So Arjan liked the early bird. But I still did not. We continued to suffer from his raucous musical renditions.

I had almost got myself committed to the early rise and the care-fully planned murder when he—no doubt by that extrasensory percep-tion so common in India—divined my evil plans and moved to a far distant tree, scarcely within hearing. We settled down to peace-ful morning slumbers again. Within three days he was back. But now the weather had grown hotter; I could no longer be roused to irritable sensitivity by his performance, and his call served merely to wake me up a little and let me know how nice it was to be in bed. This, I thought, is what India will do to me in every department if I stay long enough.

The lizards who policed our walls had already given me some intimation of the immortality to be attained by inertness. Side by side with us moderns they live their antediluvian lives—motionless for hours, then stimulated to a mechanic waddle by some passing insect which they never seem to catch; masters in the art of immobility, able to live through several winter months without appearing or eating at all; surviving by the strategy of inertness. Human existence is but a moment in the long life of the lizard. He will no doubt be here after man has blasted himself to eternity—still surviving by knowing how to conserve effort and reduce metabolism below the line of perceptibility; living by almost ceasing to live; surviving not by conspicuous consumption but by inconspicuous nonconsumption.

This, in a way, is the Gandhian ideal—the Indian ideal of learning to live without, reducing demands to a level scarcely able to sustain life. Yogis have often demonstrated their power to suspend life lizard-fashion, and have even had themselves buried and then dug up alive days later. The lizard only italicizes what Gandhi preached— the loincloth, the meager diet, the abstention from sex, the low productivity of a nearly machineless industry.

Yet who really wants to be a lizard?

Not, apparently, the goat. Goats in India as elsewhere take an aggressive hold on life and never let go.

I was sitting in the car in front of a furniture store one day watching the workers who naturally enough were doing their work on a sidewalk so completely filled up with their activities that walkers had to detour into the street. Shops are often so small that they serve mostly as storage places, while the active work is done on the sidewalk. Tethered to a telephone pole stood a small goat with a face half black, half white. A workman put aside a wickerwork bookcase which he had just finished. Behind his back the goat began nibbling over every bit of the new surface, expertly locating the tiny loose wisps of wickerwork which he pulled off with little jerks of his head and promptly swallowed.

I waited for the workmen to discover him and drive him away. He nibbled too greedily, and the case fell over. Now, I thought, his meal will end.

A workman laid down his tool, picked up the stand—and set it squarely in front of the goat who resumed work on it. He was no interloper but an employee. His job was to take all the rough edges off, and his work was his pay, for he could eat what he removed. What beautiful economy! But was this meager fare his slender hold on life? Or did he get a bonus of all the shavings and leftovers at day's end? Where the people themselves have a hard enough time to survive, how must it be with the animals?

From our point of view, it is cruel to let half-starved dogs and cattle roam the streets until they drop dead. And it is cruel to overload the little horses and beat them up a hill. So, in fact, a Fulbright professor told his class one day when he walked in from some fresh affront to his sensibilities. When he had finished his tirade, one of his students said:

"And when does America plan to become vegetarian?"

The professor had no answer to that one. Our feelings are so different, developing out of such completely opposite life views, that we really are not able to communicate on this issue. The best way to make this clear is to quote, verbatim, a few news items:

JODHPUR—A retired policeman was gored to death by a bull yesterday in the presence of a number of people near the fort here. Even after its victim was dead the bull continued to trample and tear at the body for some time.

Police Jeeps chased the bull, knocked it down, and tied it to a tree. By this time nearly 10,000 people had gathered and the situation threatened to get out of hand. The crowd was angry that the bull had been hurt and the Superintendent of Police had to pacify them by saying that the bull had been bitten by a rabid dog and would have caused much harm if let loose. The bull died of its injuries later.

ALLAHABAD—While maintaining the conviction of 10 Muslims on the charge of slaughtering a cow, Mr. Justice Broome of the High Court yesterday set aside the sentence of six months' rigorous imprisonment passed on them by the Sessions judge and instead fined each 200 rupees.

DELHI—One day last month 79 stray cattle were rounded up in the Chandni-Chowk area. A total catch of about 10,000 during the past twelve months gives an indication of the stray cattle menace.

Keeping cattle is such a profitable business, particularly in areas where there is an acute shortage of milk, that this nuisance has defied solution. Unauthorized dairies, which are stated to be about 1500 in the city, have aggravated the problem. Owners of stray cattle play on the sentiments of the people. Last year the municipal staff engaged in rounding up stray cattle were mercilessly beaten by the residents in Subzimandi, Gur-ki-Mandi, Hauz Kazi, Paharganj and Kashmere Gate areas.

Catching a cow, incidentally, is no easy operation. It will run away if it can. If cornered, it will promptly sit down and practice ahimsa (nonviolence). Gandhi perhaps got his inspiration from watching India's cows. How can you deal with a cow practicing nonviolent resistance? It weighs too much.

As for the illegal dairies:

NEW DELHI—Three senior members of the Municipal Committee have formed a committee to deliberate whether cows and buffaloes should be chased off the colonies under its jurisdiction.

"These street-corner dairies," said Mrs. Pushpa Mehta, Junior Vice President, "are a source of dirt and disease rather than of better nutrition. Let us get rid of them."

As other members appeared to agree to get rid of this filth, Mr. K. L. Rathee dropped a bombshell.

"All of us are becoming health-minded but our minds and health are deteriorating. There is nothing wrong with these dairies being where they are," he said. "If anything, cow dung is an antiseptic."

As eyebrows were raised, Mr. Rathee said blandly: "I have lived with cows and buffaloes in the same room and I should know."

A suggestion was then mooted that these unlicensed dairies should be made to pay more tax. "That would only mean more water in our milk," said the Director of Education.

Mr. Rathee is probably an astute politician who was making his play for votes. For there is no easier way to get votes than to indicate an affection for a cow or hatred for a man who has insulted one. And he was surely on the side of the majority in claiming medicinal benefits for cow dung and in having slept in the same room with cattle, which is what much of village India does.

So, we might remind ourselves, did Jesus.

The affection for animals is not limited to sparrows and cattle. It embraces all animals with an abundant regard for the unity of life.

DELHI—A five-foot-long cobra, shot with a police gun, was buried with ceremonial rites on Sunday night in the garden of a Joint Secretary of the Government.

The presence of the deadly reptile in the pantry was first noticed by the Secretary's son who raised an alarm which brought the dog of the house to the spot. The dog gave the venomous creature a threatening look but kept a respectful distance. The cobra was locked up in the pantry.

The Secretary telephoned the Flying Squad which arrived half an hour later. But the constables, who were armed with mere lathis [sticks] were too scared to open the door. The police officer in charge then rang up the Superintendent of Police and got permission to shoot the snake.

When the cobra was killed, the carcase was handed over to the servants at their request. A grave was dug, milk and fruits were thrown into it and the cobra was laid to rest.

Where it takes the official sanction of the Superintendent of Police to kill a cobra, who would dare approve the killing of a cow?

JIND—A grove of trees on the right bank of the Bulla tank here has suddenly become sacred to the devotees of Lord Shiva following the exodus of some 2,000 snakes from the hollow stump of a tree some laborers had just cut.

The snakes were six to seven feet long. As they emerged, hundreds were killed by the laborers. But some orthodox Hindus protested, as the snakes were doing no harm. The killing ended, but a thousand more crawled out.

Some old people thought the snakes were guarding buried treasure. The devout plan to build a Shiva temple at the grove.

DELHI—The New Delhi Municipal Committee, which has so far failed to check the growing monkey nuisance in the Capital by all the means at its disposal, is now considering the purchase of an air gun.
The committee feels that the gun may help to frighten away the monkeys without killing them.

Meanwhile the monkeys of India, estimated at over fifty million, are playing havoc with the food supply.

JABALPUR—An excited elephant yesterday charged a bus at Demoh and pushed the vehicle back an eighth of a mile before it was brought under control by the mahout. The bus was damaged but no one was hurt.

Two days later:

JABALPUR—The business community of Demoh observed hartal [work stoppage] yesterday in protest against the "brutal murder" of an elephant, stated to be lunatic, by the Collector's order.
The killing of the pachyderm during the Ganesh Utsava—a festival of special significance to the elephants—aroused much resentment. Several hundred people took out a procession and held a meeting at Tilak Grounds. The speakers vehemently criticized the Collector's order alleging he had intentionally injured the feelings and sentiments of the religiously-minded people during the festival.

Perhaps the simplest way to explain the Hindu attitude toward the animal kingdom is by a parable from real life.
Ants are intimate members of many if not all households. Devout Hindus provide them with a daily ration of sugar. We used to have regular visitations from a nation of ants who somehow found their way up through our solid brick house, emerging out of the concrete floor into our bathroom and crawling with the scatterbrained, haphazard single-mindedness of ants to the ceiling where they again dis-

appeared in some imperceptible crevice. We tried various un-Hindu ways of scattering them with absolutely no result. Finally we appealed to our landlord for help or advice.

"As for me, I'm a Hindu," he said. "But for you I would suggest Flit."

Speaking of insects, we remember the month we spent in Bangalore chiefly for the mango midge, a microscopic item who can dance endlessly before your eyes and whine incessantly at your ears without your being able to do anything about it. He is small enough to be uncatchable and large enough to be totally irritating, and if you use Flit, it knocks you out before perceptibly slowing him down. Since our hostel did not believe in window screens ("They keep out the air"), we retreated to bed after tucking in our mosquito nets all around. The mango midge penetrates mosquito nets without slowing down, except occasionally to do a few quick pull-ups as he passes through. When his time comes, the midge will go as he came, without permission. We would gladly have given ours.

And finally, the parable of the bees.

A smiling chap rode up to our door on his bicycle one day, dismounted, and asked us if we would like to have him take the honey from one of the lovely bougainvilleas which climbed up the front of our bungalow.

"What honey?" we said.

He led us to the bush and pointed up into the branches. At first we saw nothing, but ultimately he persuaded us that the inconsiderable bunch in a crotch was a honeycomb.

"I will buy it from you for eight annas," he said (that would be ten cents), "or I will get it down for you for a rupee" (twenty cents).

We took the larger bet, and stood by to watch. So did Arjan, Ashok our bearer, Mohanji our sweeper, the gardener, and assorted children from household and neighborhood. It is easy to get a crowd in crowded India. Perhaps that is why snake charmers, bear trainers and monkey men are indigenous there, though I could never understand why a people surrounded by livestock should support so many animal trainers.

Our honey man took a piece of rotten cloth in one hand, climbed the rickety ladder we provided, lighted the cloth and thrust it smoking among the branches. He then arranged a dirty cloth over a battered pot on the ground. When my wife learned that this was what he proposed to collect the honey in, she sent for a clean cloth and a pot of our own, and back he went up the ladder.

By this time tiny bees the size of flies were swarming out of the hive bent upon mayhem. Our man ignored them. With bees buzzing in his ears and burrowing in his hair and crawling all over his bare arms, he went to work with a small crescent-shaped knife, separating the comb from the bush and putting it on the cloth in the pot. Then with the bees still swarming though somewhat stunned, he brought it down. He was about to squeeze the honey through the cloth into the pot when Marion, with a look at his hands, volunteered to do the job herself. For twenty cents we had probably acquired all of fifteen cents' worth of honey. But it was our very own—apart from the bees—and it somehow helped to balance the accounts against all that sweetness devout Hindus were dispensing to their insect friends. It also made us feel that for once we were getting something back from the animal world in exchange for the home we were providing for ants, bees, hornets, pigeons, sparrows, lizards and mice—not to mention the jackals who raided our refuse bin and the cows who occasionally strayed in for a dessert of our luscious grass.

But we wondered about the honey man. How many hives could he locate in a day? How many times can he then find a proprietor on the spot who will strike a bargain with him? How many children does he support on this precarious venture?

And we wondered whether there was any service or task an Indian has not thought of, in order to get his little bit of sustenance from an overcrowded world.

TEN

The Tyranny of the Machine

One of our favorite indoor sports was telephoning. Telephones in Delhi are not automatons—they have personality, initiative, and for all I know the right of referendum and recall. They would sometimes ring when no one was at the other end of the line. So it was only fair and natural that sometimes they would not ring when you were at one end of a line trying to get them to do so.

The adventure begins when you pick up the phone. Someone with whom you are not even distantly connected (except telephonically) may be talking on the line. You may hear only one end of the conversation or both. The only thing you can do is hang up and try again.

If you are lucky, you will get the dial tone, though this is not certain. If you get it and dial, the tone stops, but nothing else happens. You dial again, and again. Suddenly you are in the midst of another conversation.

"Is this 54314?" you ask.

They don't speak English. In any case they don't appreciate the interruption. You hang up and try again. Busy signal. But after a while you learn that a busy signal does not necessarily mean anything. Perhaps the telephone system has learned a trick from the government clerks who hold elaborately casual and lengthy conversations behind the counter when you come to do business. It is not busy, but resting.

So you dial again immediately. The telephone rings. The person who answers speaks English, but you can't understand what he says. There is a general impression that the telephone is at best an implausible instrument, not to be counted upon to carry the human voice along its fragile wires. So the best procedure is to talk fast, repeat several times, and hang up before the machine can strike back. A conversation therefore goes like this:

"Hello, is this 54314?"

"Who is calling please?"

"Bradford Smith."

"Who please?"

"Smith. Mr. SMITH." (Long silence.)

"Your name please?"

"Smith. S-m-i-t-h." Turns out that Smith is the most difficult name in the English language.

"Who [sic] are you wishing to speak to please?"

"Mr. Malik."

"Who is calling him please?"

"Jones." Silence.

"Mr. Malik is out of station please." Click. Dial tone returns.

If you are lucky enough to get somewhat further, however, you find that the supposition of not being able to understand infects you too. And pretty soon you have two people throwing signals at each other, talking louder and louder and not listening, as if neither could hear the other fellow at all.

Here is a verbatim transcript of one such conversation, incoming call.

"Hello, this is Marion Smith."

"24818?"

"Yes, this is 24818."

"What number?"

"24818."

"Mr. Smith is there?"

"Yes, just a minute please; I'll call him."

I stepped to the phone. "Hello?"

"Mr. Smith is there?"

"Yes, speaking."

"When he will come back?"

"This is Mr. Smith."

"He is not there now?"

"Yes, I am Smith."

"All right then, I call back later, thank you." Click. Dial tone.

I conclude that the telephone does not speak English. Or that I don't. In this world of illusion, who can tell?

John Galbraith, shortly before he was appointed Ambassador to India, criticized the Indian Socialists who he said with their post-office mentality were preventing any acceleration in the economy. We knew what he meant, because we had been trying for fourteen months to get a slight change made in our telephone (a government monopoly).

We had telephones both upstairs and down, but the one upstairs could not be used without throwing a switch downstairs, whereupon the downstairs phone became inactive. We wanted the two phones to ring simultaneously, so that we could answer or phone out from either one.

Several visitations and lengthy consultations occurred, the outcome of which was that it could not be done. I offered to do it myself with a pair of pliers, but this suggestion was viewed with horror and rejection—as if I had offered to remove my mother's gall bladder with a set of carpenter's tools. The final determination was that we must apply for a model D7. There was some mystery about D7 at the time, but we complied.

The months rolled by, and a good share of my exercise came from running up and down that long double flight of stairs whenever I forgot to switch the phone up or down. Then came a bill from the telephone office for ten dollars. What for? For refusing the installation. We wrote back that we had not refused it; in fact, we were waiting for it to happen. Two months later the same bill, the same response. Finally, months later, came the word that the instruments were available but no wire. If we would buy the wire on the market, they would install. But we had already paid in advance for the wire, the installation, and the instruments. We declined the proposition. Why more wire was needed when the instruments were not to be moved anyway was not clear to me, but Arjan had advised me to pay for it. We were only staying in India two years.

The great day came, and so did the work crew—an inconsiderable array of only four men. The new instruments were quite impressive, with a row of push buttons we didn't want and a buzzer system. The buttons did wonderful things like holding and switching calls around, but specialized in losing incoming calls for us when the uninitiated answered the phone. I don't know yet why they wouldn't hook up two phones in parallel.

One more humble example of post-office mentality.

Our water meter, which lay in a negligent hole in the unpaved sidewalk before our house, was broken. The glass dial was gone and so was one of the hands. The whole face of it was clogged tight with dirt. We reported it, and after a dignified lapse of time (several months) an official appeared on his bicycle, glanced at the meter, and advised us that it was in fine condition, working perfectly.

"How about the missing hand?" I asked.

"That's only the testing hand; it doesn't measure anyway. You ought to see some of our other meters!"

"Would you consider installing a new meter, and putting it inside our wall where it would be safe?"

"If you want to move it, you can get a plumber to place it inside. Then we will replace it."

"Why not do it all at once? We'll get our plumber to make the preparations, and you can put in the new meter."

"It's not done that way," he said, and got on his bicycle and went away.

The tyranny of the machine is most conspicuous when you take to the road. For there the madness engendered by horsepower under a hood is seen at its rawest. We soon learned, for instance, to drive down the middle of the road like everyone else, leaving the sides to pedestrians, oxcarts, playing children, people sleeping, two-wheeled horse taxis, funeral processions on foot—the corpse borne aloft on a string bed—and bicycles. The trouble was that they didn't stay on the sides either; they preferred the middle. As for the three-wheel motorcycle taxis, they careened mostly down the wrong side of the road, or wove their way through traffic wherever they could find an open spot. Since they, like most of the taxis, were ancient mechanisms patched together with tape, baling wire and prayer, the hazards to travel seemed immense. Whenever a three-wheeler needed repairing, its owner would careen it up against a telephone pole and let it sit there looking like a dog with one leg lifted while he patched and tinkered with its underbelly.

We learned to sit softly in a taxi, for its tired springs collapsed quickly under moderate weight. Its body would often sigh and groan and it would pop automatically out of gear in hopes of a rest, or list gently to starboard as one of its patched tires gave way. It is sad to be in a country which desperately wants to industrialize, but can't afford it.

Our own little car of European make and Indian assembly seemed more like a toy than a car and, although it had been neither abused nor driven very far, managed to have something wrong with it every week or so.

The chief difficulty about driving in India, really, is that people have not yet accepted the motorcar as a reality. They step in front or behind a moving vehicle as if it were a bullock cart. When they take to bicycles, they turn directly in front of you, cross your path so that you can neither swerve nor avoid, and sometimes just fall in front of you.

If an accident occurs, the driver of a motor vehicle is always wrong. If a child runs out in front of a truck and gets killed, the driver, if he is well-advised, will get out and start running. If he doesn't, a crowd will be on hand within a minute to stone him. But if he kills a cow, he's in really serious trouble. In that case, the crowd may overturn his vehicle with him in it, or set it afire also with him in it.

It is easier to deal with the herds of buffalo than with the people. For the water buffalo stick their necks straight out and then follow where their nostrils point without ever deviating. They do not veer suddenly like a bicycle or squat unexpectedly on the pavement like a person, or keep stubbornly in the middle like a truck, or pass you when a car is coming the other way and there is absolutely no space to spare as do the scooters, or stand in the middle of the road with a loaded basket on the head, or spread out grain for the wheels to thresh. They, fortunately, have no minds to change without notice.

So with them you can calculate your clearance to half an inch. You may occasionally wipe their noses against your fender, but even then they will not deviate. With them around, you can pay some heed to the potholes you are forever having to dodge so that your car bobs and bounces like a boat.

Driving in India is neither a convenience nor a means of conveyance. It is a sport, and everyone plays it that way. The first rule is that you blow your horn before you charge an enemy. A vehicle can practically get along without a motor, but it could never do without a horn.

It is the desperate shortage of materials that makes India's mechanics so precarious. Labor is cheap, materials expensive. Around the beautiful Jama Masjid, India's largest mosque, sit hundreds of vendors patiently hammering out rusty nails and bits of metal, dealing in old bottles, newspaper, rags. Anything has marketable value. Our sweeper saved every scrap of paper, every old bottle he could lay his hands on. Tin cans and metal objects of any sort are salable. Also around the Jama Masjid sit workmen who will come and patch up your household equipment so that it will run again. You never buy a new thing until the old falls hopelessly to pieces.

True, our bathtub faucet leaks. It has been packed half a dozen times and immediately starts dripping again. True, the stem is bent so that you can't turn it on or off with any ease. But there is a hole in the corner of the room to let the water out, isn't there?

The shower valve was badly designed to start with. I became so resigned to hitting it with a shoe every time I took a shower that I still look around for a shoe before stepping into the bathroom.

The old crafts of stone and clay and loom are still pursued with skill, but it will take another generation to assimilate mechanics. Living then will become more comfortable. But it will not be half as much fun.

ELEVEN

Joining a Joint Family

Packing ourselves and a large basket of fruit into the little car, we set off one day for the Punjab and the home of a farmer we had come to know, eager to see what life was like in an Indian household.

His bungalow, a one-story affair with two stairwells and a chimney jutting up above the flat roof, looked exactly like a ferryboat. Somehow the whitewash and red trim confirmed the impression. So did the flag flying on the roof. But the illusion ended where the dry and dusty earth began. As we walked to the door, little clouds of dust rose around our feet. Only a few bunches of dried and withered grass remained to show where a lawn had struggled against drought and stray cattle and then expired.

Our host greeted us warmly at the door and thanked us for the gift of fruit without indicating either by grimace or voice tone that—as we soon learned—he was operating a fruit farm. Three little daughters coiled themselves about his legs or peered out from behind just like a temple carving.

The welcome was warm but casual. No one asked us to bring in our bags, or showed us to our room, or asked whether we wanted a wash or a rest or a glass of water after our three-hour drive.

Perhaps this was because of the excitement over the celebration of Lord Krishna's day which was already proceeding on the veranda. It had begun the previous evening and would continue for twenty-four hours without stopping.

95

We had heard the chanting of a dozen voices as we drove in. As we approached, it grew louder, naturally enough, but also more cacophonous. Pitch means little. As often as we heard the national anthem sung, we never heard a group who sang together in the same key. Each chose his own pitch and ploughed bravely through to the end—true as to intervals, independent as to tone. Maybe there is a moral here.

"Halé Krishna, halé Krishna, Krishna Krishna, halé, halé."

That was the chant. Accompanied by a drum and two pairs of tiny cymbals, it never stopped or varied for the next twelve hours. Since we were usually sitting right beside it in the living room, or trying to sleep in the adjoining bedroom, it wore a deep groove in my brain and still lies there, somewhat overgrown but unforgotten.

The chanters were squatting on the veranda in front of an alcove where an old coat rack had been covered with the garish lithographs of the gods India so delights in. There was Radha, Krishna's consort, her jacket bursting with the burden of her overfull breasts. And there was Krishna himself, looking as always so effeminate that we could not be sure at first whether he was man or woman. I never learned why the gods were pictured this way—unless to suggest as Indian thought is always doing that there is no absolute separation of opposites and that one is always contained in the other.

Bits of flowers and paper decorations surrounded the pictures, and an archway had been formed of banana stalks, a fertility symbol. Radha's buxomness and the amatory poses in all the pictures suggested that the whole thing derived from some ancient fertility rite.

The house we entered was that of a well-to-do farmer—not a villager. Therefore the living room had a three piece "suite" of squarish, deep overstuffed furniture, and the dining room a table and chairs. This was luxury. Yet the windows had never been washed, for the idea of keeping windows clean is a foreign anomaly. This was not of much consequence since glass had been used only in the high vent windows or in the doors between rooms. The main window holes were barred, but not glazed. Cobwebs occupied the corners. The walls were smudged or peeling.

A swing hung from the ceiling of the inner veranda looking out onto the courtyard at the back. Here the children had strewn their flotsam of toys, a sewing machine sat in the corner, and odd bits of farm equipment rested where they could find space.

Accompanied by the little girls who had now adopted us, we went on into the courtyard. A woman of ample proportions arose from the dark little closet where she had been squatting and came out to greet us. Our friend Gopal did not introduce her, but gradually we came to the conclusion that she must be his wife. In the same way we came to know the rest of the household—Gopal's mother, a semi-invalid, a brother and his recently married wife. Another brother was away at college and two sisters having married had left the family home. Since his father's death two years ago, Gopal had been head of the family. This, by Indian standards, was a small joint family.

Mrs. Gopal had returned to the closet which, it turned out, was her kitchen. We asked if we might see it. A small mortar with ground spices stood by the door. A clutter of pans and foods occupied the floor. Mrs. Gopal was cooking chapatti, assisted by 234,459 flies. They alighted on everything, including a greasy rag with which she smeared the shallow pan before placing the dough in it. They continued to alight on us for the rest of our stay, and if they don't bite, something else did, for my arms were soon covered with welts.

Marion watched the cooking in amazement. It was all done on a small brazier in sooted iron pans, and often by immersion in hot oil. All the preparations were made and the cooking done from a squatting position. Every spice had to be hand-pounded—and Indian cooking demands large quantities and varieties of spices. Everything was managed with a maximum of inconvenience guaranteed to lead a Western woman to immediate revolt—or radical reorganization.

Several hours later, around midafternoon, we were invited to a meal of puris and another fried cake made with potatoes and vegetables. As we had not eaten since breakfast, the meal was welcome. Our generous and genial host asked whether we would like tea or coffee. Neither came. After a long wait, we asked whether we might rest a while. The midday rest was one of the hot-country habits we had learned to cherish. So now our bags came in—we of course were not permitted to carry them—and we retired to "our" room—a bare, four-square cell furnished with two string cots and a crib.

By this time I was interested in other facilities too. Cautiously I opened an inner door. It led into a closet-sized room, the floor of which was strewn with green pears. Beyond this was another door. I opened it, again tentatively, and found myself in a smaller closet equipped with a bucket, a small brass pot, and a small hole in the floor. Still not what I wanted. Beyond this stood another door which led to a still smaller closet equipped with nothing but a cement floor with two humps fashioned in the shape of feet in the middle. Also a small hole in one corner. Also a small untouchable girl who would come when called to clean the floor after you had defecated on it. I chose instead to go outside to urinate, and reserved all other activity until we returned to Delhi.

We lay down on our cots for a while, but a procession of unannounced visitors ultimately discouraged us. They came to sweep, to use the toilet or washroom, to get pears, to clean the toilet, and perhaps to see whether any long-lost relatives happened to be living there, which they very well might.

Aided and encouraged by the chanting next door, we arose and went forth.

Gopal is a trained agriculturist operating a large and profitable farm, yet it looked to us like a place that had gone out of production —its fields full of weeds, fruit trees widely spaced, an apparent waste of land instead of intensive cultivation. This was the impression we were always getting in India. Why, in a land where there is a food shortage and a surplus labor force, does so much land lie idle? One answer, of course, is the lack of water. Gopal was beginning to get water from the huge Bhakra dam, but not enough to put him on a year-round basis. Other difficulties are worn-out land and shortage of fertilizer. But at the root of all India's land problem is ownership —large holdings, high rents.

We managed to get almost beyond the sound of the chanting before a hot sun and lack of any shade drove us back. Despite India's jungles, vast reaches of the country are bare and shadeless. Near the house, though, we found trees, and under these slept such workers as were not chanting.

"Indian farmers have the hardest of lives," Gopal told us. "They hardly have five dollars a month income, and on this they must care for their families. My men are well off. They get nine dollars a month, a house to live in, all the fruit they can eat besides what they can steal and sell in the market, and some vegetables."

Not to mention the festival of Lord Krishna.

On festal days Gopal let his workers and their families have the run of the house. In addition to Gopal's three little girls, their baby brother who rode about on the left hip of a servant girl not much bigger than himself, the girl who cleaned the toilets and floors, and an indeterminate number of other servants, a constant stream of farm children flowed like a human river through the living room, regarded us with large soot-blackened eyes, and passed on. Every few hours the sweeping girl would come back to rearrange the dust they brought in on their bare feet.

Apparently the festival called for fasting, though some time after dark we had a casual sort of meal. Finally around midnight we were invited out to the veranda. An old man sitting on a box near the hat rack interminably told his beads though we could never hear what he told them because of the chanting. This went on for another two hours while we squatted, or rather sat with our legs bent up in front of us. When the pain of it grew past bearing we inched our way to the wall and leaned back, and knew the meaning of bliss.

Gopal now took over the position of honor at the little fire. As he fed it with bits of sticks, incense and libations of ghee (purified butter), the pace of the chanting picked up and a couple of drummers began to weave intricate rhythms around the voices. Then suddenly the chanting stopped, Gopal made a short speech, and a big bucket appeared, out of which something like curd was dipped and placed in each hand. By now there must have been nearly a hundred people on the veranda or as near as they could get to it. After the curd came fruit and sweets, served on banana leaves. We then went to bed and battled the flies until morning.

We were glad when Gopal invited us to attend morning prayers, leading us to a drab little room where the grandmother was already breaking sticks into a small fire, then scattering spices on it from a small ladle and throwing in ghee. All the while she kept up a recitation from the sacred books, spelled occasionally by her son, while various members of the household wandered in and out.

After a casual breakfast of fried things, tea—and no fruit, we joined the reassembled crowd in front of the house to celebrate Independence Day.

Gopal had climbed up to the roof with his oldest daughter in his arms, and while we all watched she held the flag as her father pulled the rope. When the flag opened, a shower of marigold petals fell out and we all sang the national anthem in our various pitches. The two younger girls, meanwhile, leaned on the parapet like Michelangelo cherubs, only their heads and chubby arms showing. Then Gopal came down and passed among us with a bucket, handing out *prashad*—something like Cream of Wheat, though thicker. Associated with temples and festivals, it constituted a sort of communion.

And that was our introduction to family life.

As we came to know other families, we became accustomed to the informality and relaxation of the household—the perpetual clutter of piled boxes, of animals wandering in, birds flying in the window and scolding to find you there, and the simple equipment with which a large household can be fed.

We learned how to enjoy an Indian bath, which requires only a waist-high tap (if there is running water), a hole in the floor, a tin cup—and you. If you turn on the tap and squat under it, you end by bruising your back and shoulders. If you use the cup, you end by spraying the whole floor. If you get soaped up, you may find that the water has meanwhile stopped running and you're left in a lather. If, out of consideration for your foreignness, the family has given you a tin tub (reminder of the British) to sit in, you are likely to find when you try to get up that the tub, being small, will come with you. You can then qualify as a turtle, but this leaves the southern view rather exposed. All baths are cold baths, and in a hot country tap water usually feels cold. On the other hand, our Delhi house had a roof tank which delivered cold water so hot at midday that you had to jump back when you turned the tap on.

A friend of ours remembers that when her grandmother bathed every morning she would say as she poured a cup of water over herself, "This is from the Ganges," then "This is from the Jumna," naming each of the rivers of India.

Many Indians prefer to go to a river to bathe if there is one nearby, or to a tank. A woman can bathe in public in perfect modesty (among the common folk exposure of the breasts is not immodest, especially in the south) and somehow change her sari when she is through.

The effect of informality in the household is also produced by that center of the house, the courtyard, onto which many of the rooms open and where much of the living is done. Here the children play safely, the wife grinds her spices and starts her evening fire, the grandparent dozes in the sun. Open to the sky, it makes a cool sleeping place in the hot weather for the whole family.

The courtyard provides a safety, an intimacy, a togetherness which must get confining at times, but which looks attractive. People live together—they do not shut themselves apart from each other in separate rooms. Their relationships must be based upon full knowledge and no illusions. But how do they ever find the privacy to get all the babies?

Raised in such a large family, the children find a kind of security unknown to us. They may be nearly as close to grandmother and several aunts as they are to their own mother. There is always someone to care for them, to carry them about. It is a common sight to see small children toting on their hips a baby not much smaller than themselves. Babies are never left alone, can nurse when they like and may be given the breast until they are four years old.

Children not only get plenty of attention and care; they have no need to compete. Nor are they encouraged to "stand up for themselves" against other children. Where an American parent regards stealing as the worst form of behavior, an Indian mother would think fighting the worst. We never saw children fight.

In the joint family there is always someone to take care of you, someone to make your decisions. The result is that even grown men remain under the dominance of their fathers and can make no important decisions for themselves. This has results throughout the society which we shall look at later.

Indian men are even more dependent on their mothers. Children are taught first that mother is god, then that father is god, then that teacher is god. God and man are never held conceptually apart as with us. This makes the religious sensibility more immediate and personal than ours. It also underscores the importance of the family relationships. The Indian mother shackles her son, asserts an anthropologist, crushing his rebellion before adolescence. So it becomes sublimated to a worship of the mother as goddess, ending in a hungry dependence and an unconquerable distrust of women. So men rely on their mothers to care for them until they are married, an interesting by-result being that when students come to America to study they usually manage to find a landlady who becomes a surrogate mother. After marriage, they expect their wives to mother them.

Their gentle upbringing may make the men uncompetitive. "With us it is the woman who is often the materialist," an Indian wife told us. "She will push her man ahead even if he is an idealist, in order to get what she wants for her family. Even so, a girl is trained to do everything to satisfy the man she marries. Though marriages are not for love, the man is so charmed by the attention and care he gets that he ends by loving the girl anyway."

The women indeed often strike one as strong characters. Not particularly pretty by our standards (noses, at least in the north, tend to be more prominent than we like them, while heaviness is thought to be sexually attractive), they are sometimes striking or handsome. The ideal—as one can see it pictured in the miniature paintings of the Mogul period—calls for elongated eyes with deeply curving brows, high round full breasts, slim waist and ample hips, and long supple fingers. Alas, the ideal comes to reality no more frequently in India than elsewhere.

One often detects masculinity in the females and feminity in the males—a mixup which we have already noted in the way the gods are pictured. Something in Indian society permits the men to be soft and requires the women to be aggressive. The roots are in the permissive child rearing and in the high regard for ahimsa—nonviolence—which omits training in competition and aggressiveness. But I feel that it goes deeper than this—that in keeping with the philosophical outlook which sees opposites turning into the same thing and all things merged into one, sexual differentiation also gets modified. Mothers put make-up on the eyes of their little boys. Men often wear robes that suggest female attire.

Educated women often appear to be rather aggressively insistent and strenuous, but this may be only because they were long denied the same opportunities as men.

The ideal of female behavior calls for constancy, purity, endurance, and understanding. Living in a joint family must make large demands upon all of these.

A woman must show no tenderness towards her husband in the presence of his parents. How she manages this while at the same time giving him all that attention which captivates him is a mystery.

But these contradictions are somehow met and dealt with. As in the attitude toward sex. There is a strong vein of asceticism in Indian life, as everyone knows. One of Gandhi's ideals was the ancient Hindu brahmacharya, or complete sexual abstention. The orthodox physiology teaches that the loss of semen is debilitating since "it takes forty drops of blood to make one drop of semen." A village study by a British doctor showed this fear of weakness through intercourse to be universally present. Yet deeply embedded in the religion is a worship of fertility reaching back to sexual orgies which were carried on in some communities until very recent times. The Kama Sutra, a complete treatise on sexual techniques, is readily available.

So far as I know, there has not yet been a thorough study along Freudian lines of this strong tension between asceticism and sexuality. Obviously the strong tie to the mother would be a factor, also the fact that the wife who supplies sexual satisfaction is at the same time a mother-substitute. Closeness to the mother's body, so prolonged in childhood, must remain strong in the memory and somehow get mixed in with the new closeness to the wife's body. Indians are as obsessed with breasts—symbol of motherhood—as we are.

This, no doubt, is what gives rise to the coquetry of the sari. One end of the sari is thrown over the left shoulder in such a way that it never quite stays there, is always on the point of slipping down and thus exposing the rondure under the tight-fitting little bodice and the bare midriff. Indian girls are constantly letting the sari fall, catching your eye, and then replacing the sari. No exposure is involved, of course, but the game is played as if something had happened and you are a naughty man. This way you both have your sex and don't have it—you advance and withdraw, entice and forbid, assert and deny.

The mythology is full of sexuality, sometimes disguised, sometimes open in the stories about Krishna the great lover. Often you will see pictures of Krishna and his favorite Radha in various amatory poses, while the story of Krishna stealing all the clothes of the milkmaids while they were bathing in the river is delightedly repeated in art.

The Ramayana, the most popular of Indian epics, is supposed to teach the proper behavior of son to father, brother to brother, husband to wife, and all other family relationships. When a foreigner reads the story, he gets one message over and again: you cannot trust a woman.

"No, no—that is not the point," a very orthodox friend protested. Maybe not, but it keeps saying so. It says, as most epics do, that you cannot trust a woman because you have to—because you are dependent on her not only for life itself and for the lives of your children; you are at her mercy throughout life. The goddess Kali illustrates this. She is both mother goddess and goddess of destruction. From her womb comes life, but into that mysterious place she can somehow also withdraw life. Statues of Kali show her as a woman both sexy and terrible—attractive but capable of destroying man even as she lures him. No doubt the fear of the loss of potency from engaging in intercourse also fits in here. It in turn may be allied to a sense of guilt which comes from the incestuous confusion of wife with mother.

From the head of the household on down, every member has his place according to age and rank. Below the family come the servants with their ranking. Everyone except the head has someone above and someone below him. We wondered about the youngest female child of our sweeper until we discovered that she had a dog. And no doubt he chases cats. Hierarchy must be constraining, but at least you know where you stand.

"Family life was very secure in the old days," an old Brahman told me. "Our whole village area was like one big family. When we were children, we all played together in the big compound, and there was always an old man there whom we feared and respected, who saw that no harm came to us. If anyone needed buttermilk or mango pickles, he knew he could get them free from my father. But now? All this has broken down. The desire for material things and personal gain has taken its place."

We, on the other hand, found that strong family loyalties still exist, dominating in fact the lives of the members. One of our friends had to leave college and take over the management of his family when his father died at forty-five. He picked up the family business and improved it so much that he was able to bring up the eight children, put them all through college, marry off the four sisters, send two of his brothers abroad for graduate work.

"I did it by working from six in the morning until ten at night," he said—not with regret, but proudly. "So now I'm a successful textile merchant. But," he said a little ruefully, "what I wanted to be was a scholar."

Perhaps it was better for him too, for we knew of one scholar—badly underpaid like most teachers—who was trying to support a family of two daughters—one of them married and with three children—his wife, his mother and a sister.

"True, we have very little," he said. "But what does it matter? We love one another."

This sense of the richly shared warmth and affection of a large family, lost to many in the West with the loss first of the economic ties which bound a family together, then of propinquity, and finally of the affection itself seems to be passing in India too, or so the older Indians think. What can replace it?

We in the West have learned to institutionalize some of the old family functions. We join voluntary associations which meet some of our social, economic, political or religious needs. But Indians have not yet learned to do this. Their system is so based upon birth, both for family and caste, that they do not regard voluntary association very seriously. You have to be born into an association if it is to have power. Their sense of the individual is linear rather than interwoven, or rather it is interwoven with family members but not with the wider community. They think of themselves as proceeding out of a former life and passing on eventually to another. We think of ourselves as related to everyone around us—not just to the family but to friends, co-workers, neighbors, schoolmates, even strangers.

So the Hindu's debt and responsibility are to his own past and future, not to society at large. When he does good works it is to assure his future rather than out of a brotherly sense of responsibility for strangers. It appears as if he can both give alms and accept bribes without the same sense of guilt a Westerner feels. Indians are as much individualists as we are, but in a different way. They are quite insistent in getting what they want and they like to monopolize attention—a hang-over no doubt from the days when as children they got all they wanted. Instead of joining others on an equal basis they prefer to start a project of their own, however small. Though the joint family is breaking down, they have not yet found a substitute, as we have, by identifying with and supporting institutions—church, club, welfare organization. This institutionalizing of loyalties for social ends is one of the great achievements of the West which is not yet really assimilated in the East.

So the Indian who grew up in a joint family, but finds himself taking a job far away from it, is somewhat at loose ends. If he is Westernized, he may enjoy the new freedom, the home for himself and his wife, the privacy. If not, he probably feels lonely, isolated, unprotected by the warmth of the family group.

I remember a family party we were invited to in Delhi. When we entered the Western-style living room with its full row of chairs all around the wall, half a dozen people rose to greet us. Others kept coming in until all the chairs and most of the floor had been occupied. Our host kept introducing us:

"My brother—my son's wife—my daughter's son—my aunt's son's daughter—" until we all began laughing and the introduction stopped. Our host was accurate in his introductions, but most Indians find such work difficult because to them cousins are brothers or sisters, so close is the relationship in a joint family.

We never did get that roomful of people very straight in our minds, but essentially it was a family of two brothers and their children's families. One of the brothers had five children, some of whom were already married with children; the other, four. The youngest child of the younger brother was not very different in age from the oldest grandchild of the older brother. In such a family a young man may get the feeling of being very close to the attractive bride of a newly married cousin; in fact, the joint family somewhat makes up for what is denied orthodox Hindus in the way of social contact with the opposite sex.

So we sat in the comfortably, happily crowded room while tea was brought, with no lack of womenfolk to serve it. We ate the hot *pecoras*, the balls of spongy white stuff dripping with syrup, the sturdy squares of milk boiled into candy, the peppery things that look like crumbs of cold cereal.

Then the seven-month-old baby agreed to come to me. He explored my features with a clutching hand. When I handed the baby on, he was passed rapidly about the circle after a brief dandling by each, as if we were passing a dish at table. When the tea things had been cleared away it was easy to tell from the expectant hush that some sort of plan had been concerted. The children's eyes kept sliding from us, their chief focus of interest, to our host. So we knew the signal would come from him.

"Kalyan, can you do a dance for us?" he said.

A dark-eyed boy with a handsome clear brown skin rose from the floor with a smile of pure joy. We had seen enough of India's wonderful dancing to want more. Would it be classical—perhaps Kathakali—or in some modern idiom, we wondered.

Kalyan rose gracefully, effortlessly as a dancer should. The room quieted in anticipation as he took a position with hips cast sideways and arms lifted in graceful curves. "Yes, Kathakali," I decided.

Then he began to move, with arm movements that were purely classical. He also began to sing. It was a moment before I caught up with his accent and made certain. Yes, the words were familiar: "Rock and roll." While the arms continued their graceful gestures, the hips expressed unadulterated Elvis Presley.

Well, we are always being told that we live in an international world, a world without borders. Yet it is still a bit of a shock at times to meet it head-on.

When Kalyan, after many repetitions of those magic words, sank beaming to the floor, eyes turned towards a plain-looking girl in her teens who like many teen-agers wore Punjabi dress—pajamalike pants, a long smock coming below the knees, and a piece of extraneous cloth thrown one way or another around the neck, but used like the end of the sari to keep men interested. It would have taken more than an extraneous piece of cloth to interest men in this girl. But she rose and began to sing. Somehow her plainness dissolved into tenderness. Her voice had thin edges and little depth, but it was soft and plaintive. Her eyes softened with the song, her lips quivered —the contrast between this inner sensitiveness and the outer plainness struck me as terribly sad, sweet and pathetic.

"What was she saying?" I asked when the clapping died down, for her song had been in Hindi.

Our host gave an embarrassed laugh. "She was saying, 'Why do you, unfaithful lover, come back to me in my dreams when you have forsaken me and gone far away?' "

It seemed for her a prophetic song.

Then there was a young fellow with some magic tricks, and a little girl in her school uniform who recited something which I supposed was in Hindi until I at last caught the glimmer of a twinkling little star.

The air had been relaxed by this galaxy of talent; the stiffness between us had gone. We felt ourselves surrounded by the warmth and solidarity of all these good people who so obviously delighted in being a family, in possessing all these talents, in sharing them with the Americans.

"You have a large family?" our host asked us.

"Only one son," we had to confess. But we added, "Our parents lived with us until they died." Indians think Americans heartless. They have heard somewhere that we forsake our parents, who live out their last years in feeble and lonely helplessness. Every Indian I know has sooner or later indicated that he believes this.

As for the one-child family, that is hard for them to understand, too. A Hindu must have a son to survive him and perform the funeral rites. Until very recently child mortality was heavy, and in an economy that is still overwhelmingly agricultural, children are the only form of social security. The more children, the more likelihood of being well cared for in your old age. To have six or more children, therefore, was a sound investment.

The Rockefeller team which undertook an investigation of birth control began by handing out foam tablets all around and instructing women in the use of them as contraceptives. They accepted the tablets and went away. Several months later, when the same women were interviewed again, they were asked:

"You have used the tablets?"

"No."

"Why not?"

"I have only three children. I must have five."

The problem of birth control in India is not one of techniques but of motivation—a fact which has been ignored by most of the writing and much of the programming of birth control. Indians want babies—just like Americans, who on a per capita basis are at this moment slightly ahead of Indians in the world-wide race to overpopulate the globe. In the past fifty years India's population has shot up from 235,000,000 to 438,000,000. At the present rate it will *double* in the next twenty-five years, by which time it will be beyond any possibility of control except the grim one of famine.

Even if present-day contraceptives were available, most Indians would be too poor to buy them, or too uneducated to use them if provided free. Male sterilization is being encouraged and in some areas—Madras and Bombay and Kashmir, for example—has made good headway. Those submitting to the operation get it free, together with a cash bonus, six days' vacation if they work for the government, and free transportation.

Having recently sponsored a meeting with India's head man on birth control, Colonel Bishen Lal Raina, as our speaker, we decided to see what could be done with our sweeper, a man thrice married and with unnumbered children by the first two, six by the third. The sixth having just arrived, we thought it a strategic time to suggest sterilization.

"I couldn't do that," he said. "With all those children depending on me, I can't take chances with my health. But I'll ask my wife if she would do it." Wives in his experience were apparently more expendable. The next day he came back with the answer.

"She wouldn't think of it," he said. "She wants lots more babies."

That, rather than methodology, is the real problem. She wouldn't use the rhythm method or a pill. She wants babies.

The only solution to this, and perhaps to the world situation, is a chemical which, added to staple foods, would affect us all. But powerful forces would be arrayed against it. Meanwhile India is doomed to ever-deepening poverty, depletion of resources and rising unemployment, and I marvel at the ability to laugh, to relax, to live on into the next day, the next season, always with more mouths to feed, always with less food per mouth. What can we really do to help India when every advance in medicine or agriculture or industry is eroded by the rising population? Anything which does not touch this root problem seems a waste of time. We are all being engulfed, and nothing we do will have any significance or value if we continue to let the flood wash over us as it is now doing. But we don't want to lower our birth rate either, so how can we ask it of others?

A sense of this heightened the poignancy of our afternoon with that big family, so warm in its togetherness, so eagerly sharing what it had with us, so happy in bridging the gap between one culture and another. This is one of the real privileges of life in our time, far outweighing the awkward moments when you are not sure whether it is polite to refuse something, or whether you should shake hands with the women, or make a joke of something which may turn out to be sacrosanct. Yet in India it seems always safe to use humor—that sure cultural solvent, so able to break down barriers and create the sense of emotional unity without which there can be no cultural exchange.

Humor is in a sense a neutral emotion. It does not involve us, as for instance patriotism or religious belief does, in adopting as our own, symbols which clearly belong to someone else. It does not float us into dangerous waters as love might. Or hate. It establishes at once our common humanity and our capacity for feeling and perceiving, for feeling affirmatively and at the same time perceiving critically, without committing us to agreement on a level where differing cultural backgrounds would tarnish our agreement with a slight dishonesty since we cannot out of different cultures evoke identical emotional responses. In literature, in religion, in music the background of cultures varies too widely for complete transference of response. But with humor, especially nonverbal humor, we do come close to a universal language—one which mixes emotional warmth with a sharper edge of intellectual shrewdness.

So, because we had laughed together over the antics of the children and shared that deeper humor which wells up out of simple good feeling when even the belch of a baby or the knocking over of a picture by a sudden breeze may seem funny, we felt that we had been gathered into this family, been warmed by its care and allowed to look in upon its firm, enduring bonds of love.

In India the family is often the world—the effective universe of its members. They may move out into the world of strangers or business associates or classmates. But the family is always there to return to— a womb of comfort, a mothering embrace.

TWELVE

A Pretty Homely Virgin

WANTED—I read in the Sunday paper (the major news-papers are written in English):

Well settled Punjabi Khatri match for fair-skinned, pretty, homely, foreign-educated virgin, 22, appearing B.A. final, healthy & well-versed in household affairs, sewing & embroidery, from respect-able vegetarian family. Dowry-seekers please need not contact. Box 4003.

It was only one among several hundred such ads; every Sunday paper runs several pages of them. They make far more fascinating and instructive reading than the front page.

You learn, for instance, that caste and region are still important, that education must be precisely described because couples have to be carefully matched in this respect, that the dowry system is still in operation, that vegetarianism conveys status, and that a girl can be both pretty and homely at the same time. Homely, of course, means a good homemaker.

But why do beautiful virgins have to be advertised? Far as we have carried the art of advertising in the United States, we have not yet turned this product over to Madison Avenue.

We had the good fortune to make friends with a young man who had just returned from several years of study in England and who was about to go through the agony of marriage, so our view of Indian marriage customs became intimate, though without the terror of personal involvement.

The moment he returned from England Arun's family began pressing him to marry. He was not in a hurry, and he kept trying to put them off. But they insisted. When the proper time comes, you get married. Not to do so reflects on the whole family—suggests it's not good enough to attract a bride or groom.

So the search began. In fact it had begun long before Arun left England though he didn't know it. For in a country where young people don't date or even walk down the street together, finding a mate is the family's job.

The family considers everything—health, appearance, height, education, caste of course, temperament, recreational interests, family background. Skin color is important in a country where the variation goes all the way from "wheat-colored" to black, with a premium on fairness. A mother, introducing her little sons to us, said "This is the light one—and this is the dark one." Color-consciousness is ever-present, the sensitivity to slightly different shades surprising. So the bride, if possible, should be fair. If not, her father will probably have to pay a bigger dowry.

Arun came to us in misery one day to say that his family had found a girl.

"What's so bad about that?" we asked.

"I have to go and meet her tonight."

"You don't like meeting girls?"

"Well, mostly it's her family I'll meet. They may bring her in or they may not. If they do, we have to talk to each other in their presence. After twenty minutes or so—maybe less—she'll leave."

"Well, that's not too bad for the first time." We had taken on the role of encouragers—apparently this was what Arun needed from us.

"What do you mean, first time?" he said. "It's the last time too. The next time I see her will be when we walk around the marriage fire." Then he exploded over the barbarity of the old marriage customs.

With our urging, he went off to the ordeal. The next day he phoned to say that he had turned her down. "They lied when they said she spoke English," he said. "Her English is worse than my Hindi." Arun was proud of his English, as he had a right to be, and no doubt exaggerated his lack of Hindi.

So the family went to work again, and in a week or two Arun came back to be fortified against the next interview. This time he had insisted on having a private talk with the girl, and for a wonder had won his point.

He phoned us the next day. "She wants to have five children, and she has no interest in going to England." Arun hoped to return to work in England some day. So that took care of number two.

After that we lost count. Sometimes Arun had to go to Lucknow or Allahabad now, for apparently the family was running out of candidates nearby. As word got around of Arun's rejections, it was no doubt harder to find a compliant family, because a girl who was turned down this way would lose value on the market and be harder to dispose of. Also her dowry would have to be raised.

Finally we were sitting over a cup of tea one Sunday afternoon when I tossed the paper to him.

"Why don't you look through these?" I said, indicating the ads.

I thought he would throw the paper at me. Instead, he picked it up, gave a casual glance, and then began to study it with respectful attention.

"Here's one," he read. " 'English-educated B.A. virgin of Agrawal Goya family—' no, that won't do. Wrong subcaste."

He worked his way down through the columns.

"Why don't you put an ad in yourself?" I suggested. "Something like this: 'Wanted for handsome, English-educated, M.A. Agrawal who has already turned down sixteen pretty homely virgins, a buxom wealthy widow who wants to take him back to England with her.' "

Arun didn't think it was funny. In fact he wasn't even listening.

"Are you through with this paper?" he asked.

"I'm through with that page anyway," I assured him. "I've already got a wife."

He dropped us a line during the week to say that he wouldn't see us the following week end as he was going to Ahmedabad to look over a prospect.

"What happened to that one?" we asked when he returned.

"Our horoscopes didn't work out."

"Horoscopes?"

"I know you think it silly," he said, "but the families would never permit a marriage where the horoscopes were so hopeless as ours. My stars and hers didn't mix at all. Too bad, really. She was quite a nice girl."

Every week now we read the ads diligently, hoping to find the right girl for Arun. The more we read, the greater the hazards appeared. Not only caste, subcaste, color, education, language, horoscope, birthplace and all the rest, but also diet. No matter how pretty the girl, you have to find out: Does she eat meat? For eating meat is regarded as filthy by Brahmans, and vegetarianism seems to be growing as other groups attempt to raise their status by adding these marks of high caste to their own customs. Many a potential marriage must be wrecked over a weakness for flesh—not of woman, but of animal.

Then, one Sunday evening, came a call from Arun.

"Well, I did it," he said, sounding like someone who had just murdered his mother. "I told her all the reasons why she should refuse me, but she took me anyway." She had said little but yes or no, he complained, and after fifteen minutes he had had to decide whether she was his partner for life.

"Is she a pretty homely virgin?" we said, using the phrase that had become standard in our work as marriage counselors.

"Not very," he said.

"Not very which?"

"I don't see how I can go through with it," he said. "What do I know about her, after all?"

"Why don't you write to her? At least you can get to know each other that way."

"Are you kidding? That would be tantamount to—to—well, I don't know what. No decent couple have *any* contact with each other until they are married."

So he continued to agonize and to threaten all sorts of mad things —fleeing to England, pleading incurable illness, bankruptcy or loss of caste; until the family got him so involved in preparations that his jitters were channeled into constant activity. He had to visit all his relatives, consult on the selection of presents, discuss finances, look for an apartment (he had insisted that they live alone), buy clothes, draw up lists of invitees. We got the impression that after his long exile in England and his long resistance, he was enjoying this return to the favor and warmth of the family and the central importance he now had in their affairs. His manner was changed from that of the bored man of the world to that of the wide-eyed novice—even of the little boy a week before Christmas.

Several weeks later he invited us to his engagement party.

"Wonderful," we said. "Now we'll have a chance to meet the bride."

"You will not. The bride will be at home where she belongs. This will be at my father's house."

After weaving our way through several narrow alleys, we came to the spacious old brick bungalow where Arun's family lived. Indian Gothic in style, it was a relic of Queen Victoria's days. People were swarming over the veranda when we arrived, walking in and out of the house, drinking soft drinks out of bottles and in general acting like people who felt at home—which they were, since most of them belonged to Arun's family. Arun himself darted out to meet us, introduced us to his father, and darted off again. We noticed now that only the men were in evidence. But a cackling from a nearby room made it clear that the women had their own assembly.

An hour or two passed. We walked out to the garden and back, held a few conversations with people we did not know, went back to the veranda.

At last a car drove up, loaded inside and out with bundles. A youngish man got out, then an obese man in a dhoti who turned out to be a priest, and a chap in a dirty shirt who must have been a servant since he did all the carrying. Out came basket after basket of food—fruits, nuts, sweet cakes. Then more baskets and bundles, all carried into a small room, the floor of which had been covered with sheets and a blanketlike rug. They piled the foods in high pyramids on metal trays, then placed all the other gifts—a complete outfit of clothes for Arun, a radio, floor fan, jewelry.

We were now invited in for the ceremony and sat chockablock on the floor, garlanded as we entered. Arun, garlanded and with a Gandhi cap set jauntily on his head, sat cross-legged at one end, looking both nervous and somehow pleased. The priest began chanting, Arun's father handed cold drinks to any who would take them, and the chatting and smoking went on unabated. Meanwhile the priest broke up a flower which he scattered over Arun, then passed more petals around to the chief mourners who also had a go at him. Now the priest with his thumb put a tilak mark with red powder on Arun's forehead, then tied a thread to his wrist. Arun tied one on his—for the girl, presumably.

The ladies of the household had meanwhile come to the door behind Arun and crowded into the space behind the screen in front of which he was sitting. They had not slackened the pace nor volume of their chatter, so no one heard what the priest was saying.

Arun, who seemed to be both amused and embarrassed by it all, managed to create the impression that he had simply happened in on the show and was in no way involved in it—even when they placed before him a tray containing several thousand rupees in crisp new notes.

"We didn't ask for any dowry," he told us later, "but they would have been ashamed not to give one."

Dowries often run fantastically high compared to the family's means, for it is the man who has to be wooed, pursued, cornered and caught. Even poor village families habitually spend from six months' to a year's income marrying off a daughter. Even one daughter is a burden; several can be a disaster.

The engagement party with its elaborate gifts was only a warm-up for the wedding which followed several weeks later. The bride's home had been transformed as if for a carnival. Strings of colored lights led the way from the street up the driveway, past a huge tent of gaily colored canvas filled with hundreds of seats, and up to the house itself, the front of which was covered with lights, as were the trees before it. It was just turning dusk when we arrived. The lights came on as if to greet us, transforming the old bungalow into a storybook palace. Since every occasion—a wedding, an embassy reception, a public festival, a cornerstone laying—calls for the tent and the lighted trees, Delhi always seems to be in a carnival mood. At times all the trees in the big circular park, Connaught Place, are lighted in colors from tip to trunk, as if every tree were a Christmas tree.

Some of the lights on the house began to flash and simulate the whirling of pinwheels. We stood there, admiring them like children. Suddenly we jumped and whirled around as if we had been shot.

A bagpipe band in full regalia—in kilts and with the tiger-skin covering which is regulation for the bass drummer—had struck up its opening tune. The tune was as authentic as the kilts—pure Scotch. After playing a few pieces, it departed toward the road. We followed, because we knew it would be escorting Arun to the house.

At the road the band joined a group of men who bore upon their heads large acetylene lamps decorated with glass bangles. We all straggled down the street a block or two to where Arun had just left the questionable safety of a Delhi taxi for the dubious refuge of a white horse's back. At least he was trying to get onto its back. Having never mounted a horse before, he nearly ended up by getting aboard wrong way to. Someone handed him a child. It appears to be auspicious to have one ride with the groom.

We all formed into a ragged procession, including the usual mob of street urchins, and with pipes skirling and lights held high we pranced down the middle of the road, stopping traffic, drawing people out of their houses, and attracting every barking dog in the neighborhood. When the youngsters had infiltrated until they had command of the whole procession, someone shooed them away. But it was like waving flies away from sugar—they were soon in charge again, and each time they came back there seemed to be twice as many.

By the time we had stopped for several musical renditions the sudden night had come on, and the bungalow threw a blaze of light to the sky as we approached. Its crenelated roof line gave it the look of a castle and one could for a moment imagine the ancient warrior-groom riding up for a bride who would be won half as booty, half as a pledge of peace between uneasy neighbors.

As Arun got off his horse he practically fell into the arms of the bride's father. The two families were meeting and greeting in a pattern so elaborate that we could not be quite sure what was happening. (In other weddings they opened the festivities by pinning money on each other, but that did not happen here.) Caught up in the general hospitality we were swept into the great shamiana (tent), where we were garlanded with marigolds and seated in overstuffed chairs among the honored guests.

Several shabbily dressed priests got hold of Arun, reddened his forehead, and led him to the front of the tent where they handed him bits of flowers and other things we could not identify. No one paid any attention. A loud-speaker was blaring music, and members of the bride's family were passing around cigarettes, pan and tasty seeds.

Suddenly everything stopped and a recess for tea was declared. It was served from a long table loaded with the usual goodies—pepper-hot cakes fried in deep fat, balls dripping with syrup, mounds of cashew nuts.

Arun himself saw to it that we had seats on the front row before the temporary arbor of banana leaves and marigolds where the marriage would take place. There seemed to be no competition for these seats, as most of the guests went back into the tent and ignored the ceremony.

To get an idea of the wedding from here on, you have to imagine a church where the bride and groom are seated in the chancel with priests mumbling around them, the choir singing simultaneously, and the congregation with its backs turned to the altar, watching a troupe of cabaret entertainers singing and dancing in the vestibule.

The bedraggled priests squatted in the arbor and began chanting, meanwhile playing with matches until they finally lit a fire of little sticks which they kept dousing with ghee. The bride now came out of the house in a gorgeous green-and-gold sari with which she had covered up her head and most of her face. She also squatted in the arbor, but no one paid any attention to her. The guests had seen too many weddings before. Meanwhile the bride and groom had to be prompted every moment by the priests who otherwise were chanting in Sanskrit which no one understood. Children ran up to look at the fire or thrust their faces between bride and groom; waiters wandered in and out with glasses of water; members of the family kept pressing cigarettes and pan upon the guests, and in one corner of the tent someone started a card game.

Arun had told us that the ceremony usually went on for six or eight hours, but he had given strict orders that he wanted this one as short as it could be cut. So after no more than half an hour or so of the chanting and fire-building, the bride and groom rose and began to walk around the fire while the smoke billowed in their faces. The bride went first, then Arun took the lead, holding a scarf tied to the end of her sari. Several times the hem of her diaphanous sari scuffed the ashes of the fire and I wondered whether we were going to combine wedding with suttee.

Then she disappeared into the house again. The wedding was over. We were allowed to visit her for a moment in the room where she sat surrounded with her feminine relatives and the pots, pans clothes, household linens, lithographs of the gods and other items which she would carry with her. She looked scared and, in accordance with tradition, behaved as if she were attending the funeral of a close relative.

We emerged in time to be led to another tent where an elaborate wedding dinner was to be served. We were lucky to make the first sitting. To discourage large expenditures on weddings, government has decreed that only fifty may be seated at dinner. So they seat fifty—once, twice, if necessary three times. Arun himself came and sat at our table.

"Don't you have other duties?" we asked. "Please don't bother about us."

He insisted he had no other duties. We had felt that he was rather detached from the proceedings anyway—not only because he had lived abroad but because since marriage was so importantly a union of families the role of the groom seemed to be rather symbolic than essential. The marriage might be his, but the wedding belonged to the family.

And what could we learn from the tone in which the wedding had been pitched? With us a wedding, though brief, is sacred. No disturbance, no ugliness must mar its holy perfection. But a fourth of these sacred obligations end in divorce. In India a wedding seems like a unit of only slightly organized chaos. There is great show and display and vast hospitality, but little sanctity, dignity or good order. These, obviously, are not important. What matters is to assemble friends and relatives and treat them generously; they are more important than the bride and groom; to make them welcome and do everything for them is somehow or other the purpose of the gathering. A fourth of these marriages will *not* end in divorce. (I did see one village study, however, which asserted that 89 out of 300 marriages had ended in separation and/or extralegal reshufflings.)

The wedding was not over when this party ended. A family celebration would follow at the groom's home. Then after several days the bride would return to her home. The groom must go after her—apparently to prove he really wanted her—and only then would he take her to their own home. By then I should think he would be too exhausted to care; especially when you remember that all this has gone on as between strangers, the couple having never had a decent chat before being thrown together in public.

We went home wondering what sort of marriage this would be. How could the first congress be anything but horrible, without any foundation of common interest and nothing but fear and strangeness?

"You are supposed to be in love before marriage; we learn to love each other after marriage—that is the only difference," a friend told us. We thought it a sundering difference.

A week later Arun brought his Shanti to call on us. It was really our first look at her, and we were happy to see she was not wearing the heavy nose jewelry and other disfiguring facial adornments which a bride must put on. We sensed immediately that they were pleased with each other, had learned the saving grace of humor as a way to accommodate themselves, had found life together much less fearful than they had feared (Indian girls generally get no sex instruction), and wanted us to know that all was well.

"After all, I could never have picked so well for myself," Arun said to me in private.

"Pretty homely virgin?" I wanted to ask him. But I thought I had better not.

THIRTEEN

Land of Living Saints

In India I met my first saint. He became, as he is to hundreds all over that vast and yearning land, a friend.

How shall I put Gurdial on paper? Put him on a page and he would rise and walk away—to greet a friend, to care for someone who needs him, to retire to meditation.

Rather, watch him come into a room—his thin khadi trousers and long flowing smock of faded saffron, his white beard and halo of white hair encircling a rosy face still young with wonder and joy but mostly with love, his arms outstretched to greet you and his big deep voice booming out of a small body. His is the face of a cherubic Santa Claus—a role which he played to perfection for us when we gathered the twenty children of our household for a Christmas party. It is, in fact, perpetual Christmas when he is in the house. He carries that kind of joy with him, and spreads it, and infects everyone else. To be with him is a religious experience.

Gurdial spent twenty-two years as a teacher at Santiniketan, Rabindranath Tagore's college. The way he entered into this work gives a true hint of the man.

As he entered the commons room of the college where he was studying, a crowd of boys were reading a paper which had just come in, one of them holding it high overhead so that all could see. Gurdial glanced at it as he passed by, was caught by the face of a man peering out from the page. The man was Tagore, world-famous poet, educator, internationalist.

124

"I must attach myself to that man," Gurdial heard his inner self saying.

With the kind of impulse which he was to recognize later on as divinely guided, he wrote to Tagore, who invited him to come all the way to Bengal, over a thousand miles away. But Gurdial's father felt unable to spare him; he had to finish college and begin to earn.

Then he became sick "unto death." They had placed him on the floor for the final washing when his father said, "Is there any last wish we can fulfill for you?"

"That I may be allowed to visit Tagore if I live," said Gurdial.

The promise was given, Gurdial miraculously recovered, and he did make the long trip. But after he had reached Santiniketan, it was not easy to see Tagore. Gurdial had arranged to be away from home only a few days. He had his return ticket. The days quickly slipped away, and from day to day he was put off. Finally he packed his bag and was ready to leave for the station when he was told to come—Tagore could see him for five minutes.

He went into a room where Tagore sat at one end, bearded, white-robed, remote. Gurdial waited in the middle of the room. Tagore looked up and remained looking. Time went by—one, two, three, four minutes. Gurdial was shaking with embarrassment and disappointment. The secretary said, "One minute more."

Then Tagore, stretching out his arms, said:

"I have long known you. Come and stay with me."

After returning home to settle his affairs, Gurdial came back to Santiniketan, spent twenty-two years there as a teacher, and became the bridge (as both men told him) between Gandhi and Tagore. Gandhi often called him out to help with rural training programs and other village work.

"What was the difference between the two men?" I once asked him. The answer, true as it was, showed as much of Gurdial as of the two men he loved.

"With Gandhi it was the love of truth. With Tagore, the truth of love." With Gurdial, I think, it is both. He has helped thousands of young people, in a time when orthodox religion is eroding, to understand the deeper roots of spirit. His kind of spirit cannot be displaced or uprooted by truth—it is only strengthened. His outgoing, all-embracing love calls for no metaphysic; it is so spontaneous, so much himself that even the most disillusioned of university students cannot fail to see authentic divinity in it and thus know that whatever he feels within himself, there is true religion in others. Born a Hindu and retaining all the depth and richness of that religion, Gurdial was so attracted to the Christian emphasis upon love and service that he became a Quaker. In him the two religions flow together in one clear, sparkling stream, giving us a glimpse of what may happen some day when the great religions learn to support and reinforce one another.

From both streams Gurdial has drunk the full draught of God's presence in life. He has given up all property, traveling from place to place as he is called (those who can do so send him carfare), staying wherever he is invited, eating his modest bit of food wherever he may be, devoting himself entirely to the things of the mind and spirit. Most Indian holy men are rather severe or forbidding or withdrawn, but Gurdial's outgoing, enveloping love is his own. It comes in part from his literal acceptance of the Christian doctrine of love, unhampered by any overlay of Western custom which may keep us from fully expressing the love we are invited to join and share as Christians. Though an intellectual, Gurdial has that direct intuition of God which requires no intellectual justification. This again, though deep in Hindu tradition, has been strengthened by the Quaker insight which also looks directly to experience rather than to rite, priest or book for religious understanding.

God speaks directly to Gurdial, and has ever since he was a young man. He has never courted this or made anything of it; many perhaps who know Gurdial do not know of the voice which comes to him. Like this:

He is awakened in the middle of the night—suddenly, completely, as if a voice has just called him. He rises up on his bed. "Get up, Gurdial," a voice seems to be saying. Still in his pajama suit (pajamas are also worn outdoors in India), he walks down the two flights of steps, outdoors, through narrow alleys this way and that, not knowing where he is, never having been here before, to a house strange to him where he climbs two flights to a closed door.

Here he hesitates. But the voice tells him to knock, and he knocks. After a silence, a harsh voice calls out: "What do you want?"

"A weary traveler is at your door."

"Why must you bother me at this hour?" But the custom of giving food or rest to a pilgrim is strong. A woman opens the door and peers out.

"Water, please," says Gurdial, still not knowing for what purpose he has come.

She lets him in and goes off to another room for the water. As he sits waiting, Gurdial looks in another direction towards an inner room where, in a dim light, a younger woman is trying to hang herself with a rope. He rushes in and pulls her down.

"Let me die, let me die," she says. "Have I not been miserable enough?"

Reluctantly she and her mother then told him how she had been victimized by a man who had married and abandoned her for another woman.

"Promise that you will wait twenty-four hours before going through with this," Gurdial said. Then he went off to a hospital where he thought he might get her in as a student nurse. The class was just being closed, there was one vacancy, and the course would start the next day. But forty rupees must be paid in advance. Gurdial had no forty rupees. He borrowed the money, enrolled the girl, and returned to tell her.

"My daughter handle bedpans!" said the mother. But the girl wanted to go. She turned out to be an excellent nurse.

Gurdial often receives messages, as if they were written on a blackboard in silver, about people he has never heard of. A certain man has tried everywhere to get the five thousand rupees he needs to save his business. To Gurdial comes his name, and that of a man in another city who will lend him the money. Gurdial sends off a telegram to this effect—and the man gets the money.

One day when he was working as an editor, he had just finished and sent off his copy and was relaxing in his chair when suddenly he jumped up to push back a car that was about to go over a cliff. The experience was as real to him as if it had happened. A few days later he had a letter from a cousin:

"Thank you for saving my life. I was learning to drive and nearly went over the edge of a cliff when I saw you rise up in front of me and turn me back."

To snatch these few small stories out of the whole depth and breadth of Gurdial's life is unfair and somehow cheapening. They belong with all the rest of him; they must be read within the full text. They are the by-products of a life that is lived in the strength of the spirit.

"How do you account for these experiences?" I asked him.

"I don't account for them. Better people, far more spiritual and worthy, lack this power. Why does it come to me? I can only say that the all-knowing power somehow, on these occasions, communicates to and through me. I am the channel but not the stream; I am the wire but not the current."

I do not want to pretend that there are many people like Gurdial in India, for to me Gurdial is unique—a man in whom God has built a nest. Yet this is not unique either, for in India as elsewhere God has built his nest in every man. Only most of us do not sing, we do not fly, as if this were so. Gurdial has the song (he sings beautifully, by the way—songs that come to him by the same intuition) and the arching flight. He provides the bird—the live, warm singing body—by which we know the nest is there.

God seems very close in India, an experience that may at first be unsettling to Westerners. It is not the temples with their butter-smeared idols and their offerings of flowers and food, nor the way-side stones marking some hang-over from the worship of snakes, nor the frequent and colorful festivals which draw their millions of celebrants. It is rather in the matter-of-fact way in which the people

take God for granted—not wondering, speculating, defining, an-
alyzing, doubting, studying, learning, hoping, and then beginning
the cycle all over again. No, in India religion is felt, not debated.
And in the end this is the only way religion can be taken.

"In India, God and man are not severed as they are in the West,"
Mr. Nehru once said to me.

When my wife took care of the gardener's wife during some minor
illness and cured her, Mali said simply to Arjan, without selfcon-
sciousness or any sense of the unusual: "Ah, she is a god."

Indian culture assumes God without intellectual difficulty. There
is a mental set toward wholeness, universality and oneness which
gathers everything into the Godhead without embarrassment. In
the West we adopted the law, stated by William of Ockham in the
fourteenth century, that "Plurality is not to be admitted save in case
of necessity," and with it forged our science. In India, the law sub-
sumes all things under God with equal applicability.

Here religion drives inward and with a rich emotional environing
where ours drives outward toward good works. If a man does good,
we credit him with religion without probing his motives or feelings.
Indians regard the inner feeling, the emotional involvement, as the
real thing. If they find that, they do not look too much for outer
manifestations such as works. They think of religion in its personal,
individual significance where we tend to value it in its institutional
form—in the church, the congregation, the Sunday school, the social
service work, the ethical teaching as applied to life and its problems.

Perhaps, then, only India could nurture such a man as Gurdial.
For first he must be what he is—a man of God. That in itself is a
great thing. But there must also be a society which takes the man
of God for granted—which recognizes him when he appears, believes in the possibility of his appearance, and honors him. In India
there is this comfortable environment, this acceptance. For Gurdial,
yes, but also for all kinds of holy men, most of whom would seem
dubious to us and whom we would reject as cranks and crackpots.

One day while we were at lunch a sudden trumpet blew right behind me on the veranda. What was it? A holy man dressed in a

few rags, his forehead covered with markings, a begging bowl in his hand. I felt as if the last trumpet had really sounded for me; I was incensed at this invasion of privacy. Instead, I should have been grateful for the opportunity the visit of this holy man afforded to make a gift and gain merit in the future.

Wherever Gurdial goes, or other holy men, families feel it an honor to take him in. Rest houses have been built all over India by families concerned that pilgrims and holy men should have places to stay. And pilgrimages to holy places are as common in India today as they were in Europe in Chaucer's day.

The quest for religious truth still goes on. The whole concept of life is based upon the assumption that men seek religious truth. So life is divided into four ashramas, or periods. The first (brahmacharya) is that of a student studying under a guru (teacher) and living with him in an ashram (retreat) where there are no sexual stimuli. The second (grihastha) is that of the active worker and householder who marries and raises a family. In the third stage one becomes a vanaprastha, or hermit of the forest, renouncing sex though perhaps accompanied by a wife, but engaged in religious seeking. In the final stage one becomes a sannyasi, severing all ties with society and dwelling in constant contemplation.

The search goes on everywhere and always. A student came and talked to me, as if he were possessed, about his search for God. He had so much to say that he could not speak very coherently, and much of what he said sounded orthodox and commonplace, but to him it was obviously revelation. He talked steadily for hours, stayed to supper and still talked—and all the while spoke about overcoming the ego!

In a city not far from Delhi, a young college instructor who was not very happy in his work took a notion to sit under a tree and think about the meaning of life. With anyone who came along he would discuss God and the gods (for there are many in India) and the next life. Soon he had quite a following. Then he decided not to talk at all. The following grew larger.

"What a shame," his mother would say to the neighbors, "my boy sitting there in touch with the gods and no shelter."

So they built him a shelter. Still he sat. After a while he began to talk again and to perform pujas (rituals). By now his following was immense. His fame as a holy man had spread round about. The faithful built an ashram so that they might live with him, and a temple for his rites, and a horribly effective public address system with which he bombards the ears of faithful and indifferent alike for miles around at daylight and at dusk.

Everywhere you see men who have entered the third phase of life. They have retired from work, turned over the family responsibilities to the eldest son, entered an ashram—there are thousands of them throughout India—put on the saffron robe, and now, as one old man told me "are learning how to die." Spindly but spry, his forehead covered with yellow powder, he lived in an ashram near our house. As we came to know him, he shared with us ideas which are so typical of the religious approach that they will serve for all.

"I rise at three in the ashram," he told us. "Then I walk down to the river in the dark and bathe. I bring water back from the Jumna to pour on the lingam in our temple. The lingam [a stone phallus] in our temple represents Shiva, the god of destruction. But Brahma and Vishnu, the creator and preserver, are there as well as the destroyer. The three go together, like your Trinity of father, son and virgin mother."

There was no time to correct his error, for the account ran on:

"After pouring the water I meditate in my cell, have a cup of hot milk for breakfast, and read the Gita. At noon I have my regular meal of vegetables, and at night a cup of milk again."

"How do you meditate?"

"By thinking of the nothingness that was before man, which is God. The perfect form of God is the void before life was, and to this all will return. Life is only a dream, an illusion, from which we pass into the reality of nothingness."

"Do you think of Shiva as a person or a symbol?"

"As a symbol—not a historic person. God is in everything; God is everything, but one can worship him in many forms. Since God is all, how does it matter in what form we worship him?"

This is the crux of the eclectic, permissive Indian mind which hospitably sees the one in the all, welcomes religious insight from every quarter, and readily assimilates all beliefs. Thus the bewildering Olympus of gods great and small, of creators who in turn had to be created, of destroyers who are also creators, of gods suddenly dissolving before your eyes from one thing into another even in the process of being described. Every form of religious practice is current in India, from the most abstract and intellectual philosophizing of Dr. Radhakrishnan to animal sacrifice and orgies reaching their summit in sexual intercourse and in a communion in which all partake of the "male and female semen."

"What iss Hinduism?" we heard a lecturer propose to himself and to us.

"Iss not ritual, iss not church, iss not savior, iss not personal god, iss not creed."

What iss? We came away from the lecture still not knowing.

One evening a group of college instructors gathered with us for a talk about the universals in religion. It never got off the ground. At the first sally the group got to arguing about Hinduism—whether or not it is a religion. I had expected them to take their own religion as known and to go on to something else. Not at all. They fought every inch of the ground and could hardly bear to listen to one another. Usually half a dozen were talking rapidly and continuously. The group never did agree that Hinduism either is or is not a religion, that it includes belief in God or what gods it includes, or that it is or is not exclusively Indian. (Of course they knew it had spread long ago to South Asia, but in argument you never concede points easily!) So it is apparently about as impossible for Hindus as for Christians to agree on what or who they are, or on what or whom they stand for. They accepted with some enthusiasm Toynbee's suggestion that Hinduism is an inclusive religion as contrasted with the exclusivism of Christianity and Islam, but when I inquired why, then, it was often impossible for a Christian or even a Hindu untouchable to enter a Hindu temple, they traced this to ignorance.

The group was still warming up for what looked like a major explosion when we left around midnight, but although no agreements had been reached, we concluded that most of them would accept as Hindu the basic ideas of Karma (the moral economy which says that you pay for your deeds or are rewarded for them, even though this may happen in a future life), dharma (the moral law), Brahma (creator god), in the Vedas as holy books, in certain universal rituals (basically concerned with pollution and purification, it seems to me), and India as the motherland. Clearly, Hinduism has kept its contact with the days when religion and state were one, under a king-priest whose semidivine nature guaranteed safety to the people and the land. The continuing concern with pollution and purity (to be looked at later under ideas of health) also suggests the fear, so common in human history, of losing grace and power and bringing down misfortune on the land.

The day after the discussion, one of the instructors told me: "We all like to argue, but we know well enough what the fundamentals of Hinduism are—ahimsa (nonviolence), the oneness of the world and the presence of God in all, the renewal of life through rebirth, the way of giving up the world and retiring to a simple life of contemplation."

Said a wise old man: "If Jesus were asked which Christian sect he acknowledged, he would say all, since all try to follow him. So God, with all religions and with atheists. They may disown him, but he will not—he cannot—disown them, for they are a part of him." That comes closer to catching the spirit of Hinduism—indeed of all religion—than any further defining is likely to bring us.

To summarize anything as ancient, as complicated and as contradictory—perhaps purposely contradictory for philosophical reasons as well as out of plain confusion—as Hinduism is clearly impossible. At the village level there is a confused mingling of primitive animism, superstition and belief in magic mixed together with the worship of local as well as the major gods. The better educated reject the magic, the anthropomorphic conceptions, the superstition, and concentrate upon devotional exercises of prayer and meditation.

A compulsion towards cleanliness inevitably leads the deeply religious to ascetic practices—celibacy or abstention from sexual intercourse, fasting, rigid diet free of meat, going without sleep, the practice of yoga (more about this under the subject of health). It is widely believed that a truly holy man who practices all the austerities can see what is happening afar off, transfer himself by thought to another place, even make an airplane fall from the sky.

Of course one expects more from a holy man than this. A true dharmatma (righteous man) is expected to be pious, careful in the observation of ritual, and given to visiting holy places. But he is also expected to do something for the unfortunates of this world, too—to give food to the poor, take good care of his family, be hospitable to guests, and look out for the welfare of the neighborhood and society. Piety and practical virtue should travel together.

One great difference between Indian charity and Western is that in India the thing is still personal, not institutionalized. We tend to make our contribution through some organization or society set up to perform a certain kind of good work. Because salvation is so personal a thing, and because it is tied to karma and the wheel of rebirth, an Indian sees his duty much more personally. Beggars flourish only where there are people to give to them. To place a copper among the filthy rags in the leper's cart is probably more satisfactory than to give ten rupees to someone who is collecting for a leprosarium which you may never see and which possibly your money will never reach. So each man is likely to start his own charity—whether he goes out to do penitential street sweeping in the slums, or feeds the birds or ants, or starts a little ashram, or begins to edit his own little religious paper. The country is full of these things. As a Quaker who has been accustomed to having a "concern" I found it a little unsettling to be in a country where everyone had one! Which led me to be grateful, among other things, for the fact that there is no country that is all Quakers.

Another difference is that life being of one web, there are no artificial barriers separating religion from aesthetics, from health rules, from politics, from caste, from occupation. The false compartmentalizations of the West have no acceptance here. Thus it is possible for an erotic dance, defecation (as part of purification), fasting, avoiding contact with untouchables, giving alms, reading the holy books, joining a religiously-aligned political party—all to be drawn together. We have refined and etherealized religion until we have refined the life out of it. (Revivals prove the point.) Indians still feel religion in their bowels. Religion is not only part of life; it is life.

Because India is an ancient land, it has known every form of religious experience. At each stage of enlightenment the previous form has been incorporated, not discarded. All the principal gods have their animals which temple sculpture shows them riding upon—an anthropomorphic conception of deity imposed upon an earlier animistic one. So every religious idea rides upon the back of another. The richness of Indian religion is one of accretion, not of a harmonious or consistent system. In the Upanishads, God

1) creates the universe from his own substance and then enters into it as a spider presides over his web
2) pervades the universe as salt does the ocean
3) is identical with the universe
4) is identical with the human soul.

"Which is true?" we ask. And the Hindu replies, "All are true. All the things we can say about God are true, and then all the things we are not capable even of imagining. For if God were not greater than the mind of man, he would not be God."

In his *Discovery of India*, Mr. Nehru distinguishes six systems of Indian philosophy. They include polytheism, idealism, realism, theism which embraces the idea of a personal God, pure monism, and an evolutionary theory which gets along without positing God.

To an educated Indian, God may be all these things together, for God would not be God unless he could admit and embrace contrarieties. He is impersonal Brahma, dancing Shiva, radiant Vishnu; he is the life of renunciation and hermitage, the constant cycle of rebirth, the childlike myths of Ram and Sita or of Krishna and the milkmaids, the oneness of all life.

The oneness. In Atman, the absolute soul, lies the ultimate reality. The true end and aim of human life is self-realization which leads the individual to an experience of oneness with the absolute, the universal soul. This, in oversimplification, is the core of Hinduism. But the roads are many.

One of these is ritual cleanliness and good order. Hinduism is very broad and tolerant as to doctrine, but firm about ritual duties. Observance of rituals constitutes the dharma (law, duty) or appropriate way of life. It assures the welfare of the family, the caste, the community, even the life or lives that must be lived after death. Karma, the cosmic moral law, will punish or reward the individual according to the way he has fulfilled his duties.

The concept of ritualistic cleanliness is central to the daily practice of religion. It is quite obvious to the outsider that food is at the core of it all. One authority claims that the source of division into castes was the question of whom one could dine with or accept food from. The fewer you eat with, the higher your status, the purer you are, the more fit to serve as the community's intermediary with the gods. Preserving this cleanliness becomes the central preoccupation of ritual.

Before the body is considered fit to receive food in the morning it must be cleansed—by defecation, bathing, and the most remarkable scouring of the throat and nasal passages I have ever observed—as noisy as it is thorough. Yogis also "cleanse" their stomachs by swallowing and regurgitating water. A really accomplished yogi can draw water up through his penis and expel it.

The next concern is for the cleanliness of the food to be eaten. Preoccupation with diet is common. Perhaps the minister of state who sends his menu to you if he agrees to come and dine is only following Gandhi, a great food faddist, but it reads like that of a ruminant animal:

"A. B. takes for his dinner some pieces of sugar cane, curds, pulses, warm milk with jaggery (unrefined sugar), nuts, dried and fresh fruits."

Wherever an international group of students gathers, it will always be the Indians who show the most concern about their food and who have the greatest difficulty in adjusting to what is served.

Does food, then, symbolize something buried deep in the personality? Does the preoccupation with it indicate a desire to be tended like a child—to return to the happy days of being nursed whenever you were hungry, of being guarded and mothered by aunts and sisters? Is a system which ritualistically prevents dining with all but a favored few an attempt to retain the restricted child-world and shut all else out? Is caste itself a symbolic family which both assures the purity of food and preserves the child-world? And does there perhaps lie beneath all this a fantasy of incest—of retaining the mother and the permissive sister-in-law to cater forever and exclusively to one's needs?

These questions are of more than academic importance because the compulsion towards ritual cleanliness is a political fact of great importance. Although the constitution has abolished caste distinctions in law, they still exist in society. They are beginning to break down in the cities. But as caste erodes, it begins to appear that the habit of mind, the need which produced caste, may seek some other outlet. The battle over languages and linguistic states is another way of organizing society on an exclusive rather than an inclusive principle.

There seems to be in Indian society (as in all societies) a force which keeps throwing the elements of it apart, keeps insisting upon a new division. Ritual has regularized and controlled this force until now, and caste has. If these go, what will take their place?

The young intellectuals think they cannot go soon enough.

"Religion is nothing but food habits and rituals," one of them explained to us. "In India, religion is the source of divisions, riots, strife of all kinds, but of nothing good. The best thing to do with it is to abolish it."

"But don't religious organizations help to promote better government, or make better citizens, or help to train the children?"

"Nothing of that sort. When I applied for a passport I wrote 'no religion.'

" 'How can this be, a man with no religion?' the clerk asked. He refused to give me my passport. 'We have a state with no religion,' I told him. 'Why not a man?' That satisfied him."

Among the university students in the group, all but one or two said they had no religion or had renounced Hinduism.

These young men seemed to know or care little about the re-interpretation of Hinduism through which Gandhi had drawn a whole nation to him and prepared it for independence, or of the way Vinoba Bhave has shown the ethical value of action, or the work of the Ramakrishna Mission or the Aurobindo Ashram in providing an authentic Hindu base for religiously motivated activism.

The problem in India is how to overcome ritual exclusivism, how to make ethics universal rather than a matter of caste loyalty. Each caste has its own code; there is therefore no absolute sin, but only a ritual offense against the dharma of the caste. How to move from this to the universal ethic which a unified and integrated society requires is one of India's basic problems. A caste ethic makes a virtue of nepotism.

The old sister of the President of India was dying, and she had come to the vast presidential palace to spend her last days with her brother. As she lay in one of the big upper rooms, she asked that she might take hold of a cow's tail.

One reason why Hindus think a cow sacred is that when you come to the shore of the river of death, you must hold on to a cow's tail in order to get safely across.

But how could a cow be conveyed into the presidential palace, and up the long stairs to the upper room?

One of the braided officials had a bright idea. He had a cow brought into the courtyard, let a string down from the window of the room, and when it had been tied to the cow's tail, gave the other end to the old lady.

This seemed to satisfy her. But another official, perhaps still more braided, had an even brighter idea. He went and got a little calf and carried it up in his arms. So the old lady died with two firm grips on eternity.

Hindus believe that there is an ethereal as well as a corporeal body, and that it only gradually withdraws during a period of seven or eight hours after death, carrying with it all unfulfilled desires, all thoughts and ideas.

"This body goes to a place of spirits," Gurdial told us, "but it is likely to hover around the earthly home up to nine months. In the spirit home it may have to wait for fifty to a hundred years to be reborn, though innocent babes can be reborn very quickly—perhaps in six months. That people may ever go back to animals is only a superstition. Even a bad man will still be reborn a man."

This explanation helped me to understand the allegation I had frequently heard—that occasionally young children could recall a previous life, would recognize former parents or home or brother or sister, and would even insist on being taken back to the former home.

Belief in reincarnation is widespread. When a psychologist remarked that heredity and environment were the only factors responsible for personality, a student asked:

"Is not reincarnation also a factor?"

"This is a subject psychology has not yet investigated," he said.

When a person dies, the corpse, wrapped tight in cloth and placed on a string bed, is carried through the streets to the burning ghat on the shoulders of family members, possibly with a few balloons tied to it, or decorated with flowers.

We once stayed for two weeks across the river from a burning ghat. Nearly every day a procession would come, and a pile of wood be prepared on the concrete platform, and the body placed on it, and more wood. In the old days it was the custom to crack the skull in order to let the spirit out—a privilege reserved for the eldest son. Now a coconut is sometimes cracked and thrown into the fire.

"The eldest son also gets the opportunity of lighting his father's funeral pyre," a friend wryly remarked. "But he has to wait a long time."

It takes about four hours for the fire to burn out. When the ashes are cool enough to handle, someone takes them up and carries them down the broad flight of steps and tosses them into the narrow stream. A wind blows a cloud of them back in his face and up the stairs to take a last farewell of the watchers. Meanwhile the water buffalo graze quietly in the meadow which fills most of the stream bed, or sink into the shallow stream while the cowherd splashes and rubs them all over, from curling horns to tufted tail. The mourners, meanwhile, will pick up odds and ends of shoulder- and breast-bone that are never destroyed by the fire and will carry them home. Some member of the family, after keeping them for a month, will make a journey to a more sacred river—the Ganges if possible—and drop them in.

The temples India has built to its gods are as numerous, as various, as crowded with carvings and sculptures and objects of worship as the literature about them is confusingly rich. Since paradoxes are at home in India, it is safe to say that despite poverty, profusion is the national keynote. India pulses with life. There is an impression of surplus. In the bazaars the foods and goods are piled high in stall after stall, block after block, street after street. There is a surplus of cattle, of birds, of children, of laborers, of vehicles. And of temples. And on the temples, of carvings.

An Indian temple—I am thinking now of the finest, whether at Khajuraho or Bhubaneswar or Konarak or Madurai—overwhelms with its surplus. From a distance, the high pyramidal towers look black and crumbled with age. But when you come close enough to see the detail, you find that all those meaningless dents and crenellations are objects—are men and women and animals mostly, but sometimes vegetative or geometric designs.

You try to study one tower with care, but have to give it up because the carvings escape skyward as you follow them up, or run around a cornice and disappear. When you step inside the gate—if you are allowed inside—another gallery of art awaits you. There is the back of the tower, as elaborately carved as the other sides and perhaps a gallery of statues around the courtyard. Inside the temple itself again every inch is likely to be decorated.

At Konarak and Khajuraho the decorations take the form of couples in loving embrace or in the act of intercourse in all sorts of positions, sometimes with assistance of interesting sorts from a third party. It is as if the already overwhelming profusion is being multiplied before our eyes, the very stone itself engaging in the creative act so that the supply of stone figures, also copulating, shall be endless to eternity.

This is the other side of India's religious inspiration, which runs all the way from extreme asceticism and self-denial and saintliness to the blood sacrifice, copulation as a fertility rite, and an art which frankly and joyously expresses the delights of sex. It is hard for the Western mind with its microscope and measuring stick, its simple polarities of good and evil or black and white, and its habit of breaking things down by analysis, to enter into a world where opposites are true and where ambiguity and contradiction are accepted as inescapable aspects of truth. Yet this is one of the strengths of Hindu culture, and it is everywhere illustrated by the bewildering variety of religious practices and beliefs.

We have said nothing, as yet, about those sturdy offshoots of Hinduism—the Jains, the Sikhs and the Buddhists. Nor is there space to deal properly with them. Buddhism, which flourishes throughout Asia, is no longer important in India. Some of the great monuments to its Indian founder are there, of course, and are visited by devout Buddhists from all parts of Asia. Tibetan refugees have now brought their special brand with them.

The Jains, though small in numbers, trace their origin back to Mahavira in the sixth century B.C. But according to tradition he was only the last of twenty-four saviors. The message of the Jains is love for all life expressed in nonviolence. The world is not an illusion but reality—dynamic, creative, infinite in power and variety and change —in which the interaction of soul and matter gives dynamism and drama. From this viewpoint comes a belief in equality, pacifism, abstemiousness, self-control. Orthodox Jains used to wear masks over their mouths to avoid breathing in insects, swept the earth ahead of them to avoid stepping on them, filtered their water to avoid drinking them, and cooked their meals by daylight to avoid killing any small creature. Mahavira is always pictured naked, though the relation between nonviolence and nudity is not quite clear to me. Perhaps naked men are less likely to pursue one another violently. Or possibly it had something to do with the use of animal fibres for covering—though why not try cotton? Anyhow, most Jains wear clothes now. They are a very gentle, hard-working, and successful business community for the most part, and in their case nonviolence has paid off. But I cannot always agree with their arguments. At one of the many Jain meetings I attended, a speaker told us how we are all descended from fish, and monkeys don't eat meat, so why should we? The answer, I thought, was obvious: we don't particularly want to be like monkeys.

Contrasted with the gentle Jains, the Sikhs have a reputation as warriors. They are largely Jats, descended originally it is said from Scythians and Parthians, and the British used them as soldiers. Many of them are in the Indian army today. Concentrated in the Punjab, they have spread throughout India and seem to have a corner on the taxicab business everywhere, with a reputation also for being good mechanics.

The founder of Sikhism, Guru Nanak (1469-1538), wanted to abolish caste, establish equality, and raise the Hindus out of the apathy into which they had fallen under Muslim rule. He taught that there was one deity, God of the universe, of all men and all religions. In the seventeenth century the Sikhs found that they had to fight to retain their religion. Under Govind Singh, who was Guru from 1675 to 1708 they extended their power and ultimately controlled northwestern India until the British came. The Sikh movement is to Hinduism what the Protestant movement was to Christianity, and developed many of the same virtues—equalitarianism, skill in commerce and mechanics, aggressive drive. Orthodox Hindus regard the Sikhs as rude, uncouth, yet strong and energetic, clever mechanically but weak in abstract thought. This stereotype results from the fact that many Sikhs are still country people, while whose who have come to the city have taken to mechanical trades—but also to medicine, law, the army and everything else.

There are fewer than two million Jains, somewhat over six million Sikhs. The Christians, somewhat over eight million, outnumber the Jains and Sikhs combined. They are concentrated in the south—especially in Kerala—where tradition says Saint Thomas, one of the twelve apostles, landed near Cochin in the year 52 and began to preach. An ancient Syriac work called the *Acts of Thomas* asserts that when lots were cast after the Ascension, India fell to Thomas. But Thomas was unwilling to go. Jesus therefore appeared to a merchant from India, named Habban, offering to sell him a carpenter for his king, Gudnaphar, who was planning to build a great palace. Purchased for twenty pieces of silver, Thomas was taken to India and set to work. But instead of building, Thomas visited the poor, preaching the Gospel and giving away the money the king had entrusted to him. When the angry king inquired for his palace, Thomas told him that he had built him one in heaven.

When the king shut Thomas up in prison, his brother Gad fell ill and had a dream in which he was shown the palace in heaven. When he heard the dream, Gudnaphar was convinced. Both he and his brother were baptized and Thomas was allowed to go on with his preaching. He was later killed while preaching in another Indian kingdom.

This charming legend has gained some reliability of late with the discovery that there was indeed such a king. Many early Christian writings describe Thomas as the apostle to India and Parthia, while early church fathers like Dorotheus, Bishop of Tyre (245-313), assert that he suffered martyrdom there. A Bishop John, Metropolitan of Persia and Great India, attended the great Council of Nicaea in 325. And to this day the Indian church is referred to as "Syrian" or more properly Syriac, from the language of its ritual. In the state of Kerala family names like Mathai (Matthew), Joseph and Thomas are very common.

Indian Christians have a strong sense of being a minority, and a deep conviction that in an era of change when social controls are being lost, Christianity with its strong social conscience, its practical ethics, and its congregationalism is the only answer.

"Hinduism is mostly an amorphous hodgepodge of beliefs and customs with no central truth," an earnest Christian remarked. (All Indian Christians struck me as earnest.) "Up-and-coming Hindu groups like the Ramakrishna Mission have to borrow Christian ideas —even recognize Jesus as a great teacher. But they can't provide the real thing, because Christ is the unique son of God, and only Christians have that."

This uniqueness, plus the rejection of Christians by orthodox Hindus who will not even accept a glass of water from them, has ironically enough made the Christians into another caste.

"When I was a boy," one Christian friend of ours remembered, "if I took a drink of water at a Hindu friend's house, the metal cup had to be burned in the fire right away to purify it. That's what Hindus think of us. We don't gain anything by fraternizing with them—religiously, I mean. One day their eyes will be opened; then let them come to us."

Christians think of themselves as a group apart. No doubt as a result of past rejections, and because they cannot build a completely different social framework, they are a community—just like the Sikhs, the Jains, the Parsees. Where Christians are numerous, they have even preserved the caste distinctions which their families had as Hindus, and some churches refuse to accept any but a Brahman as pastor—strange parody of the message of Jesus! (The American parallel is our racially segregated churches.)

Independent India is very sensitive to Christian influence from outside and has ruled that although retiring missionaries may be replaced, there can be no increase in their numbers. Missionaries have been active among some of the twelve million tribal peoples whose languages and customs are very different from those of the majority. Mission education has resulted in a sense of cultural identity and even in a demand for outright independence which has been embarrassing to India.

Thus the hill peoples of Assam, who feel themselves to have been mistreated by Hindus, became Christians because they found a spirit of love and acceptance in the missionaries, mostly Baptist, who settled among them. Yet the government now accuses the missionaries of political meddling when they had simply given good treatment to a despised group.

The conflict of attitudes appears in the following conversation:

"You should be appointing Indian bishops, not foreigners," said a government official to a Christian leader who called on him.

"We are doing that."

"You ought to give up this money you're getting from America. We are independent now—we ought not to be leaning on foreigners."

"I am perfectly willing to do so," he answered, "the moment you give up the loans you are getting from the United States."

"Christianity is new to our country," the official persisted. "It does not fit into our culture."

"We have been here two thousand years. How long have you Muslims been here?"

In most parts of India the relatively few Christians still depend on overseas support. In Delhi alone there are some thirty thousand Christians, many of them out of work. They complain bitterly of discrimination.

"Hindus get the preference everywhere," said a man who had been seeking work. "Christians are passed over when government posts are being filled. Even untouchables get special privileges, but Christians have no protection. Those who recant and become Hindus can get jobs that are otherwise closed to them."

What to do about it?

"We must start a factory that will employ only Christians. We must have a daily newspaper—a good one—that will expose all the mistreatment we are receiving. The missionaries and pastors say they can do nothing for us—they can minister only to spiritual needs. But we need bread and work, too."

But there are Christians in government posts, good ones. Because they tend to be better educated, Christians probably have influence well beyond their numbers. It is paradoxical that in Kerala, where Christians are most numerous and have the highest literacy rate in India, communism has got its firmest foothold.

But by far the most numerous religious group after the Hindus is the Muslims, who make up about a tenth of the population, even after the partition of Pakistan. Communal riots are still all too common, yet the Muslims, who have been in India for over twelve hundred years, are an ineradicable part of its life.

Our friend Malik Sahib, a Muslim educator, typifies the best that Islam has given India. A large, quiet, dignified and fun-loving man, he tells his students:

"When I was a graduate student, I thought I knew everything, and I thought there could be no God. But now I believe in God. I believe that God knows about me and takes an interest in my welfare."

To students who find themselves adrift in a society which is losing faith in old ways and rituals, he is a solid and reassuring rock.

"In the Jama Masjid," I heard a student say to him, "there is a huge footprint in stone which they say was made by Mohammed. Do you believe this?"

Malik Sahib placed the tips of his big fingers together while his wrists rested against his well-rounded middle.

"Mohammed was a man, and no man could make such an imprint," he said. "He always said that he was like other men, except that God had given him a message to bring to men. As for the stone, I, too, knew such a stone in my youth. It was said that if you drank water from the depression, you would be enlightened. I drank a lot of that water."

India has much to gain from its Muslims. But until the terrible wounds of partition with its mass murders and its millions of refugees can be dimmed by time, their situation will remain uneasy.

But there is one advantage Muslims still have over Hindus. They may have four wives. Any man who wants to take an extra wife may become a Muslim simply by repeating a sentence which acknowledges Allah. Indian law also permits divorce if one party changes his religion. Becoming a Muslim (or a Christian) is therefore a way of getting a divorce.

The possibilities in polygamy were pointed out to me by none other than Dr. Radhakrishnan, the distinguished scholar and Vice President (now President) of India.

"The emperor Akbar had a Muslim, a Christian, a Hindu and a Parsee wife," he said. "He truly believed in practicing peaceful co-existence."

Nothing is more revealing of a culture than its invention of ways for people to gather together: think of the Greek theater, the Roman coliseum, the Spanish bull ring, the American baseball park and cocktail bar—and church. In India it is the ashram—a severely simple living place, often remote, designed for living at a minimal level of intake and comfort, the inhabitants doing their own work, with life so designed that a maximum of time is left for prayer and contemplation after getting rid of material things so far as possible.

We Americans seek to produce more and more material and to make it more and more generally available on the assumption (unproved) that it is a good in itself. India seeks to suppress needs almost to the starvation point on the assumption (unproved) that spirit and matter are hostile.

Yet a visit to an ashram is an edifying, even an uplifting experience to a Westerner. Such a suppression of the material does leave rich meadows of time for the contemplative to walk in. An American viewpoint on these thousands of ashrams would be: But wouldn't you do more good if you set up a service to help the poor or the uneducated or the sick? The Indian answer might be: You have been doing that for a long time. But look at your mentally sick. Wouldn't you be better off with a few thousand ashrams?

Our word "divine" comes from a Sanskrit root meaning radiance. Living in India, I came to see that it is the radiance both inward and outward which characterizes true religion, and that you may find it anywhere. Religions differ as to the symbols through which they express the truth they see, but in substance all are the same. Hindus sense this universality of the religious impulse and welcome it; they do not claim unique access to the truth. That is one reason why God seems to be at home in India. Whatever you assert as your belief, a Hindu is likely to agree that he believes the same. And no doubt he does, for Hinduism embraces all the religious concepts man's ingenuity has been able to devise.

The aim, however, as Dr. Radhakrishnan pointed out to me, is a working upwards from the world of matter and emotions through intellect and contemplation.

"The human is incomplete, but working towards individual perfection, towards the attainment of the world of spirit. As long as the cosmic sun continues to shine, people have their functions to fulfill. When it ceases to shine, then the oneness of the individual and the Absolute will be achieved."

"Does this mean the end of human life?" I asked.

"When someone asked Saint Augustine what God was doing before he created the earth, he answered that he was creating a hell for the curious. There are still mysteries—we don't know all."

India embraces those mysteries which so exasperate a Western mind. In India all mysteries find a home.

FOURTEEN

Holi, Holi, Holi

In India almost any time of the year is festival time, though there is a saying that "Tij comes and sows the seeds of festivals; Holi comes and takes away the festivals in her shawl." Since Tij (prettily celebrated by hanging swings in trees for girls) comes in July and Holi (the Indian Halloween) in February or March, that covers a good part of the year. No month lacks a holiday of some sort—the public holidays number about twenty-five—and since the public calendar has to aim at impartiality, Christmas and Good Friday are recognized as well as Sikh, Muslim and Hindu days.

The festival is at home in India, where tradition still has the upper hand. Amazing outlays of money and energy go to maintain the old enactments of godly intervention in the affairs of men. It is through the festivals that the people keep green that sense of godly presence, of an intermixing which leaves no sharp division between god and man.

Is Ram a god or a man? What of Krishna, with his fondness for women? In the festivals, these god-men come to life in a way which brings the godly down to the human plane and lifts the human up.

To arrive in India in late September or early October is to be thrust into the midst of the liveliest festival of the year. It is, in fact, several festivals celebrated together or in quick succession, and with varying emphasis in different parts of the country.

All are related in one way or another to the worship of Sakti or power as symbolized by the goddess Durga, consort of Shiva. But

149

Durga is also known as Parvati, Devi, Kali, Uma and by a good many other names, while Shiva may be Mahadeva, Hara, Mahesa and a thousand others.

The Dussera festival (the name indicates a ten-day celebration) commemorates Durga's struggle against a monster. But in northern India, Durga is rather overlooked in favor of Ram (or Rama), a devotee of the goddess, who also fought a demon called Ravana. In either case the battle is symbolic of the struggle between good and evil, ending of course in a triumphant celebration which coincides with the feast of lights.

Every sizable town has at least one Ramlila celebration, and sometimes several going on at the same time. Ram-lila means the sport or play of Ram, but in Hindu thought all the divine acts of creation are sports—the joyful creativity of a Supreme Being who had no need to produce anything since he was already perfect. In this sense the play of Ram is very serious work indeed, since he has to overcome whole armies of demons.

The typical Ramlila is an elaborate thing which runs for ten or even more than twenty days, unfolding night after night the drama of the young prince Ram who came to earth to destroy evil, who first revealed his strength by breaking the bow no other princes had been able to bend, thus winning his Sita and starting the long series of adventures and misadventures which include the abduction of Sita by demons, the aid given by the monkeys who reach Sita in her captivity, the final great battle and destruction of the demons, and Ram's triumphant return to his land and throne.

Based upon the revered Ramayana and on the *Ramcharit-manas* of Tulsi Das, the play reproduces only the dramatic parts of the epic. But it does so in a truly epic fashion, often by shifting to different parts of town for major changes of scene. Local committees raise funds, find actors and musicians, and provide the costumes and stage settings for the elaborate drama. The undertaking is so vast that there is never time to perfect the acting, the sets or the coordination of all the elements. A real folk drama, it must resemble the medieval miracle plays of England.

Delhi in recent years has been treated to a new version of Ramlila planned and acted by professional dancers and musicians who have produced a beautiful three-hour dance-drama, blending the most expressive pantomime and dance with a stirring orchestral accompaniment to voices that come from the orchestra rather than the stage.

Since it never rains in October (or in half of the remaining months either), the play takes place outdoors on a stage a hundred feet wide. From the moment the curtain opens, brilliant color combines with grace of movement and music to accentuate the drama. The costumes are in the flaming colors India loves—shocking in their brilliance, suggesting motion and evoking response even before the dancers begin to move. The dance pantomime makes the story perfectly clear, and when the high moments come—the monkeys in their delightful masks and motions, the breaking of the bow, the battle with the demons, the triumphal return and enthronement—the stage is a wonderful world of color in motion. As the drama of good against evil seizes upon these tangible forms and speaks through them, the very source and purpose of ancient ritual makes itself felt.

The orchestra with its drums, flutes, reeds, and string instruments with long necks and huge bowl-shaped bodies is used with telling effect to heighten dramatic tension. Mostly it plays in unison, or echoes the singer's voice a bar or two behind. The voices sing the narrative of Tulsi Das, but in the dramatic passages they sing the words the actors are supposed to be saying.

How often the whole thing suggests Wagner!—the river journey, the trial of strength, the forest idyl when Ram and Sita are exiled through the plotting of evil women, the fight with demons, the ultimate victory and return. Ram seems a very Wagnerian hero—rather pompously good and superior, yet managing to do some stupid things. Imprisoned within the tradition which requires him to act as he does, he seems a little stiff, yet somehow at the same time refreshingly young and noble and good.

This handsome spectacle is only one part of the elaborate celebrations around the figure of Ram. Down Chandni Chauk—that historic street where Mogul emperors led their victorious processions —on a certain evening comes a parade that recalls these vanished glories. The street itself no longer gleams with the splendor it once had—in fact it looks drab, cluttered and tired, its drooping wooden buildings plastered over with merchant's signs, at all heights and angles. Friends led us up a sagging narrow stairway, through a bedroom where we had to step over a sleeping man, and onto a balcony heaped with rubbish which however directly overlooked the street. We waited over an hour for the procession, entertained meanwhile by a nine-year-old boy who spoke torrents of English. When the parade came at last, he explained every float to me, but the din from the brass bands was such that I could hear nothing he said.

Cart after cart went by with tableaux which told the story of Ram, lighted by acetylene chandeliers born on the heads of men walking alongside. The most elaborate floats were lighted electrically from a generator carried on a following ox-drawn cart.

Then came carts full of armed men who jumped down into the street and fought with swords or sticks, surrounded by a crowd which often had to leap nimbly out of the way when the fighters hopped back or fell on each other.

Despite the frightening realism of the battles, much of the color was on the sidelines—the peddlers' carts piled high with every conceivable kind of food, the rows of bullock carts which had brought the villagers into the city, the hundreds who had come all this way only to sleep through all the din on carts, window ledges, doorways, or in the dust of the street. That they should be sleepy was understandable, for it was two-thirty in the morning before the last cart went by and Chandni Chauk suddenly filled solid with the thousands of spectators who had been standing along the sides or crowding the balconies.

On the last day of Dussera huge effigies of wood and paper are erected in the public parks—Ravana himself and his chief helpers Kumbakarn and Meghdoot. Thirty feet tall, brightly colored, their innards stuffed with firecrackers, they await the moment of sunset when a mock battle is staged, a flaming arrow goes flying at the figures, and the whole erection goes up in flame and explosions amidst the rejoicing of the thousands of spectators.

Village people walk for miles to see these spectacles, or ride patiently behind a slow-plodding bullock. We happened to be on the road one year when they were on their way, an endless stream of them on foot or in carts, in three-wheel rickshaws or on bicycles loaded fore and aft. We saw them go and we saw them return, walking for miles to enjoy this moment of Ram's greatest triumph.

For hundreds—even thousands—of years, foreign invaders have imposed their rule upon India—the Aryans themselves, the Greeks under Alexander the Great, the Parthians and Persians and White Huns and Turks and Afghans, then the great Mogul emperors Tamerlane (Timur), Akbar, Shah Jahan who built the Taj Mahal, the ruthless Aurangzeb. And finally, after the Portuguese and Dutch, the British. What must it do to a people to be conquered by one foreign ruler after another?

But in Ram, India had the ideal ruler, its own hero who year after year conquered the evil intruder and restored beauty and order to the land. So Ramlila, like ancient Greek tragedy, was as much ritual as art. It not only imitated, it re-created the return of the god-king to rule his people. Muslim or Briton might rule the land with his armies and his laws, but Ram had his yearly triumph. He was indestructible, for his rule was in the heart.

One of the great popular scenes of Ramlila is that in which Hanuman, the devoted monkey, to prove his loyalty rips open his breast to show that the name of Ram is carved upon his very heart. This is how India—at least north India—feels about the epic of Ram. The feeling is somewhat different in the south where it is felt that the monkey people are an insulting Aryan-drawn portrait of the Dravidians.

Immediately after Dussera comes Diwali, the festival of lights which marks Ram's victorious return and enthronement after overcoming Ravana.

In preparation, houses get a fresh coat of color wash, rooms are cleaned and rubbish carted out. The chatter of fireworks, intermittent for several weeks past, grows to a rapid dialogue. On the morning of Diwali, families rise early (when do they not, in India?), put on new clothes, and visit friends and relatives to exchange greetings and gifts. The boom and crack of fireworks continues like some erratic clockwork to mark the running of time towards the evening climax.

At dusk each family will light a row of little earthen oil lamps in the best room of the house, and before a simple altar of flowers will make offerings and sing songs to Lakshmi, the goddess of wealth.

As darkness comes on, each household will fill hundreds of the little lamps with a spoonful of oil, drop a piece of twisted cotton in for a wick, and place them in rows a foot or two apart all along the veranda steps, at the windows, and around the edge of the flat roof. In downtown New Delhi, thousands of colored electric lights also glow in the trees of the central park, while the great dome of the presidential palace sparkles with row upon row of lights like jewels, and the hundred-foot-long front steps after being covered with bricks and sand to protect them from oil, are crowded with lamps. At a distance the lights twinkle like stars—the effect of hot air arising from the parliament house nearby, according to a cynical friend. But as we approached, the electric lights were switched off. Was it economy, or failure of the electric supply, or was the President tired and wanting it dark so he could sleep? It was only nine-thirty. We never learned.

We drove on through streets lined with lighted bungalows, the little oil lamps sending out a soft yellow glow.

Here was the climax of the struggle between good and evil. Here on what is considered the darkest night of the year, light triumphs. How wonderful a symbol of man's optimism! The longing for purity and perfection, so deeply planted in Indian culture, comes closest to realization at this moment.

DIWALI GREETINGS,

said a very remarkable card we received one Diwali day.

SWEET GODLY REMEMBRANCES
AND GODLY INVITATION

for the Forth Coming True Diwali in New Bharat (India) in the New Golden-aged Satyugi Deity World or Ram-Rajya of 100% Purity, Non-violence, Peace & Prosperity being Re-established incognito by the Most Beloved Incorporeal God Sermonizer of Gita—TRIMURTI SHIVA through Godly Knowledge & Yoga, like Kalpa (5000 years ago).

When I asked about the meaning of Diwali, I got a different answer from each informant. The age, depth and variety of Indian culture make it quite possible for half a dozen different answers to be given, and for all to be right. But it makes for confusion.

I asked a student about Diwali, and he began to tell me the story of Ram, which he took literally. I began to explain how all cultures have feasts of lights deriving from primitive times. And I mentioned the yule log as a survival of an ancient celebration of the winter solstice which had been grafted onto Christmas. He didn't get it.

"Why does Diwali take place on the darkest night?" I asked.

"No such a thing," he said. "No Indian would say this." Several had. The books also say it.

"Mahavira, who founded the Jains, died on this day," someone else offered.

"Not at all—he received the message of ahimsa this day."

Even the government was confused. On Tuesday evening it suddenly decided that the Diwali holiday should be on Wednesday instead of Thursday, thus throwing the whole country into a tailspin. India still has several calendars in use, and the calculation of festivals according to one of the ancient reckonings is apparently full of pitfalls.

As we drove through the quietly glowing streets on Diwali night it struck me that everyone—Jew, Christian, Muslim, Hindu, Buddhist —celebrates with a festival of lights his longing for a world which shall be pure and peaceful and good. Could we not, I wondered, bring all these feasts of lights together? Is there some way we might focus all this light upon a common goal, attaching to it a vigorous sentiment for world fellowship?

We are all seekers of light. We know that it comes from one source. We share one human longing. Only our nomenclature is different. Instincts unite, but words divide us. Perhaps we should light more lamps together, in silence.

Next to the complex that is Dussera-Ramlila-Diwali, Holi is the most popular of festivals. It comes in February or March, and obviously it has some connection with an ancient rite of spring.

The story goes that Krishna had a bad uncle who wanted to get him, and who ordered all his nephews killed for fear that they would succeed him. The uncle sent Holika, an ogress, to set fire to the house and burn Krishna. But he, knowing what she was up to, arranged it so that he escaped and she burned up. Other versions have Krishna as an infant preserved in Holika's lap while she sits in the blazing pyre, or tell of a cruel father who wants to murder his son but fails.

In all of them, as in the Christian story of Herod, there are clear remnants of a primitive drama of the year king, the old trying to kill but being killed himself, and of sun worship connected with the increasing heat of spring. Fire and blood undergird this popular festival, and it is interesting to see how they have been civilized.

In villages, a month of preparation leads up to Holi, with singing of songs and collection of wood for the bonfire. On the eve of Holi, everyone goes to the big pyre in clean but ragged clothes. As the flames mount, the children set off firecrackers, the women sing, and then everyone starts to throw colored water or rub red powder into the face and clothes of his friends.

The mayhem goes on until after noon of the following day. Not only children, but grown men approach each other smiling, take handfuls of colored powder out of a bag, and rub it gently but firmly into each other's cheeks, foreheads, hair, chests. Then they embrace to show it's all in good fun—and smear each other's backs. New refinements are being introduced. One year the colored water was dispensed in squirt guns; the next it was ejected from plastic bottles and thrown at cars in small balloons. Little groups parade the streets, pounding on drums, singing, dancing a bit, coming to the door to collect tribute.

On the edge of town the enterprising set up roadblocks and stop cars with the threat, Pay or Spray. The bandits themselves are dripping with color, their faces smeared thick with red, blue, green, yellow; their hair dripping colored dust, their clothes streaked and soaked. Great fun.

It is all in a spirit of brotherly love and friendship, they say. For this is a day when there is no high or low—all are equal. The need of such release in a country where people live on narrow margins is clear enough, and perhaps healthy. But the origin is steeped in blood, as the red splashings show. The red water is an innocent survival of the days when blood sacrifices were frequent (they still exist in parts of India), the amiable smearing of a time when men embraced each other not in fun but in mortal combat. It is fascinating to see how an ancient civilization can modify old ways, turning them to modern needs. The roadblock, the splash of color, the smeared face are a cheap price to pay as replacements for the bloody and sacrificial past.

We think of India as a poor country. But the splendors of its past live on, so that no nation can exceed or perhaps even equal it in the magnificence of its pageants. And none is more magnificent than Republic Day when on January 26 this young democracy celebrates its era of the common man with the pomp and circumstance of royalty.

Even the vast open spaces of New Delhi's Rajpath (*raj* means rule and *path*, pronounced paht, is the Sanskrit origin of our own "path") and the park stretching from India Gate to the presidential palace are too small for the hundreds of thousands who pour into the city from all parts of India, by plane and train, by car and bicycle and bullock cart, to see the President ride to the reviewing stand in his state coach.

The army runs the show, and it is therefore run efficiently. We had tickets to the guest stand, together with elaborate directions how to get there, a parking ticket for the car, a map of the approach route. Everything except word that they would close the road at eight o'clock. The show was to start at ten, so we arrived at eight-thirty. Since the ticketless crowd had now been let into the India Gate area, we could not get within half a mile of our seats. We walked back to Curzon Road where I found a big army truck parked at the head of the street where the parade would pass, got permission to sit on its high flat fender, and saw the whole parade from a front seat.

Parades are much alike the world over. The tanks and guns and military bands and the files of soldiers, cadets, and sailors offered nothing new. By now we were accustomed even to the Scotch bagpipe bands, and their drummers covered with tiger skins. But then came the elephants—colorwashed belowdecks, covered with flaming gay trappings above. And the camels, also brightly bedecked, sneering their knowing sneer at the little world of men below. And the floats —one from every state and union territory. Some of them bespoke the new India of hydroelectric dams and steel-making, but the most attractive portrayed in accurate yet somehow romantic detail the simple straw houses, the cottage industries, the trades and occupations. Most colorful of all was a float in the shape of a shrine, completely covered with brilliant marigolds.

As interesting as the parade were the incidental scenes. Beggars sat in the dust covered with ash, squirming, writhing, yelling, or exposing maimed limbs to tease a few coppers out of passers-by. Children swarmed at their parents' heels, or rode upon a parental hip, or nursed at a street corner, or defecated in the gutter. Spectators in search of a better spot crashed into a private yard and literally climbed the outside of the building to stand on the roof, smirching the whitewash as they went. Nobody complained; it was Republic Day.

The holiday spirit continues three more days as the folk dancers bring their varied styles and costumes from all over India to display them in the stadium. Dark faces from the south follow oriental features from the northeast, and each troupe seems more brilliantly costumed than the one before. India is not only a subcontinent, but an ethnic museum. The hill tribes—copper-skinned and Mongoloid, with huge brass decorations at their breasts, ears and noses—are as alien to Delhi as they would be to Washington. When the dancing was over, all the groups came back onto the stage to stand, row upon row, in front of the President and Prime Minister while the national anthem was sung in a tongue which belonged to none of them. It was a thrilling sight, for what other nation can show so dramatic a contrast of folkways and costumes and tongues? What government, though, has the skill and wisdom to make one nation of these so varied peoples?

The fourth day brought the spectacle known as Beating the Retreat, an elaborate show of horsemanship, military music and drill when the flag is taken down in the presence of the President and other dignitaries.

Indian pageantry appears to be a blend of old tradition and British influence—a confluence of Akbar the Great with Queen Victoria.

If no one thought to warn us of an imminent holiday, we could usually detect one by a kind of flurry in the household when we came down in the morning. Since each holiday called for its special paraphernalia, food, and frame of mind, we had to feel our way.

On a morning in August we knew something was afoot when Mohanji the sweeper scurried out of the living room as soon as he saw us on the stairs, and made for the back of the house. In a moment his wife, who had never been in the house except for the staff Christmas party, appeared in the hall. She was a handsome woman—very dark of skin, with broad nostrils and high cheekbones and big dark eyes that somehow managed to suggest both motherhood and sexuality. This morning she was wearing a sari of blood red and gold, the end respectfully forming a hood.

We murmured "Namaste," placing our flattened palms under our chin, and waited.

Mohanji, grinning with pleasure in the background, stepped forward and pointed at my wrist. Ashok the bearer had also joined the party by this time and had added his infectious grin to the occasion, but even his English was not adequate to explain a thing so alien to the tongue.

Mohanji's wife held out a strange thing of thread and tinsel and a cheap celluloid imitation of a watch.

"She will put it on your wrist," said Ashok.

She put it on my wrist—tied it on, then made another Namaste to which I responded, still not sure what was going on. She had a decoration for Marion, too.

We could hardly wait for Arjan to come to find out what had happened to us.

"Ah, that is a *ponchi*," he said, smiling his beneficent smile. "Long ago the god Indra was defeated by demons. When he returned home his wife Sachi tied a sacred thread around his wrist, and he went back and defeated them all."

"But I haven't been defeated by any demons," I said. "Unless it's that customs inspector who made me pay duty on the package of my own old clothes. Or the bank that wouldn't open an account with a check unless I also gave them twenty-five rupees in cash."

"Nowadays a sister always ties such a thread on her brothers," he said.

"Then I have become her brother?"

"Not really. She asks you to be her protector this way—like a brother. There is another story, about a queen whose country was about to be attacked by the emperor—I think it was Akbar. She sent him a *ponchi*, then of course he could not attack her, as he had to become her protector instead."

I had by now had enough experience of festivals to realize that I no doubt had incurred an obligation.

"What should I do in return?" I asked Arjan.

"The brother always gives a present in cash," he said.

When that had been attended to, Arjan said:

"There is another story about this festival—we call it Raksha-bandhan—you might like to hear. Krishna had a real sister and a sister-in-law. His real sister was always complaining that he favored the other. 'I do not discriminate,' he would tell her. 'I only return what I receive.' One day when he cut his wrist, the real sister went off to look for a rag, but the other ripped a piece from her beautiful sari and bound up his wrist. When the real sister returned, she understood."

"A very nice story," we agreed.

But how about that celluloid watch?

The usual thread, we discovered, was a simple thing of red (in memory of Krishna's bleeding), and I had been treated to a deluxe modern version of a sort Brahmans no doubt would despise. But I did not need to worry about that, for I had become the brother of an untouchable. Nothing in India, I think, made me feel prouder.

A book could not begin to contain the full story of India's festivals, varying as they do from place to place and numerous beyond remembering. On many festal occasions, the chief activity is to go for a dip in some sacred river or tank, and when these occasions are important enough, they are combined with a mela, or fair.

Kurukshetra, less than a hundred miles from Delhi, is noted as the battleground where according to the Bhagavad-Gita, the lord Krishna gave his famous advice to Arjuna who, about to enter battle, was dismayed by the fact that he would be fighting members of his own family and thought it better to give up. The passage is famous as an expression of the essence of the Vedas—a sort of Hindu Sermon on the Mount, and one to which Gandhi was always turning.

The essence of the long dialogue is that by overcoming desire one attains peace, and that in the end no one is really killed since men's souls live on forever. Arjuna, therefore, should proceed with the battle and do his duty.

The argument appears tendentious, even suspect, to a Western mind and hardly conformable to ahimsa, but Gandhi was able to find in it a call to disinterested action.

Kurukshetra becomes an especially holy place when there is an eclipse of the sun there, and on such a day we went off to see what a holy fair and a holy immersion were like.

Once we left our car in the designated lot, we were swept up in a crowd which moved forward like a flow of lava—slow, massive, inescapable. Humanity seen wholesale is a little frightening, especially in India where people are often trampled and crushed to death. So we flowed with the stream, surrounded by country people in their flowing rags, the men with turbans piled high, the women in the bright reds they love best.

Small shops made of odds and ends had sprung up along the roadside to sell everything a pilgrim might want—trinkets, toys, cakes, great mounds of puffed rice to give in handfuls to the beggars.

The beggars—it seemed as if the eclipse had been engineered solely for them. Some exposed big, evil-looking, raw sores. Others had precise red spots arranged in perfectly even rows as if they had been painted there or produced by chemical burning. Lepers exposed their stubs of hands, or a stump of leg wrapped in a filthy rag. The victims of filariasis—elephantiasis—arranged themselves so that we would not miss their gruesome exaggerations. Boys all but naked and swabbed with ashes lay upon piles of thorns. Sadhus—holy men—their roped hair rubbed stiff with cow dung, hid within their heaps of rags and ragged beards, their foreheads daubed thick with paint and ash.

The fair itself turned out to be a tawdry row of side shows not very different from our country carnivals. Big canvases illustrated in crude paintings the half-human beasts or half-bestial humans who might be seen within. Bedraggled dancers stood on a platform while nearby a motordrome vibrated with the churning of the cycles inside. Over the vast grounds spilled a complete circus, a tent movie, animal shows, games of chance, and crowds so crushing that one could have a preview of that intriguing experience promised for the year 2065 when humanity will become so numerous that we shall all be crushed to death.

So at last, pushing our way past shows and beggars and encampments of people who had apparently spent the night here, we arrived at the tank—a huge body of somewhat liquefied mud in which a few crocodiles had been spotted the day before. Police patrolled it in motorboats, their guns ready to pot any crocodile who tried to snatch a limb from an immersing pilgrim.

The pilgrims meanwhile waited expectantly on the bank, lined thick and deep all around. Some had already undressed so that they might be the first in, the women not very fussy about nakedness abovedecks, though preserving modesty below. Old sadhus dressed in rags and paint and dirt awaited the moment, their eyes cocked at the sun.

Then a horn sounded and the immersion began, each pilgrim having his own ritual. One woman came all the way out, quite naked, and all the way back in three times. Others stood naked to the waist in the water and offered a handful of it to the sun. A woman kept crouching and jumping up, her large breasts rising out of the water and going on up as she came to a standing position, then riding down again. With all this activity and with these thousands of people, a strange quiet pervaded the place as if one were looking at a silent movie. Perhaps the crowds of India know that if they were as noisy as they are numerous, they would frighten each other to death.

The largest crowd we ever saw was that which greeted President Eisenhower at a public reception in Delhi. Half a million people turned out to see him, sitting close together on the ground in ordered rows and in perfect silence. When he appeared, some thousands of American flags waved at him, but still in silence. The silence, though unexpected, was somehow more impressive and no doubt more respectful than a roar of welcome.

An Indian crowd comes to see a great man in order to have, as they say, his darshan. To see him is to receive some of his strength and virtue. Hardly a week is without its festal day, but an Indian community will gladly make another at any time, to receive the darshan of a Nehru, a Vinoba Bhave, an Eisenhower, and will endow the event with religious significance. For religion is still at home in India. And therefore India is still a land of festivals.

FIFTEEN

A Gallery of Miniatures

Most of the world's travelers go abroad to see cathedrals, palaces, lakes, mountains and museums. It is far more fun to search out people. India with its rich human variety provides a continuing pageant of profiles and personalities, from turbaned Sikh taxi drivers and gowned Tibetans to handsomely costumed maharanis and graceful dancers. In the north the sudden surprise of a Semitic nose, the long eyes of the women, the faces like Abyssinian friezes give one a sense of being plunged back into a long-forgotten course in ancient history. Eastward, Mongolian and Aryan merge imperceptibly, while in the south rounded, friendly features and mahogany bodies are common.

There is a small community of Negroes in India, the remnant of a group of slaves imported by the maharajah of Hyderabad long ago. India has its Jews, too, though hardly more than 20,000 in the whole country. They entered the country centuries ago, at first in the south. Cochin still has several thousands of them, divided in true Indian fashion into two groups which do not intermix—the "white" who have not intermarried with Indians and the "black" who, at least in the past, have.

It is not, however, the look or ethnic origin, but rather a curiosity about the sort of people they are inside that impels an interested observer into temporary exile overseas. Many of the people we came to know had sought us out in quiet desperation, hoping we could somehow lift them out of the pit of poverty they had fallen into. There was, for instance, the thin, smiling, dark-eyed man of twenty-

164

nine who came one evening, and who talked for an hour about his life and his problems. We saw many others like him.

"I'm making a mere pittance as a government clerk," he said, in that Victorian English which is one of India's charms. "In India you can get nowhere without influence, and I have no connections. The other way is by dishonesty. Most of the men I know accept bribes, but I cannot do that.

"I have a wife and three children. Going on as I am now, I can never get anywhere. But"—his eyes lit up—"if I could carry on my studies in the United States and come home with a foreign degree, then I would have a chance."

"What education do you have?" I asked.

"I failed M.A." To fail a degree conveys rank, for it shows you at least got so far as to try.

"You know many Indians have come home with foreign degrees and still can't get jobs."

His answer had an internal logic. "I dreamed of a kind foreigner who would take an interest in me. That is why I moved to Delhi—so that I could meet foreigners. Indians won't help you." He named a distant connection, a man with a good government post, who inquires about his family when they meet and invites him to bring them for a call.

"Why should I spend five rupees to get my family there, and another five for gifts, when he could come to see us in his car and by his call raise our standing in the neighborhood?"

How pathetic, when such scraps and rags of recognition must be sought after but still be beyond reach! He will never get to the United States. Perhaps all his efforts will result only in digging the pit deeper. Yet the dream itself is a kind of sustenance, and so long as he can find a foreigner to call on now and then it will not seem mere gossamer. In this world of maya, of illusion, dreams which are mind-stuff are in any case the realer reality.

Our English friend had an invitation to the Maharajah's and we had a car. These facilities fitted together very nicely with our desire to spend a week end in a maharajah's palace. No American would dare return home without having stayed in a maharajah's palace—it would be as indecent as ignoring Notre Dame in Paris or the Abbey in London.

Ours was not a big maharajah. So far as we know, he possessed no uncounted hoard of jewels like the nizam of Hyderabad. He had not given his daughter a wedding costing several hundred thousand dollars like the maharajah of Gwalior. His palace was hardly as large as Buckingham, though indeed it must have had forty or fifty rooms. But he was authentic, and a big enough maharajah for us.

We found him lounging on a big open front veranda strewn with low tables made out of the real feet and lower legs of elephants. He was reading *Punch* and the *Illustrated News*, and the red mark on his forehead was shaped exactly like a lady's hairpin. Telephone and an electric bell button on the end of a cord were at his side. He rang, and tea was brought by a couple of bearers in scarlet coats and high, starched turbans who did everything for us but drink it.

"You would like to see the birds," he said. Our friend was a bird watcher. "The Jeep will come round for you whenever you are ready."

The Jeep drove us through wilderness roads so deep in dust that the tires disappeared. So did we, in a cloud so thick that if we had been jounced out of the vehicle, which was a momentary possibility, we could have floated on it. After a ride which must have taken us to the other end of the maharajah's domain, we tumbled out onto a road running like a bridge between two stretches of water. When the cloud of dust from our clothes blew away we saw them out on the water—the pink-necked Siberian cranes which had flown direct from Mr. Khrushchev's domain to that of the maharajah. Later we went looking for a tiger, but found only his tracks.

After a bath—cold perforce, since the hot-water taps turned out to be purely ornamental—we wandered about the grounds and discovered signs of many vanished splendors—a small zoo with a lion or tiger house, an empty swimming pool, vast gardens going slowly back to nature's own indiscriminate jumble, lawns gone to seed. But as we returned toward the house the westering sun reddened the big sandstone palace until it glowed and shone like a jewel, its towers and ornate outline majestic and a little sad.

We stepped into the reception room, taking our cautious way among the large supply of furniture, the lighted cases full of trophies and mementos. The walls glowed with lighted portraits of the maharajahs, resplendent in costumes hung with ropes of pearls. A wall-to-wall carpet made of tiger skins covered the game-room floor, while tiger heads sprouted from the walls along with other unfortunate assorted heads, none human. Neither the billiard room nor the library appeared to be used much. Since his wife's death, the maharajah had devoted most of his time to devout prayers and duck shooting.

The maharajah had invited three or four other guests to join us at dinner, which was served by half a dozen bearers at a table big enough for sixty. The eight of us huddled together at one end, the maharajah and his Indian friends eating out of big silver trays with depressions of various shapes and sizes into which half a dozen different vegetarian dishes were served. They of course ate with their hands. We got a complete European-style meal which we ate with knives and forks like good little Christians.

Since the guests were university people, we talked after dinner about education mostly. In our conversations with the maharajah, I sensed that the loss of his wife and the loss of his effective power as a ruler had left him rudderless. He had tried photography, which he claimed to be no good at despite a suitcase full of fine cameras. He took an interest in his bird and game sanctuary—perhaps as a displaced ruler he felt a kinship with animals who were protected only to be picked off when it suited the protector. He of course was getting a good income from the government, which was paying a total of thirteen million dollars yearly to its more than five hundred dethroned rulers—small price for such peaceful abdications. He traveled, went shooting, and kindly entertained foreigners fulfilling their obligation to see a maharajah. Early every morning he disappeared into the private heavily gilded shrine where he sought and perhaps found the peace and purpose which had gone out of life. He was there when we left, so of course we could not disturb him.

Every American who goes to live in India, if he can manage it, spends two weeks in New Delhi at an orientation course supported by the American Technical Cooperation Mission and the Ford Foundation and presided over by Rameshwar Dayal, a prime example of the innate dignity of Indian culture allied to the British sense of responsible administration. Panditji, as we called him, had retired as Commissioner of the Delhi Corporation, but had been called back out of retirement to administer this program. His devotion to it, and his gentle but firm determination to help us understand India, were wonderful to see.

Panditji is a handsomely impressive man. Usually he dressed in white from head to foot—white turban, long white many-buttoned coat reaching to his knees, close-fitting trousers falling in wrinkles down to the feet. A piece of cloth like a short stole hung loosely around his neck. Even his moustache was white, setting off the handsome bronze of his face.

At first we thought he was wasting time—he spent an hour or so making arrangements that could have been done in minutes with mimeographed instructions and a little quick canvassing. So, when he said, "It always turns out this way—we never have time for the last item on the agenda, which is the self-introductions," we smiled. But when we came to know him better we understood the warmth and depth of his concern for us, his personal interest in seeing that to each of us the right door was opened upon India. The speeches and demonstrations he arranged were almost without exception first-rate. But I have forgotten most of the details. What I retain from that two weeks is the character and person of Panditji—a man of the old school who could combine immense dignity with a personal attention to our most trivial or most specialized needs and interests, who found nothing too much trouble, whose appearance alone would have been enough to dignify the school but who added to this the unpurchasable increment of his loving care.

Mohandas Nehra came often to our place, and we became good friends. Powerful-looking as to build where many Indians are slight, he had thinning black hair and a broad face usually lighted by an open, friendly, alert, and at the same time contented smile. He was not wrapped up in himself; rather he was always looking for ways to be of use to society, and it was over some work in an orphanage which we shared that we became friends.

Mohandas had been brought up, after the early death of his parents, by a rich uncle who wanted to make him an engineer and put him to work in his factory. But Mohandas had ideas of his own. He registered for the arts course, and when his uncle found out about it, he left him to shift for himself. So he often went hungry, but he also learned to rely on himself—a rather unusual thing in India where everyone has a family to lean on.

After graduation he went to Assam as a teacher. When war came, most of the teachers returned to their homes but he stayed on "to see what the Japanese would be like." They never did reach the place where he was, but the fear of shortages led to hoarding and profiteering. With only a few hundred rupees he and a friend opened a shop which advertised goods for sale at legal government prices. Only then did the public realize how outrageously they had been cheated by the rest of the merchants. Now all the business flowed to Mohandas, the little shop was thronged, and Mohandas hadn't enough capital to buy stock to meet the demand. Well-to-do citizens, impressed by his honesty, loaned him funds without interest and the business prospered. Even with the modest markup, he made what was for him a small fortune. He placed it all in a bank which failed. (One of the largest banks of India failed while we were there, wiping out the savings of thousands of small depositors.)

Ever since that one venture into business, Mohandas has stuck to teaching—teaching Hindi to foreigners. His hobby is social work.

He visits orphanages to teach sports to the boys, or goes into the *bastis* to help alleviate a little the rough conditions there, or helps a neighborhood clean itself up and make a park or recreational facilities where there was only a trash-littered wasteland. He lives alone in a small freshly whitewashed apartment where he cooks for himself and keeps house with a simplicity that appears monastic.

"Why have you never married?" I asked him.

"Who would marry me?" he smiled. "I have no family, no fixed job. The only woman I could get would be someone I wouldn't want. And why should I marry?—" with that upward lilt of the voice which is so appealing a part of the way Indians speak English. "I am happy. I am busy. I have so many good friends. Who can tell what might happen?" He gave his head that Indian side-shake, as if to say, "Let things be as they are."

Every Sunday well over a thousand people flock to hear Swami Ranganathananda at the beautiful, chaste stone buildings of the Ramakrishna Mission in New Delhi. They cannot all crowd into the big hall, but loud-speakers carry his voice if not his handsome presence out to the surrounding lawns. Swamiji is an impressive person on all counts—fine-looking, with a well-shaped, close-cropped head, wearing the simple but effective saffron robe, and speaking impeccable English. His audiences are largely made up of intellectuals, particularly of those who have found temple Hinduism unsatisfying and who want the kind of brilliant metaphysical exposition he can give them.

Our first meeting with him was in his own small but comfortable reception room at the Mission. He began in his eloquent way to say how all paths to God are equally good since they lead to the same Absolute, no matter what religion one starts from. But then in the most winning manner he began to show us that Hinduism is really the best path. "The Hindus have had many gods in their midst, while Christianity has only one, Jesus," he said.

"Don't you think it rather strange," I ventured, "that God has selected only one country for these frequent visitations?"

"Indians know a god when they see one," he parried. "It may be that the Western world carried the idea of one God too far. Perhaps it doesn't want to see Him too frequently; it would be quite upsetting.

"The principles of Christianity were asserted in the Vedas long ago," he continued. "The Christian idea was good in essence, but its exclusivism made all those tortures by the Church inevitable, and made people rigid and grim. The Vedas teach us to accept God's presence wherever we find it."

After leaving him, we went to the handsome shrine nearby where the founder of the mission, or his likeness rather, sat on a dais at one end of a large and beautifully designed room. Offerings of food and drink had been spread before him, and an electric fan was blowing on him to keep him cool.

Vijaya was a girl of striking appearance, and although she came to our house perhaps a hundred times, I never saw her wear exactly the same costume twice. Sometimes it would be a sari of flaming red with a spectacular gold border, sometimes Punjabi dress with pajama-like pants and a smock coming down to the knees, and fitting so close I feared for her when she drew a deep breath or leaned over. She had striking features—big eyes with the almond shape so prized by Mogul painters, skin that she liked to call "wheat-colored," and a lively animated manner.

From her we learned all about the hazards girls face.

"No girl would ever ride alone in a taxi at night," she said. "It's not even safe by day. I always take a scooter—they're much safer." The scooter is the naturally air-conditioned three-wheel motorcycle that serves as a taxi and also unerringly blows all the street dust into your eyes.

"Why isn't a taxi safe?" we asked.

"Of course I can't ride in a taxi with an Indian boy," she said, avoiding the question, "but with an American it's all right."

She wouldn't or couldn't tell us exactly what the hazards were. We had to assume that they were of the same order as those that made a mother say to us that she would never leave a four-year-old daughter in her own house when only the male servants were there. Since we knew American girls who drove all over Delhi alone by taxi and at night, we were never sure whether the issue was safety or propriety.

When I winked at our friend one day at the culmination of some little joke, I got another lesson in propriety.

"Winking is considered very evil in India," she said. "It is very suggestive. A girl would never do it, and a boy—if a boy. . . ." It was the only time her English failed her. Apparently it is tantamount to a sexual invitation. So when you go to India, don't wink. For I cannot tell what would happen to you.

Then there was Sashi, the teen-age boy we met on one of our daily walks. He jumped off his bicycle and held us up at the point of his wheel.

"Good afternoon," he said. "May I speak you English, please?"

We assented, with that Indian nod of the head which had now become habitual with us too. He laid on his questions like a mason building a wall, one above another. Where did we live? Were we Americans? What were we doing in India? Did we like Mr. Nehru? When could he come to call on us?

I named the next Monday, and that became his regular day. His persistence, his hideous English, but most of all his lively interest in everything fascinated me. He was grasping hungrily in all directions for new contacts, new friends, new knowledge. He was taking wrestling lessons—one day he brought me a photo of himself with his biceps carefully spread to fullest capacity by the old trick of pressing them with palms placed behind folded arms. He also invited me to feel the living muscle. Fortunately he did not propose a match. I don't know why, except that he had so many things to say when he arrived that his head was spilling over with them, his eyes had the glassy look of memory overtaxed, and the words began gushing out like water over a dam with a driving wind behind.

"Mr. Bafford Smiff," he would begin, "may I ass you you like Kendy?"

"No, I don't care too much for candy," I cautiously replied, thinking he might have a sticky something or other in his pocket to offer me.

"No, no. He presdnt. He going be presdnt Uni Stayss. You more like Kendy Nixn?"

I made a noncommittal answer.

"You no afraid. I tink maybe you like Nixn; he Quaker man."

I had no time to clean up the several faults of fact and of grammar in that statement, because he was off on another tack, pouring his English over me like ghee on a temple image. I kept stopping him to correct his more atrocious errors. It irritated him at first, but I persisted until I think I managed to clear up a few basic points. Every week he would launch on an account of the past week's activities almost before he was through the door.

"Mr. Bafford Smiff, last days, no—Sunday, in Connaught Place I meet three foreigner. One Russian, two Amercan from Philadelphia. I ask them you want speak me all right, you no want speak me all right. I ask them what your name. . . ."

And so on, step by methodical step. Sashi was interested in cricket, movies, working in a neighborhood library, and in his studies. But mostly he was interested in people. He collected them the way our maharajah had collected tigers or ducks. He had a hunger to possess humanity. So every Sunday he wandered the streets looking for unwary foreigners to catch in his web, and every Monday he would proudly record his catch with me—one Russian bagged as he got off a bus, two Viennese stalked as their London to Bombay bus slowed down to a halt and neatly captured as they stepped out of it, four natives of North America caught at bay and trapped into a conversation about "Kendy." One day he confided to me that he was learning Russian from an uncle who knew some. Perhaps that explained his English. But his enthusiasm, his persistence and his gay engulfment of all experience were his own.

"Mr. Bafford Smiff," he assured me, "I want much study Amerca. Some day I think I see you there."

I don't doubt it.

Sudhir Ghosh is a handsome Bengali with a devotion to the new India, a clarity of thought, a liveliness of manner and a capacity for making friends that are wonderfully impressive. As a member of the not too influential Upper House of Parliament he perhaps feels himself a little outside the mainstream, but his gift for knowing everyone, combined with his residence in the capital—actually in an apartment where as he humorously remarks he can keep an eye on the Prime Minister just across the street—have made it possible for him to play a strategic role in Calcutta's urban renewal program.

Sudhir studied at Cambridge, then returned to a desk job in India. One day he went to the railroad station to say good-by to an English Quaker, Horace Alexander, who was going to see Gandhi.

"I wish I could go with you," said Sudhir.

"Come along," said Horace.

Sudhir jumped on the train as it was starting to move. Gandhi took a fancy to the young man. With his gift for bringing out the best in every man and using his special talents in the struggle for freedom, he made an intermediary of Sudhir, whose residence in England and whose personal attractiveness made him a good one.

When he and Horace and another Quaker, Agatha Harrison, came in together, Gandhi would say: "Here comes the Trinity. I'm busy now, so you can sit down and have a little Quaker silence."

Sudhir was in Delhi one time when the viceroy was to send a car to take him to the airport for a flight to Poona, where Gandhi was staying, in order to persuade him to come to Delhi for important negotiations. The chauffeur overslept and, when Sudhir finally got to the airport, the plane had left. Word soon came back that it had crashed, killing all aboard. Sudhir went in a special plane to urge Gandhi to come to Delhi, which he agreed to do. Gandhi always traveled by third-class train. But the viceroy was in a hurry, so a special train with only the locomotive, a first-class car and a third-class car sped him all the way from Poona to Delhi, a distance of 1,000 miles. There were thirteen people in Gandhi's party, so the old man sent Sudhir around to the viceroy's office to pay thirteen third-class fares.

"We want no pay," said the viceroy's secretary. But Gandhiji insisted. "Let him pay the twenty-five thousand it cost us, then," he said. But the matter was settled on Gandhi's terms.

Later on, when negotiations for independence were well-advanced, Gandhi chose Sudhir as his emissary to London, in response to Sir Stafford Cripps' request. Nehru angrily told Gandhi he shouldn't trust a boy without diplomatic experience. But Gandhi said, "I trust him." And that ended it. He felt in Sudhir a sympathetic under-standing of the British, and trusted this bond of the spirit more than worldly experience; that was his way.

Sudhir later spent several years in charge of Faridabad, the city near Delhi which was built to provide work and living quarters for refugees from the Punjab. He then put in five years in the Ministry of Steel, Mines and Fuel before entering the Upper House. His commanding interest these days is to see India succeed in its great democratic experiment, which means winning the battle of produc-tion.

"We must succeed within ten years or be overwhelmed by some other system," he says. "Some of our leaders make the mistake of thinking the public sector is more holy than the private. Either is good if it can produce.

"India has as many bright, capable people as any country. Our problem is one of organizing. We haven't yet found the answer. We have to find a way of making people all down the line take the initiative."

India does have its share of capable people. Even so, it could use more like Sudhir Ghosh.

Asians are deeply schooled in the wisdom of adjusting to an environment they cannot change. As foreigners in the land, we too had to learn how to adjust to customs and conditions we could not change. I felt much happier when I accepted the unwritten rule that all traffic should move down the middle of the road. I came to accept the cow, the horse, the dog, the bullock, the camel, the elephant, the jackal, the monkey, the goat and the sheep as brothers of the road, as much entitled to their path down the middle as I was. I was glad to learn that a man may wear as much or as little as he likes without being noticed, and I several times contemplated taking to a Gandhian loincloth.

I learned to accept my liking of Indians and my love of India as items of faith. I liked them even when they were trying to shake me down. The beggar children are often quite wonderful characters— good-humored, humorously persistent, chattering a language they think is English but which is pure fancy, masters in the art of pathos yet no doubt authentically destitute, too—that's the hell of it. I learned to expect child beggars to keep up a persistent campaign against my pocketbook while I sat waiting in my car at Connaught Place, and to accept their right to beg as equal to my right to sit.

I learned that when people promised to do a thing they meant it just as sincerely as if they intended to carry it through. I came to accept the love affair with words which makes Indians not only faultless speakers but wonderful builders of structures as beautiful to them as if the alleged facts really existed.

I like Indians because they are mentally alive, because they have made a virtue of poverty by discovering in themselves a superior spirituality which in fact many of them do have, because their sharpness in argument or in winning something they want is wonderful to see, and because they are a magnificent blend of humor, calculation, spirituality, imaginativeness and idealism. They have enlarged my life and my horizons, my awareness and my response. Now I know that no life is complete without India in it.

SIXTEEN

Inside India's Mind

"There's something schizoid in every Indian," an English diplomat remarked. Although the same might be said of the English or ourselves, yet to understand the sources of mental conflict is a good way of getting at the heart of any culture.

Consider my friend Govind Patill. Govind is just old enough to have taken part in the independence movement, winning that cachet without which a man cannot get anywhere in government—he was jailed by the British. He managed a year's study in England despite his hatred of the British—a hatred based upon deep respect. He gave up a profitable career in business in order to become one of Gandhi's many indispensable helpers, and he now fills a post of moderate responsibility in the government. New Delhi's bureaus are full of men in their forties or over who worked with Gandhi for independence. Now that the maharajahs have been deposed, they are India's new elite. The esteem for business and government is reversed, and almost any university graduate would prefer a career in government to one in business.

Govind is a charming person—bright of eye and quick of movement, with a handsomeness approaching that of a matinee idol though he has passed forty, full of quick enthusiasms and good ideas, a brilliant talker, knowledgeable in almost any field, a capable administrator, a reliable friend.

Govind is married to a very capable woman, a lawyer, who holds

177

a job in a cooperative, but has also managed to produce three children.

"How did you meet?" I once asked Govind.

"We didn't meet," he said. "Our families worked it out. I suppose you think that's horrible."

"Not at all. In some ways the method seems better than ours."

"Well, it's been a good marriage. I wouldn't have known how to find the right girl."

"Did they compare your horoscopes?"

"Naturally." He was on the defensive now, for Indians are sensitive about the prescientific thinking that flourishes in their culture. "It didn't do any harm, you know. After all, your papers are full of astrology too."

"Maybe there's something in it; I don't know. Why don't you come over to the house tomorrow night? Someone has promised to bring around a really scientific astrologer who's willing to explain how it's done."

Govind shot a quick glance at me to see if I might be pulling his leg.

"I mean it," I said. "I wish you'd come. I'd like your opinion."

Several other friends joined us the next evening, including the one who had promised to bring a "really scientific astrologer." The astrologer was a little man with big front teeth that had a tendency to hang out like a rabbit's, causing an ineradicable lisp.

"It is a scientific fact," he began, "that the moon affects the growth of plants and the ovulation of fish. In the same way man is also affected by the planets. So by taking a man's horoscope, we can predict the whole course of his life. There is no free will. All is determined by the astral influences."

"How were these influences determined in the first place?"

"Oh, scientifically. Long ago. We don't know who did it—our forefathers. It has all been written in books. Round features give smoothness. The triangle is intellectual, the square methodical. It is the same with the stars. The moon is a crescent—a triangle. So under the moon's influence the intellect is strong. The sun is round, which stresses the soul. Mercury combines these two with a cross. Therefore it gives mind plus soul plus energy."

I glanced at Govind, but his head was down and I could not guess his reaction.

"But what proof is there for these things?"

"It was worked out long ago. All the details. Mars has a martial influence, and Venus of course promotes love."

"Isn't that just playing with words?"

"We make predictions and they come true. Of course sometimes we fail. It is like medicine—part science, part art. We have to interpret the data. If we make the wrong calculations or forget to include one of the influences, our result will be faulty. The facts are there, but we have to interpret them. That is the big thing."

"What did you think about it?" I asked Govind when the astrologer had left.

"Mostly nonsense," he said. "But of course there might be a shred of truth in it."

"At least for fish who are ovulating," I agreed.

Yet many a weighty businessman will not conclude an important deal without the approval of his astrologer, or start out on a journey without being given a propitious day and hour. Even a scientist whose career is based upon principles of demonstrable cause and effect will consult an astrologer about his daughter's marriage with no sense of incongruity. It occurred to me now and then that the sense of incongruity was lacking in India, when I saw, for instance, a man carrying a desk and two chairs on his head stop to squat and relieve himself, or the dingy disorder inside the dignified looking government office buildings, or the strange contrasts in costume.

Through the centuries India assimilated whatever useful things the conquerors brought in. This is a rare and precious gift, but it has resulted in maintaining compartments in the mind rather than in generating an internal consistency. The habit of caste—of contiguity without intercourse—has spilled over into the intellectual life and made possible the simultaneous acceptance of things we regard as irreconcilable. But of course we may be wrong.

So, for instance, Govind assured me on several occasions that caste had been abolished in India. But it slipped out that his daughters would have to marry within their own caste and subcaste. He assured me that government appointments were free of discrimination, yet a few days later complained of a certain colleague who was always choosing Bengalis when there were openings in his office.

I began to notice these incongruities. Despite the creed of nonviolence, India is a violent land. (More on this later.) Gandhi is quoted incessantly—and ignored as often as he is quoted. Tolerance is claimed for all religions, but there is obvious discrimination against Sikhs, Christians, Muslims. Though proud of their own culture, Indian intellectuals are vaguely uneasy about it. They think it superior spiritually to the West, yet have really given up many of the suppositions it rests on. Though blaming the British for many of their problems—illiteracy, destruction of the onetime sturdy local self-government, draining instead of sparking the economy—they greatly admire the British for their skill in administering and governing and for their culture.

Educated Indians have been raised on English literature and history. Ever since Macaulay's recommendation that entrance into the Indian Civil Service be by examination in English, that has been the administrative language of the country. The Indians who speak English—hardly one per cent of the population—are the ones who rule the country. It is in English that they have done all their higher studies. But the heart and soul are in the vernacular. No wonder then if schizoid traits appear.

Govind lives in two worlds—the world of government administration and schools and cinemas which is primarily Western, and the family home which is Indian. At forty-one he still has to leave every major family decision to his father. At the office his word is a command—at least to those below him in a very rigid hierarchy. But at home, he is still a child. He may not fondle his children nor pay any attention to his wife in the presence of his parents. His father will decide where the children should go to school, and how the family income (including Govind's) should be spent.

This retention of authority in the elders may in part explain the reluctance of government officials to make decisions.

We had a caller one day from England who happened to mention that he was about to see the Prime Minister. In the brief span of a few days several other callers had also mentioned seeing Mr. Nehru, so this time we said, "What about?"

"Oh, I want to put up another factory to make biscuits."

"Does Mr. Nehru make the decisions about biscuits? Couldn't the Finance Minister perhaps take care of it—or even the sub-secretary for biscuits?"

"Oh no," he said. "It wouldn't do. If you don't see him, the next man down the line thinks you aren't very important and won't bother about you, and you never get your business done."

The concept of authority is an important one in any culture. In India it is a product of two major forces—the social system with its rigid positioning in a family, a caste, a language and a religion; and the weight of tradition—that is, the past. The past is a very weighty thing in a country which has contributed many of the truly great intellectual discoveries to human history. The ancient books—the Vedas, the Upanishads, the Gita—exert a continuing influence on the Indian mind. What they say, what they assert, must be so.

The Bhagavad-Gita tells how Sanjaya was granted the power of seeing at a distance all that happened on the battleground of Kurukshetra.

"This shows we must have had radio or television centuries ago," several people told me. Similarly it is asserted that ancient India must have had airplanes. The authority of the revered ancient book is sufficient evidence.

An accompanying effect, originating no doubt in the influence of the sacred books with their reiterations, is that if you assert a thing impressively enough it will not only be accepted as true but will be true.

How often did it happen to us in India that an acquaintance would make an assertion like this:

"The British destroyed all the panchayats in India. That is why we have no local government."

"But there was Lord Ripon. He did his best to encourage panchayats."

"That was only official policy. The facts were quite different."

"But the panchayats never died out. And the caste panchayats continued the same as ever."

And the conversation will take another turn.

The ancient books are full of reiteration—no doubt because they reflect a purely oral tradition, and a time when the learned got all their learning by rote. In the old days students first memorized the dictionary so that as they studied the sacred Sanskrit texts they could find the necessary definitions in their minds!

Oral tradition requires memory, and Indians have wonderful memories. The university entrance examinations devised by the British also put a high premium on memory, so that any educated Indian puts me to shame if I have to match my recollection against his.

But this very quality seems to have a serious side effect. When a high premium is put upon memory, logical analysis suffers. To recall and reproduce is enough. And it is enough of an effort so that it can appear to pass as an intellectual equivalent of analytical thinking. Because it is hard to do, it must be worthwhile. It must therefore be authentic. If you can produce *the* answer from the memorized authority, you have won the argument.

I spent a month of intensive seminar work with a group of brilliant university instructors and came to have the greatest respect for their intellectual capacities. And yet—

When we talked about American literature, they wanted to know:

"Who is the best American writer?"

"Is Emily Dickinson as great a poet as Walt Whitman?"

"Is American democracy fundamentally materialistic?"

The examination system has made even good minds into textbooks. It leads them to hunt for the "right" answer and to reject all precautionary modifications. This is also the only way an oral tradition can be upheld through the centuries, so the two influences keep pushing in the same direction—toward brilliant refinements and oversimplification.

One aspect, one explanation thus becomes the "right" answer. Subsidiary or conflicting evidence is ignored. Indians still speak of *the* Truth as if it were one and indivisible, without internal conflicts.

"Is character or story more important to a novel?"

"Was the European or the frontier influence more important in the development of America?" (Their answer: "The frontier, because Americans are different from Europeans.")

"Who was responsible for World War II?" (Their answer: "The United States, because it failed to invest abroad after the first World War, and thus forced other nations into economic nationalism.")

They are bound to have one simple answer to every complicated situation. The curious unstated assumption that underlay our conversations was this:

Since Truth is indivisible, every situation can be explained by one factor alone; the others can be ignored. They may fit into the picture elsewhere; they may be answers to other questions. But to every question there is one answer.

It struck me then that the admirable fluency and clarity of my young Indian colleagues had been achieved only by sacrificing wholeness and faithfulness to all the facts.

"Truth comes from realization," one of these young teachers said when I tried to explain my concern to him. "Sometimes even for a moment we reach that state of realization which is beyond intellect. This is truth."

How did he know this?

"Because the truth must be one and unchanging. We now say the earth moves around the sun, but later we may discover this is not true. Therefore what science teaches is not truth, but merely suppositions. The truth is something higher."

Truth, it turns out, is something monolithic and beyond human knowledge and experience. I got nowhere by suggesting that a thing is not merely good but good for something, that truth is relative to surrounding conditions. In the end, after a good many conversations, I had to conclude that my Indian friends would frequently reject any solution which appeared difficult or pluralistic in favor of one that ignored some of the evidence in order to provide a clearer answer. My American colleagues in the seminar were also astounded at the ease with which the group ignored facts and made sweeping assertions based on insufficient evidence, steadfastly refusing to confront the complexity of experience.

The reason this worries me is that we may see and suffer the consequences of this tendency in India's vast drive for development. If too much faith is placed in one solution instead of experimenting with many things and letting the best ideas win, costly errors may be committed on a nation-wide scale.

What puzzles me is that throughout her history India has been noted for a capacity to absorb new peoples, new religions, new ideas, new art forms, new modes of living with splendid disregard of consistency. In temple sculpture the anthropomorphic gods ride on the backs of the animals whose cults they have overcome. Unseen above them floats the Absolute, the Universal Soul which unites all and is beyond the art of the sculptor. Animism, anthropomorphism, and abstract thought inhabit the same house, the same mind. This sense of the ultimate sameness of opposites, of the oneness of all experience, crowns Indian religious thought. Why, then, has it not resulted in a sensitivity to the varieties of experience and a delight in contrariety?

The drive toward oneness seems to have produced an opposite effect. We are, on the whole, pluralists. We delight in the variety of our world and in varied approaches to understanding or coping with it. But Indians are—despite their thousands of gods, their hundreds of languages, their sophistication of many cultural origins—essentially monists. They yearn for unity. They long to be absorbed into Brahman, the Universal Soul. This is the whole point of their religious quest. Their quick acceptance of all points of view is a strategy for conquest.

"Yes, yes, that is what I believe," our Indian friends have often said to us in the midst of a religious or philosophical discussion. Their ability to welcome and absorb many cultures and religions is the thing they most often mention with pride.

But this is a universality of absorption, not of coexistence. Over and again it is the great ocean with its power of dissolving all into one which captures the Indian imagination. In primordial time God floats in the ocean which is also himself. His acts of creation are "plays"—for being All He needs nothing more to complete himself, and thus He creates only for sport, not out of need. Out of this oneness all has come, and to one all must return. This certainty undergirds all Indian thought. But it leaves us with the paradox that while it is the genius of Hindu thought to see the truth in opposites and the impossibility of black and white answers where there are many colors, yet in the end all must dissolve into one.

Yet, as soon as I have written this, I must qualify it, for I cannot accept the accuracy of any simple answer! Where Indians want a simplified answer, they are also able to accept without mental indigestion two or more ideas that may be mutually incompatible from our point of view.

"Caste has been abolished by our Constitution," we were told over and again. But caste still controls society.

"Hinduism accepts all religions. In the Ramakrishna Mission they include the teachings of Jesus and Mohammed. Everyone is welcome if he wishes to worship with Hindus."

"But I have been kept out of many Hindu temples," I pointed out. "A sign at the entrance says 'Only Hindus permitted beyond this point.' And as you know, Hindus are also kept out if they are outcastes."

It gradually became clear to me that the Indian mind delights in abstractions and sees no incongruity between an abstract idea that is consistent within itself and evidence in the workaday world that controverts it. I sat for a whole week end through a series of discussions on law and education. The university students there spoke with ease and brilliance, without ever once referring to school boards, textbooks, teachers colleges, law schools and courts and probation programs—the very tangibles which would have been the meat of such discussions with us.

I came to see that the abstract world is both more real, more valid and more prestigious than the workaday world, and that Indians are happiest when they dwell in it. Indian intellectuals are brilliant speakers, planners, devisers. They enunciate grand ideas. And because the world of ideas is the real world, the higher world, there is a feeling that to enunciate a plan is to have executed its more important part. To give birth to a thought is more important than to do an act, for action is in the realm of matter, while thought lives in the higher mansions of the spirit. American advisers report that while the government is planning brilliantly for increasing agricultural production, it fails on the practical level of sending experts out to work with small farmers and to show them how with their own small resources they can increase their yields.

Indians see the world of the mind as a real world more readily than we do. They live in it; they are at home in it; they know all its ordered turns and paths. The skill with which they can deliver an extempore speech—and in English—suggests that their minds are somehow tidier than ours, and under better control. We keep getting tangled in the embarrassment of checking ideas against reality. They see beauty in the mind and do not sully it with the world of matter. They can therefore build more stately mansions, make tidier constructs. It gives them a great advantage as debaters, as advocates, as propagandists. They can believe what we have to reject by our constant reference to experience.

I often had the feeling, when talking to a man of high intelligence and position, that he was brilliant in his analysis of causes, but fuzzy in his prescription of measures to be taken. This, of course, could be true anywhere; yet it seemed to me that the Indian mind hazes out into abstraction when it comes to grips with a problem demanding practical 1-2-3 steps for its solution. A sociologist who gave a brilliant analysis of the Akāli problem and the demand for a separate Punjabi-speaking state could produce nothing but a vague "be good" attitude when it came to recommending practical solutions.

We attended meeting after meeting, sponsored usually by religious or Gandhian organizations, where this attitude repeated itself. I came to see that there is an absolute realm of truth, beauty and goodness which seemed to be above and apart from the effort to realize tangible truth, beauty and goodness here and now. We too listen to a lot of dull sermons, but we feel uneasy unless we do something to apply these principles to our living.

Since the idea is superior to the act, it follows that saying you will do a thing is equal to—or better than—doing it. Indians are terribly friendly people. They want to be helpful and hospitable, and they are. But their eagerness to be helpful often leads them to promise more than they can possibly perform; more than they have any intention of performing. We had to learn that when they said, "Come and spend a week end with us," or "You want to go to Agra? I will get my uncle's car and take you there," what they really meant was, "I want you to like India and hope you will find it a friendly place."

These easy promises—to meet for a meal, to come and act as a guide, to help with a program of social action—are let fall and left lying loose all over the place. There are, we discovered, two kinds of promise in India, plain and pucca (pronounced puck'ah). A plain promise means nothing. If you want to be sure you have a date, you ask "Is that a pucca promise?"

A friend of ours made the mistake of taking literally a many-times-offered invitation to stay with a family he felt he knew rather well. He had not been there long when it became clear that they had really had no intention of putting him up and were not very happy about it—a fact that became painfully evident when they took no meals with him, sent his breakfast to his room, locked his door into the house so that he had to come and go by the garden, left him stranded without promised transportation, and hardly saw him except by accident in the garden. An extreme case, but helpfully illustrative. Indians, on the other hand, say that when they visit America, we are always inviting them to drop in but rarely issue a solid invitation. We hang out all the signals of real friendship, but fail to follow through.

"I was invited once to dine with a family," a student told me. "They were very cordial and we had a good time, and when I was leaving they told me to drop in any time. When I did several weeks later they weren't even sure who I was. I felt unwelcome."

Somehow we get our signals mixed. Part of the problem is that while we give our allegiance to institutions—church, service club, party, union—they reserve theirs for individuals. We prefer voluntary association—affiliating ourselves with groups we choose ourselves, while they are tied to the groups they are born into—family, caste, religion. We are always looking for causes or purposes which will unite us (as voters, workers, improvers of our neighborhood, preservers of our wild life), while they are born to a fixed position in a society which accents their differences from one another. Sociologists have noted the large amount of faction and distrust in village life. The social dynamo seems to be rotated by strong alternate forces of attraction (family, caste, religion) and repulsion (the other fellow's family, caste or religion). There is a relevant religious mythology for this too—Vishnu the preserver; Shiva the destroyer; Kali as both mother goddess and goddess of destruction.

With this social background, promises given outside the inherited responsibilities are not important. College instructors say it is hard work to get students to accept responsibility in a club or organization. They want to be officers, they want their names to appear, but they won't shoulder responsibility. If an organization is formed, the promoters are satisfied with a façade; they do not care to do the hard work that will make it alive and useful. We watched many groups form and die for lack of carry-through; for lack of a simple willingness to work which would match the original enthusiasm with which the group was formed.

I came to see that if you are raised in a hereditary society, a voluntary institution which brings strangers together is not quite bona fide. It does not strike emotional roots, does not lead to identification, does not call forth allegiance and losing oneself in the job and finding satisfaction in it. So, while we tend to escape from our born ties to those we choose voluntarily, in India it is the hereditary ties that count. The institutionalizing of loyalties for social ends has not yet taken hold.

Indians often do good works, but they do them as individuals rather than through an institution. They do this because of the strong drive towards self-realization—the high goal of Indian life and philosophy.

Self-realization implies no selfish drive for material success or happiness. Rather, it means a hard-won struggle to realize the oneness of the individual with the universal, the absolute soul. The road to self-realization is long and rocky. It demands self-denial of the most rigid sort, constant curbing of all appetites, ultimate withdrawal from the world to a life of severe contemplation. This saintly tradition runs through all Indian life and thought.

An advertisement for a novel read:

"What can withstand the power of her beauty? But lo, a new foe—the spiritual strength of an ascetic."

This is the basic conflict—between sex and sainthood, between temptress and teacher, between material and spiritual worlds. Sex is looked upon as a barrier to spiritual growth as well as a physically debilitating act. It seems to be regarded as polluting. One of the first steps in self-realization is to give up sexual intercourse, as Gandhi did.

While we tend to look upon social service as the road to personal maturity and satisfaction, an Indian will say that he must first perfect and self-discipline himself before he can undertake any worthy social service. Here again the idea of pollution, so central to Hindu thought, is at work. If one is to be a vessel of the spirit, he must first make himself clean. Gandhi, Vinoba, Jayaprakash all preach the need of reforming the individual completely from within as a step to social reform. So a man will say with all sincerity:

"I wish to practice nonviolence. But to do this fully I must renounce my family and live a life of perfect service like Vinoba. But my family needs me. I am their sole support. Therefore I cannot go, and therefore I cannot practice nonviolence. I must live in this world and live by its standards. Therefore I must strive and compete and press my competitors. But some day I shall retire and practice nonviolence."

Thus the saintly tradition, which has so strong a hold in Indian life, is to a certain extent self-defeating. For one cannot be half a saint. It is all or nothing. To us there seems to be hypocrisy in this attitude, "Since I cannot do perfectly, I will do nothing." To India *we* appear hypocritical in settling for a compromise, a second or third best, a partial solution. India is willing to admit that a man may have a perfect concept of nonviolence yet not practice it. We tend to say, "If his concept is perfect, he must at least practice it a little." We test by results, they by the concept. Our holy men are fewer, our ideas less ideal, but we do insist on results.

Yet they also yearn to do good works. Self-realization seems to require that this be done through a project originating with the projector rather than through an existing organization. So the country is full of ashrams, religious cults, yoga teachers and practitioners, food faddists, naturopaths and seekers after truth—all bent upon reaching a higher state of self-realization. I talked with many earnest people who needed nothing but financial support to enable them to do a great deal of good. Since we had come to India, we hoped, to do some good ourselves, we suddenly felt that we were looking at ourselves in a trick mirror. Might we not better go home and in Voltairean fashion cultivate our own gardens? All these concerns seemed so noble and so pathetic! Suddenly it seemed to us rather fitting that the Prime Minister began his day by standing on his head. His yoga appears symbolic of a country which can stand on its head, but can't pack a faucet; which knows a thousand paths to eternal truth, but cannot read; which plans Utopia while the beggars and the unemployed sleep and give birth in the streets. Perhaps India has turned to self-realization as the only escape from reality.

We were a little puzzled by the almost aggressive way in which favors were pressed upon us, until we learned that when you do a person a favor he is really doing you a favor, because by allowing you to gain merit he has increased your chances of a better life in the next incarnation. You therefore owe him something for having given you something. Since one must go on living life after life, it becomes really important to do some good in this one that will accrue to you personally. Work done through and for institutions or organizations seems to lack this benefit.

So when an Indian friend starts to do you a favor, watch out! Because you are really doing him one, as you may find out before it is over.

We wanted to visit a session of Parliament, a thing we could easily have managed since we knew many of its members. But we happened to mention it in the presence of someone who wanted to do us a favor. He insisted that he would get tickets for us on a certain day (we would have preferred another day when something interesting was happening), and that a cousin who had some vaguely defined function in the office of a minister of state would get them for us. We had merely to call at the minister's house. (Our own friends would have sent us the tickets or left them for us at Parliament.) We called. No cousin. No tickets. We waited half an hour. Parliament meanwhile had begun, and the first minutes are always the best when the Prime Minister appears. Peons (messengers) dashed like snails here and there to locate the cousin or the tickets. Another half hour passed and a tired car chugged in the gate, burdened with our two tickets. It had been assumed first that of course we wouldn't come on time (it's not done in India), second that we might not come at all, and third that there would be little point in applying for the tickets until we showed up.

If there is a disadvantage in being done a favor to, there is equal hazard in being sought out for a favor.

One method is a kind of obvious deviousness with which the seeker lays siege to you, so that you know you are going to be had if he can manage it. He tries to corner you and impose a favor on *you*, thus pinning on you an obligation from which there is no escape.

Or he sits. A suitor who wishes to lay siege to you is perfectly willing to sit, squat or lie on your premises for an indeterminate time (what matter, since yesterday and tomorrow are the same?) until you notice him, make the mistake of asking what he wants, and

thereupon become involved in his life and problems, of which he is
certain to have several. Where survival is a struggle and where we
are by comparison wealthy, this is natural enough. Sometimes the
request is direct: "Give me money to rent a house." "Buy me a pair
of shoes." "Give me the money to buy a new bicycle tire so that I
may look for work." Yet there appear to be no hard feelings if you
refuse.

Self-realization also seems to involve self-expression. Indians are a
volatile, lively, friendly, curious, eager people as a whole—especially
if they are Bengalis, Keralans, intellectuals, city people, country
people—or men, women or children! They respond to a smile or a
friendly word and one can quickly be on easy terms with a clerk,
a boy, a merchant, a waiter. I often sensed a rather surprised though
pleased response to a friendly opening, and I wondered whether they
were still recovering from the British. We are really more like them
—except for those of us on either side who prefer to stand on privilege
and position.

Indian behavior is often animated even to the point of nervousness.
The hand motions, for example, are quite different from ours. One,
done with fingers spread out in the graceful fashion of a dancer and
the forearm gyrating, seems to say, "No, it wasn't that way at all;
I'll tell you how it really was." Or "He didn't put anything over on
me; I saw through him from the start." Or "Let me get a word in,
can't you?"

Or there is the hand pushed forward once or twice with palm
forward, also raising it a little: "It's in the bag." "Everything is
lovely." (It probably isn't.) "It's just as you say." (Meaning: You are
a perfect liar, but I will pretend to agree with you.)

Or the fingers wriggle rapidly, pointed upward as the arm is thrust
toward the ceiling: "My mind is as active as snakes, and my speech
though rapid can hardly keep up with it." Or perhaps: "You see the
beauty of my idea; it has taken flight and left the earth."

Palm switched back and forth like a railway signal: "Comme ci,
comme ça."

Indians in a group are a lively, happy, noisy, agreeable lot. They are eager to react with each other, they love to kid—sometimes with an edge of cruelty—and they respond to the smallest sally of wit. They love talk—especially their own. When they listen to others they are likely to start up a nervous foot-jiggling which afflicts them until they can speak themselves.

But if you expect a group to reach a decision, you are in for trouble. All talk at once, each one advancing his own proposition. It becomes a point of pride to win, so the result is chaos. I never realized until I went to India how much self-restraint we have imbibed from our experiences since childhood with parliamentary procedure.

There is plenty of good talk, brilliant talk in India. The oral tradition still gives high place to the speaker, to the magic of words. There is a faith in words as objects, as reality, as acts. We are impatient of words. We grow tired of them, we mistrust them. They never do. They are in love with talk, and they can build in talk worlds that never were, but which they honestly believe in.

"In the beginning was the word." They believe this. The word is the symbol of creation; it is creation. Yet here's the rub—since speaking fluently gives status, they inevitably say more than they need to say, and therefore say less than they might say with fewer words.

This sort of thing happened too frequently to be coincidental. A charming and intelligent visitor drops in, exuding friendliness and wanting us to feel at home in India. He starts talking—brilliantly, every word perfectly chosen and placed. He continues. Your efforts to respond have each time been politely overborne or smilingly ignored. He goes on talking and you begin to realize that this is to be a monologue, not a conversation. He tells you all about himself, how important he is, what degrees he has taken, where he has traveled. He tells you about India, then about Japan, where he once spent four days. You manage to whisper that you lived there for five years, and have been back several times since. He smiles indulgently, as one would at a child's prattle, and goes on to deliver a lecture full of inaccuracies about Japan.

He has also spent eight weeks in the United States, which he proceeds to describe as if you had never been there. After an hour's steady talk, he smiles, rises, says it has been a pleasure to make our acquaintance (which he has not), and affably takes his leave—a thing which by this time we, like Hamlet, can think of nothing we would more willingly part withal.

The experience was repeated so often that I began to wonder what I had done in a previous life (I certainly had had them, now that I was in India) to deserve the bromide talkers who descended on me. They seem to specialize in stating the obvious, the redundant, the tautological.

"We have to solve the problem of poverty, because if we could solve this problem, people might become more prosperous."

"Something must be done about unemployment, because in that case people are out of work."

"What we need is more industry so that people can have those manufactured goods which you have it." (A favorite construction, one of the few consistent English errors.)

Gradually I perceived that in spite of the flow, Indian English tended to be texty and Victorian. Indeed one kept meeting the Victorian everywhere—in the over-ornate buildings, the ancient pre-war plumbing—Boer, that is, the brilliant uniforms, the old-fashioned offices with their clutter, their big ledgers, their Dickensian appointments.

After a number of these experiences I came to have the strange and unpleasant feeling that my affable callers had taken a brain cathartic and then run to favor me with the result. Why? Is it a case of the child encapsulated in the adult, still seeking the attention he enjoyed in childhood? The mind of the primitive who still sees magic in words and who possesses a powwow mentality—the longer the better? A mesmeric preoccupation with the sound of one's own voice? A fear of inferiority? Or just an innocent, exuberant overflowing?

Sometimes the talk comes out of an inner searching. One evening a young man talked to me as if he were possessed, about his search for religious truth. He had so much to say he could not speak very coherently, and much of what he did manage to say was platitude, but to him it was obviously stamped with the hallmark of eternal truth. The endless outpouring had sincerity without meaning, fluency without depth, great good will and friendliness, but never a notion that the listener might also have something to say—even though he had announced that he came to seek guidance. He had to project himself, he had to make an impression at all costs—and all this while talking steadily about overcoming the ego! I think Indians are obsessed about subduing the ego because they have so much of it; it is really their central spiritual problem. Where we have a sense of finding ourselves through service, through community, they seek self-realization. Though the goal is merging in the universal soul, I sometimes wondered whether there was not a secret hope that the operation might be reversed!

The phenomenon of compulsive talk is not restricted to private conversation. Indeed, the public meeting, of which there are many, gives the speaker a chance to spill himself onto a whole audience which by custom is expected to sit still and take it. I rather believe the story of Saint Thomas, come to think of it. No doubt he brought the gift of tongues along with him and planted it in India.

I listened one evening to a lecturer who had just returned from overseas. He spoke fluently but not well, because he repeated too many times the ideas he wanted to get over, and they were not profound ideas. Too cocky and peppery to be charming, he was not brilliant enough to do without charm. He spoke unhesitatingly for more than an hour and a quarter, shouting much of the time at that, without any sign of fatigue. He promised several times to stop, but halfway through his peroration he would think of something else he simply had to say. The burden of his speech was that Indians should practice real equality and democracy. Meanwhile he was busily demonstrating by his own behavior an uncontrollable desire to raise himself above his audience by the display of what he took for brilliance. This prima donna quality in Indian leaders is a serious matter, for it prevents the teamwork, pooling of ideas, and willingness to listen which are essential to progress.

It was my lot to hear this man make many speeches. One night he served as chairman of a meeting which was to be addressed by a distinguished American educator. But first he made an introductory speech twenty minutes long. The visitor then spoke informally and modestly for half an hour, whereupon the chairman got up and talked for another half hour, and then had the gall to thank the visitor for the hour and a half he had given them!

"I don't know why it is," Mr. Nehru said at one such meeting, "but speech-making seems to be our national vice."

We went to a vast number of these meetings, and we, like Mr. Nehru, wondered what their purpose was. Take one.

It was a meeting in honor of nonviolence, sponsored by the Jains. We had been told to arrive promptly at five, which we did. Nobody was there except a few technicians in pajamas, arranging the inevitable loud-speaker, and carefully laying out their wires for people to trip over. The meeting was to be under a huge bright-colored tent. We wandered around it, admiring the solid stretch of rugs laid down to make the floor, and contemplating the pictures of Gandhi, Buddha, and the gentleman clothed in a tree limb who must have been Mahavira. Someone led us to the front, where the most uncomfortable chairs had been placed for the honored guests.

Half an hour later someone came and led me to the stage, as I was to be one of the speakers. Other speakers, wiser about timing, began to arrive until the little stage was sagging with us. The Vice President came. We were led off for a cup of tea and a photograph. We returned to the stage to find that a dozen singers had joined us. At six o'clock the meeting got under way with a song about peace and nonviolence, after which the singers stepped gracefully upon our toes and departed.

The Vice President spoke first. After that I counted the speakers for a while, but ultimately lost track of them. The Vice President, a wise man, departed after he spoke. So did I. Only I, unfortunately, was last. As the speeches droned on, the chairman, who had had plenty of practice sleeping through speeches as speaker of the Lok Sabha (lower house of Parliament), blissfully closed his eyes and snoozed. Every once in a while his practiced ear would detect a pause, and he would carefully and economically open one eye part-way to see if the speaker had finished, then patiently close it again—for when did a speaker ever finish?

The audience was practicing nonviolence so thoroughly that they hardly ever struck their hands together. Indeed they seemed to be as wrapped in somnolence as the chairman. While the speakers extolled nonviolence, I looked up at an outside stairway of the house next door, where a crowd of children gazed directly down and in upon us. A girl turned and slapped her little brother, where-upon he promptly turned and slapped the child next to him. I thought of using it as a parable when I rose to speak. But I didn't. I was so sleepy by that time that I could barely rise to my feet. I made the shortest speech of the evening, which is no way to impress an Indian audience. Three claps could almost be heard when I finished. Those who still remained in the tent rose, stretched, yawned, and silently slunk away. Another meeting had ended. It is proof of their devotion to nonviolence, I decided, that Indians don't rise in revolt and slay their public speakers.

On another occasion we went to a meeting on Africa where the chairman arrived forty minutes late. He had not met the three African student speakers, so he told each to introduce himself. Then he got up and made a speech longer than their three put together. It was finished long before he quit. When he finally sat down, an-other character rose and thanked the chairman for the mess he had made of things, and he didn't know how to quit either.

"We are indeed fortunate, ladies and gentlemen, that we were able to persuade Mr. Chinwobble to preside over this honorable assembly. His impressive familiarity with international affairs, his gracious charm and delightful sense of humor have contributed im-measurably to the success of our function this evening." And so on. The trick is always to use a Latin word, never an Anglo-Saxon one. I thought of several plain Anglo-Saxon ones as I suffered through these meetings.

What were others doing, I wondered? For surely they were not listening; no man could endure to listen to all the speeches Indians sit through. Finally I hit upon it. They were composing the speeches they would give tomorrow. They go to other people's meetings so that others must come to theirs. And they spend the time composing beautiful speeches of their own. This way everyone is happy, for no one ever listens. I was happy that I discovered this secret early enough to make use of it for nearly two years.

But I was never able to bring myself to use the language chairmen are expected to speak. It goes something like this:

"We are profoundly indebted to you, sir, for your stimulating, thoughtful, and may I say brilliant address before this distinguished audience. We have known, sir, of your many talents, but this is the first time we have had the privilege of being addressed by your distinguished self in person. We have been deeply impressed by all that you have said to us, and will carry it away to ponder in the hours, yes even in the weeks and months to come. I need not repeat here what you have already said with such eloquence. [He then summarizes the whole speech—with amazing accuracy, too.] But I may say that I am reminded of my own experience while I was assistant to the minister of roads. [He then launches on a speech to show his importance.] But to put the matter briefly, and I must not speak any further—indeed I feel that I have already taken more than my full allotment of time—may I thank you, sir, for this stimulating, thoughtful, and may I say brilliant performance in which you have kindly consented to come and speak before us in person. And may I thank you, sir, for attending this meeting and gracing it with your noble presence, and for making our function such a success."

On one occasion Mr. Nehru was invited to speak at such a "function." He arrived to find a huge tent, several hundred chairs, preparations to serve tea to an equal number—and no one there but the man who had arranged the affair and a few staff members. Meetings are so frequent that even with the Prime Minister as bait one cannot be sure of an audience.

"It appears that the arrangements are more than adequate," remarked the Prime Minister.

According to the old legend, the Brahman was born from the cosmic being's mouth which, as the organ of speech, has magic gifts. Hindu philosophy regards sound itself as possessing metaphysical power. The hymns of the Rig-Veda properly recited have such power and can influence both gods and demons. At the creation the gods first formulated the idea, then uttered the names of things. "In the beginning was the word." Nowhere has the word such power as in India.

SEVENTEEN

Yoga—The Unseen Yoke

Dr. Sarvepalli Radhakrishnan, now the President of India,
is a professor of philosophy who taught for many years
at Oxford as Spalding Professor of Eastern Religions and Ethics.
President of UNESCO in 1952, Ambassador to Russia (1949–1952),
and author of many books on religion and philosophy, he was the
man who could best enlighten us on the Hindu view of life.

When we called on him, he was still the Vice President, living
in a modest bungalow not far from the huge presidential palace he
now inhabits. He never kept us waiting and we went without protocol into the comfortable living room with its rather heavy box-shaped
furniture and its two large Japanese dolls in glass cases. Dr. Radhakrishnan is tall, with a lean aristocratic face, gold-rimmed glasses
that reinforce the scholarly look, and an air that combines informal
friendliness with dignity. His knee-length shirt of homespun made
for informality, but the ample turban gave him a viceregal look.
Each time, a bearer served tea unobtrusively, while the talk went
on. There were no interruptions, and he never seemed under pressure or in a hurry.

"Everything that happens comes from a higher power," he remarked, and told us how this guiding hand had influenced his own
life. When he was trying to decide what subject to specialize in,
someone gave him an armful of philosophy books. They fascinated
him, and he made philosophy his career, beginning his studies at
Madras Christian College. When he was offered a scholarship for

200

England, his parents opposed it. But he took it anyway. It helped to open the way for him to the professorship of philosophy at Calcutta when the incumbent was elevated to Vice Chancellor (our equivalent of college or university president).

"Each step in my career came about as if a larger power were directing my affairs," he said.

Dr. Radhakrishnan believes that there is a religion of the spirit, an eternal religion, which informs all the established faiths, and that all must and will come ultimately to "the acceptance of fundamental unity with a free differentiation." Hinduism itself, he explained, is not a dogmatic creed, but a vast, complex—but subtly unified—mass of spiritual thought and realization. The various names of the gods, so confusing to an outsider, are ways of expressing the Absolute Reality. Thus cognition, emotion and will are symbolized in Brahma, Vishnu, Shiva—the supreme knower, the great lover, the perfect will. Every god is ultimately identified with the central Reality which is one with the deeper self of man. "Hinduism seeks the unity of religion not in a common creed but in a common quest."

"What place has Yoga in the Hindu way of life?" I asked.

"Yoga is not just putting a string up one nostril and bringing it out the other," he smiled. "Koestler came and talked with me. His book shows a Western rationalist bias in its disappointment with Yoga and Zen. Yoga is more than Koestler thinks. It is a way to higher realization. Some things cannot be explained by logic but are not inconsistent with it."

Yoga of course comes from the same root word as yoke, and is a discipline for uniting the individual with the universal soul. It can be practiced by anyone, regardless of religion, for it is a discipline— not a faith or doctrine. Or rather it is several disciplines:

Hatha Yoga—union by bodily control
Raja Yoga—union by mental control
Mantra Yoga—union by speech and special utterances
Karma Yoga—union by service—fulfilling duties and performing
      meritorious acts

Bhakti Yoga—union by love—the approach by intuition and emotion

Jnana Yoga—union by knowledge, for those who can realize the one impersonal absolute Brahman, essence of all.

Patanjali, the "father of Yoga," in a work now about two thousand years old, described eight necessary practices:

Five Yamas, or abstinences:

> nonviolence (Ahimsa)
> truthfulness (Satya)
> nonstealing (Asteya)
> chastity (Brahmacharya)
> nonreceiving (Aparigrapha)

Five Niyamas, or observances:

> purity (Saucha)
> contentment (Santosha)
> austerity (Tapa)
> study (Svadhyaya)
> worship (Ishvara Pranidhana)

Asanas, or postures—these are the well-known exercises

Pranayama, or breath control—also achieved through prescribed exercises

Pratyahara, or sense withdrawal—a discipline of detaching the mind from the sense organs

Dharana, or concentration—a discipline of focusing the mind upon an object or symbol

Dhyana, or contemplation—focusing upon the abstract

Samadhi, or self-realization—the final yoking of individual with universal soul through the practice of all the arts of Yoga.

Yoga is full of subleties and complications, but this is the gist of it. The exercises, both physical and mental, have a great deal to offer anyone who wants to be more alert, perceptive, empathic and relaxed. The difficulty for Westerners comes in some of the Yoga hygiene which is laid down as a prerequisite.

Cleanliness and religion, as we have noted before, are yoked in

Hindu thought. The important first acts of the day are bathing and defecation. But Yoga carries cleansing to a dubious extreme. It includes six purification practices: swallowing eight yards of surgical gauze to "cleanse" the stomach; cleansing the colon by drawing water in through the anus; passing a cord through a nostril and out the mouth and drawing it back and forth; staring without blinking at a flame; relaxing and contracting the abdominal muscles; and "cleansing" the breath by forcing it out with an upward tug at the abdominal muscles and diaphragm.

You can wash your stomach out, if you prefer, in this way: (I quote from a manual of Yoga hygiene.)

Take about two pints of lukewarm water and add one heaping tablespoonful of salt and sodium bicarbonate in equal proportions. Stir the contents thoroughly till evenly mixed, then begin drinking the same. Keep on drinking till the stomach can contain no more. Exhale all the breath and draw in the stomach, or really the abdomen, towards the spine. After an interval of 20 seconds, slowly take in the breath and again exhale deeply. Repeat this process for 5 to 10 times as may be found convenient. Assume either standing or squatting position. Should this not be comfortable, keep standing with the body above the waist bent forward. By now, you are sure to feel nauseated, and, if this is followed up with a slight pressure on the pit of the stomach with the palm of the right hand and with the drawing-in on the abdomen towards the spine, the contents are likely to be vomited easily. If not, push down the forefingers in the throat and touch the end of your palate, and thus slowly bring out all the water. Of course, it will come out mixed with a large quantity of what may look like mucus—really the unused, unnecessary and filthy surplus fermented juices and secretions of the stomach.

The idea that those secretions may be there for some purpose is not apparently a part of Yogic knowledge.

There are other bits of Yogic lore that strike the Westerner as nonsense. "One should never sit facing south," according to one of the many books on Yoga. "If a man always sleeps with his head to the north he soon loses his mental power."

"The meeting place of anus and the urethra canal is the seat of the dynamo of the nerve-currents," we are also told. "One should imagine a full-blown lotus of four petals at this meeting place and think that the Mother of the universe who is All-Powerful, beautiful, blissful and the very embodiment of wealth, success, wisdom and learning is standing with an effulgent body, smiling and blessing." But why does she have to get mixed up with the anus and the urethra?

Maybe because "The energy wasted in a single coition is equal to that spent in twenty-four hours of hard mental work and seventy-two hours of hard physical labor." No record is given of the experiment on which these statistics are founded.

Again: "Chronic diseases can be cured by Mantras [chants]. Chanting of Mantras generate potent spiritual waves or divine vibrations. They penetrate the physical and astral bodies of the patients and remove the root causes of sufferings. They are the best, most potent antiseptics and germicides." Again the word is the purest, most potent of vibrations.

Yet of course there is truth in it. An American physician interested "in curing the whole man" came to India to see what he could learn. We put him in touch with an Indian physician who is also a mystic. They quickly agreed that rapport between doctor and patient is the major part of healing and that human beings have emanations which are in some way similar to electrical currents or waves.

"There is something that knows us, but we do not know it," said the Indian doctor, and went on to argue for the existence of an essence that transcends the physical. "The taste buds are not taste, the brain is not the mind."

The traditional physiology on which Yoga is based, however, is rather difficult for a Westerner to accept.

"The spirit of man is in the right eye," an old holy man told me. "Press the man's eye and he will die. In sleep it moves to the throat, in deep sleep to the breast. By looking at the right eye a guru [teacher] can read a man's spirit. The vital part of a man is the 'serpent' [*kundalini*] of the backbone and brain. You can cut off a man's legs and arms and still he can live. The real life is in the spine and head."

The head comes in for special attention in India, where it is regarded as the part which belongs to God. Whenever a bit of cold weather came on, men wrapped their heads in woolen scarves, lengths of coarse homespun, towels or whatever came to hand. Anointing the hair and caring for the beard are other signs of this veneration. To keep the head warm and dry will avert diseases and prevent them from entering the body.

Dr. G. Morris Carstairs, Indian-born and thus able to speak Hindi with ease, found that his patients always felt themselves to be invaded by something evil when they were sick, and that somehow this evil spirit had to be exorcised—the old preoccupation with pollution and cleansing. The attitude is to be seen in many of the popular cures.

One day Arjan appeared at the house with a sty. The gardener told him he could cure it by taking seven mango leaves, each separately laid against the eye, then taken away and placed together like a pack of cards with a straw to hold them together. They should then be put away to dry, by which time the eye would be well. No doubt some witch doctor in the past had discovered it takes about that long for an ordinary sty to disappear by itself. When the leaves had dried, Mali came to inquire, and Arjan had to tell him it had failed. "Perhaps because I didn't have enough faith," he said, to spare gentle Mali's feelings.

The rationale behind Mali's cure was to drive out the evil thing. Similarly the cure for a headache is to drop a heavy stone down a well on a Sunday. But what if you have the headache on Monday?

In olden days many cures depended upon taking as medicine the five products of the cow—ghee, milk, curd, dung and urine. Even today these ingredients are popular, especially in the country, where a doctor of Western medicine is practically unknown and where the

Ayurvedic physician (*vaid*) or the local lore is the only recourse. So for typhoid a patient may be placed under a cover where cow's urine is dropped onto a hot brick for him to inhale. A tubercular patient may be quartered with goats, whose dung and urine are held to be curative.

Another lore is that of jewel therapy, which has been rationalized in the light of modern science as producing its benefits from cosmic rays imprisoned in the gem. "Gems have the power to cure not only physical diseases, but also psychological and psychic maladjustments," says one treatise. Gold and silver are also curative, you will remember. Here the theory is obviously the reverse of the evil influence. Imbibe a precious thing and its virtues become a part of you.

Dysentery (it says here) is caused by the displacement of the "pulse" near the navel. When it shifts up you get constipated, if down, diarrhea. A burning lamp placed precisely in the middle of the stomach and covered with a small bowl will take care of *that*. Speaking of dysentery and navels reminds me—

It is a rare Westerner who can escape dysentery for long in India. No preparations for travel into the country are complete without tucking away a paper of Enterovioform pills for amoebic dysentery and a bottle of Sulfaguanadine tablets for the bacillary type. Thanks to dysentery, I began losing weight about as soon as I reached India, acquired a whole new set of creases in my face, and transformed my own physical features in the course of getting acquainted with India's. Taking stool samples to the doctor and then taking the drug appropriate to the invader became as routine as getting up in the morning.

And now of navels. In the course of a trip south I noticed a small spot or two near the navel, but assumed that they were marks left by the predatory horde of insects which invaded my mosquito net every night. By the time we reached Bombay they were spreading across the landscape, up over what remained of the hill of my stomach, and southward. They then overleaped the long narrow ridge of my legs and began to chew at my ankles, attacking other outposts in a scattered and unpredictable way. They itched. They itched diabolically, especially in the middle of the night. I applied calamine lotion. It stopped some of the itching but did not stop or even slow down the invasion.

By the time we returned to Delhi I was ready to see a doctor. The verdict: *dhobi's* itch, a fungus infection. A *dhobi* (laundryman) in the south had thrown this in gratis when returning my laundry. *Dhobis,* since they are not particular about washing clothes in the same stream where buffalo wallow, sometimes put more into the laundry than they take out, it seems. (They would consider dung and urine cleansing agents, anyway—and perhaps they are. Maybe the stream that did me in didn't have enough dung and urine in it.) Anyhow, along with the slight grayness my shirts had begun to acquire came an invading horde of fungi who discovered in my white skin a treat the likes of which they had never before encountered. They browsed and ruminated in it like cows in a spring meadow, and they refused to leave.

Several cures were tried—perhaps a dozen. Gentian violet, which stained my clothes and fingers indelibly. Yellow salves which oozed through my shorts and socks. Still the angry red areas spread, hospitably inviting friends and neighbors in to form secondary infections. I took to my bedroom, since it was getting practically impossible to wear clothes. I stole down for meals in a loose gown, did my business by telephone, avoided callers, read vastly to keep my mind off the itching, and thought of calling in a *vaid.* This went on for weeks, for months. The infestation would seem to moderate, then take hold again. It was the only navel battle I had fought, but it was enough; I was tired of going to see. I only wanted it to go away so I would never have to look at it again.

Then my doctor happened to think of a miracle drug called grisovin (griseofulvin). You didn't daub it on like paint, or rub it in, a greasy mess. You just took a little white pill. In three days the curse had gone. Better take some grisovin with you if you go to India.

Colds are also frequent, at least in north India—nasty ones which don't leave gracefully. And why should they? Like everything else, their struggle for life is precarious and it has made them tough. No matter how you wash and scrub yourself, your foodstuffs, your dishes and your clothes, the vast armies of the microscopic unemployed are lined up and waiting, probing your defenses, quick to find an opening, ruthless in occupying territory you have always regarded as your own. Life is too plural in India to allow any patch of skin, mucous membrane or intestine to remain untenanted.

About six per cent of India's population has access to a protected water supply, half as many to a sewage system. Latrines are rare, defecation in public streets routine. There is one physician to each 6,300 people, but since three quarters of them are concentrated in cities and since three quarters of the people are outside cities, very few ever have access to modern medicine. There is a nurse to every 43,000, and a dentist to each 300,000.

Naturally quacks flourish—no one knows how many. But in a city like Delhi their pretentious shingles with phony degrees appear in every street, while others operate from the sidewalk.

Here is a fellow offering to pull your teeth without pain, without instruments and without pay. All you have to do is buy a package of his tooth powder.

And there is a holy man just returned from the sacred Himalayas —you can believe it from the matted hair and beard, the forehead painted bright yellow, the coarse heavy rags that make up his costume. He has a bottle of something that will restore your youth and potency overnight and which he will sell at less than cost out of a bountiful love for humanity. It's not his fault that the ingredients are so expensive.

There squats a gypsy with a basket of desert lizards, known since antiquity for the aphrodisiac effects of their fat. He will skin one for you fresh for a quarter or fifty cents. Aphrodisiacs seem to be greatly in demand, since any pan wallah (vendor of that aromatic chewing leaf) has them for sale. Charms and amulets also enjoy a brisk sale, as do all sorts of drugs supposed to have magic potency.

In the absence of qualified physicians, and because the indigenous systems of medicine do have some claims to authenticity, it has been impossible to devise laws that would eliminate the quacks without also hitting at herbalists and naturopaths who under present circumstances are useful.

Meanwhile the search for health is vigorously pursued, and nearly everyone has his diet, his set of ablutions and exercises and incantations—all based upon the idea that ritual cleanliness lies at the root of health, that abstinence strengthens and purifies, that the body must be continuously scoured and emptied and punished for its failure to be pure spirit.

One day a card came to us from a student we knew slightly.

"Do Americans believe that semen is made by blood? Is it bad to discharge it?"

We never answered. If physiology remains in the realm of faith, we decided, we had better remain agnostics.

EIGHTEEN

The Roots of Violence

Mr. Nehru's military exploit in Goa awakened the Western world to the realization that India is not, after all, committed to a policy of nonviolence on the Gandhian pattern—a fact which has long been demonstrated in Kashmir. Perhaps Goa will provide a useful corrective to our image of India as the land where nonviolence determines behavior. The fact is that India is both a land where nonviolence is regarded as the highest ethical value and where bloody conflict breaks out with frightening frequency.

The course which the idea of nonviolence took in becoming the spiritual center of Gandhi's campaign for a free India is one of the most fascinating examples of cultural migration in human history, and proof that we do indeed live in one world.

The idea of resisting evil by nonviolent means first occurred to the forest sages of India living in the Himalayas, perhaps as long ago as 2000 B.C. Fifteen hundred years later Buddha made it a part of his teaching, and it spread throughout Asia. In the late eighteenth and early nineteenth centuries British scholars discovered and translated the great religious books of India, so that they flowed into the European cultural stream.

These books in their English translations were placed in the library of Harvard College where Henry David Thoreau found them. He borrowed and attentively read the Bhagavad-Gita, the Upanishads, some of the Puranas. And they were clearly in his mind
210

when, protesting the war against Mexico, he wrote his famous essay on *The Virtue of Civil Disobedience* in 1849.

In 1908 a young Indian lawyer living in South Africa was jailed for passively resisting the inequitable laws against his countrymen there. In the jail library he found a copy of Thoreau's essay. The young man, of course, was Gandhi, who immediately responded to the phrase "civil disobedience," adopting it and the idea behind it in his struggle to get justice for the Indian laborers in Africa. Returning to India in 1915, he took it with him, and thus nearly four thousand years after it had got its start there, it returned to begin the campaign which would free India from colonial rule.

In our own time Gandhi's exploitation of this Indian-American idea, and his enlargement of it for use as an instrument of mass disobedience, has made another journey across the world to be used in our South by Martin Luther King and others who have studied and applied Gandhiji's methods towards racial integration. Racial discrimination in the United States and caste in India have many common factors, and now a common strategy of attack—the method of nonviolent resistance conceived in India four thousand years ago.

When Gandhi, defying the British salt tax, marched to the sea, saying, "I go to the ocean of God, and I make salt with my hands, and the foreign government will arrest me for it, but this is my truth and I will die for it," he was dramatizing with his own particular genius the whole concept of nonviolent resistance. For nearly half a century Gandhi gave the world its most inspiring demonstration of victory by love since early Christian days. Vinoba Bhave, following his master, has not only gained land for the landless but received the surrender of dacoits—armed bandits—who had terrorized the country and eluded the police for many years.

Hundreds of organizations hold meetings, such as the one I spoke at, in praise of ahimsa, and if most of the speeches with their lofty sentiments perish at the moment of utterance, there are other organizations like the Sarva Seva Sangh whose workers, living on a meager vegetarian diet, doing all their own dirty work and strictly limiting even their sleeping time, are devotedly putting these principles into practice in village or slum.

Yet India is plagued with situations which abound in conflict. Like any country, it has its crimes of violence. But in addition it is subject to outbursts of mass violence which often get beyond the power of the police to control. No day passes without some news of a mob conflict. For example:

SEVEN KILLED IN FACTION FIGHT

GARGAON—Seven people, including two women, were killed and one man was seriously injured in a clash between two factions of Ahirs belonging to the villages of Dhani Kulana and Dhani Shorsa, according to a report received here yesterday. It is stated that a land dispute led to the clash.

NAGPUR RIOTS

BOMBAY—Damage to the extent of Rs 195,000 ($40,000) to private property and about Rs 27,000 ($5,600) to public property was caused by the violent demonstrations organized by the Nag-Vidarbja Andolan Samiti in Nagpur. The demonstrations were a protest against the decision of the Nagpur Congress Committee to celebrate the 48th birthday of the Chief Minister.

In all, 34 people were injured, of whom one died in hospital, nine were injured in the police firing, two by tear gas, and the remaining 23 by the lathi-charge [a police drive with poles].

YOUTH THROWN INTO BONFIRE PERISHES

JODHPUR—A Jat young man of Kolhapur was bodily lifted and thrown into a bonfire by some men and was burnt alive. It is stated that while the youth was working in a field, about 15 people of his own community who had enmity with him, caught him, collected the crop stubble, lighted it and threw him in.

SIX SHOT DEAD

ALIGARH—Six people were shot dead on March 6 in Sakariya village, allegedly as a result of panchayat election rivalries.

MOB ATTACKS MAGISTERIAL PARTY

JAMALPUR—A mob of about 500 persons attacked a magisterial checking party of the Jamalpur railway station yesterday and rescued

50 persons arrested for ticketless traveling. The mob hurled missiles and brickbats on members of the checking party, including policemen, injured six of them and damaged a State transport bus waiting to carry the arrested persons. Being outnumbered, the magisterial party withdrew.

Why does violence erupt on a mass scale, causing millions of dollars' worth of damage each year to say nothing of the lives lost?

"We think we are civilized," Dr. Radhakrishnan said when we were discussing this subject, "but suddenly we lose the varnish of civilization and we see the brutality beneath."

Divisive influences were fostered, he explained, by the struggle for independence which encouraged resistance to the government when the government was British. With the British gone, the same kind of resistance to constituted authority keeps cropping up when people feel aggrieved.

When we talked with Mr. Nehru, he stressed the point that all these internal conflicts are natural to a country made up of many cultures.

"It's correct to say that India has not that whole genius compared to England or France, but if challenged there is fierce nationalism; otherwise, subnationalism."

When Gandhi announced his "Quit India" campaign, our beloved Gurdial had a terrible vision in which he saw rivers of blood. Seized with the feeling that he had had a strong visitation of the spirit, he wrote Gandhi that the campaign would bring terrible bloodshed and begged him to give it up. Such a negative approach, he felt, would bring an evil harvest. Today's strikes, riots and other disorders, he feels, grew out of the long habit of resisting British authority and the attitude of praise for those who were " 'agin' the government."

But with the British gone, what are the roots of this continuing conflict?

The most important are these:
   1. Caste, along with its subcastes and factions
   2. Religion
   3. Language

4. Economic factors

5. Ignorance

It has struck me that since Indians all belong to minorities—not one but several—they are continually fearful of being overrun by the "others."

Suppose in an American city each ethnic group remained to itself—Italians, Irish, French Catholics, Negroes, Spaniards, Jews, Poles, Germans and all the rest. Each had its own community—its own streets, shops, clubs. Members of one group could never sit down to eat with another. Their children could never play together or intermarry. They would vote only for their own members. They were further rigidly divided into the three major religious groups—Protestants, Catholics, and Jews—which never came together and which interfered with each other's ceremonies and festivals. Then imagine that each of these groups clings tenaciously to its old language, and that furthermore the country is divided into more than a dozen areas, each one of which has one of these languages as its official tongue. English is spoken by the educated elite, French is being pushed as the official language, and at the same time those youngsters fortunate enough to go to school are being taught in their regional language.

Imagine all this, and you get a partial idea of what life is like for Indians. They all suffer from the minority mentality. No one caste outnumbers all the others. That means you are born into a minority you can never escape from. No language has a clear majority, so everyone belongs to a linguistic minority, too. Hindus make a religious majority, but they are, again, broken up into many sects and practices. There is no ecclesiastical hierarchy. Furthermore, their sense of membership in caste and language group is much stronger than their sense of belonging to a united religious group. The other religious groups feel very keenly their minority status. The Dravidians in the south feel themselves to be a minority opposed to the Aryans of the north.

The word "community" is vaguely used in India to apply to all or any of these groupings. To caste, language, religion and ethnic group a man is born, and from them he cannot as a rule escape. Hindus wanting to keep more than one wife have been known to become Muslims, since Muslims can have four. Dr. Ambedkar, aroused by the failure of untouchables to win fair treatment, led 200,000 of them into Buddhism. But such a change is the exception.

Dr. Carstairs, in his fascinating study of Indian mentality, *The Twice-Born*, notes that people seemed quite calm and at ease in their behavior toward one another within the prescribed relationships of caste and family. But relationships depending on spontaneous feelings and emotional exchanges were precarious. Paranoid anxiety seemed to alternate with flashes of trustfulness in most personal relationships. When open quarrels broke out, adults let themselves go completely in a pattern like that of the child's temper tantrum.

Prisoned in their hereditary groups which they sense as minorities subject to mistreatment, and removed by inexorable time from the indulgence and care of childhood, Indians in a crisis find no way out but the violence which lashes out with childlike surrender of all control against groups and forces they regard as implacably opposed to them.

In recent years the worst outbreaks have been based on linguistic differences. Under Gandhi, the Congress committees were organized by language areas. After independence this structure remained. Thus political opportunists have played upon these linguistic differences. Disturbances in Bombay state became so serious that it was divided into two states, Maharashtra and Gujarat, on the basis of language. The vastly destructive Assam riots of 1960 were directed against those who spoke Bengali. The reasons behind the frightful conflict include economic and political factors, but it was as a linguistic group that Bengalis were identified and attacked. The Naga hill tribes, revolting against the central government, demanded independence but have been granted a separate state with their own language. And in the Punjab the Sikhs, feeling themselves to be a politically ineffective minority, have demanded another bifurcation along language lines—Hindi in the south, Punjabi in the north. Their demand includes the teaching of Punjabi in the schools, and in the Gurmukhi script in which the Granth Sahib, their holy book, is written. Here the linguistic difference is only a pretense for the formation of a separate state in which Sikhs would wield political power. The Hindus, though they actually speak Punjabi at home, to confound the Sikhs are insisting on the teaching of Hindi.

Language in India seems to be a unifying force which assumes that all those who speak a language are of a culture distinct from others and should have a geographically defined region of their own within which they will wield political power. The trouble with this is that India has 845 languages and dialects and only 15 states and 6 union territories.

India's dilemma is that for leadership at the local level the local language must be used, yet at the national level a common language is needed. The national government was built by harnessing the forces of regionalism, but this very force now threatens as a disruptive rather than a unifying one.

When West Bengal and Bihar got into a border dispute, Mr. Nehru had to tell them to "stop behaving like two independent countries on the brink of war." The separation of states on linguistic lines often sharpens the conflict instead of ending it. Andhra, after winning separate statehood through Potti Sriramulu's fasting to death, discovered that the conflict between the two castes of Kammas and Reddis who had been lost in the larger state of Madras could now upset the state. Near Madurai lives a group of 225,000 weavers whose ancestors migrated there 800 years ago. They still speak Gujarati.

Obviously people must speak their mother tongues. But what about a national language?

Hindi has been declared the national language, but over bitter protests from the south.

DEMONSTRATION BY STUDENTS

MADRAS—Students of two colleges in the city abstained from their classes yesterday and took out a procession to express their "dissatisfaction" at the President's Independence Day speech. The students demonstrated before the Secretariat shouting slogans like "Down with Hindi imperialism."

Five students met Mr. Kamaraj, the Chief Minister, and represented to him that the people of the State would be at a "great disadvantage" if Hindi were made the official language of the Supreme Court and if the All-India competitive examinations were permitted to be answered in Hindi. The Chief Minister is said to have assured them that he was aware of the difficulties the people of the State might face if Hindi became the official language.

While the north argues that Hindi is the language of nearly 42% of the total population, southerners reply that if you deduct the Muslim and Sikh users of the related languages, Urdu and Punjabi, the Hindi-speaking people total only 31%. Furthermore, they do not all speak the same Hindi—there are many regional variations.

It was Gandhi's intent that Hindustani, a combination of Urdu and Hindi, would become the national tongue. But Urdu is the language of Pakistan; therefore it had to be eliminated. Independence, moreover, brought with it a natural thrust toward indigenous things. Sanskritization occurred not only in language but in a revival, for the most part healthy, of old customs and arts. But when Sanskrit attempted to deal with the technological world, it came out with *thrichakara manushya vahana* for rickshaw and *sravana yantra* for telephone. Obviously it was not the instrument for a great country in the midst of one of the great technological developments of history. Technical textbooks in Hindi appear to be an impossibility.

A member of Parliament who worked on a committee to convert the Indian Constitution from English into Hindi told me that after months of hard work it was sent to the Prime Minister, who struggled with it for a while and tossed it aside, saying, "This is sheer nonsense." Since Hindi had no vocabulary for the ideas involved, one had to be invented. By now the words used in the Constitution have grown into use and even Mr. Nehru himself has accepted them. But to do this for every science and technical subject is a task that appears impossible.

What the non-Hindi speakers fear is that once Hindi becomes the official language, displacing English, all non-Hindi speaking people will suffer under a heavy handicap in the vital government examinations on which so many careers depend. English, now the official language, is at least neutral—nearly everyone except a few Anglo-Indians has to learn it from scratch. If Hindi became the official language, all whose mother tongue was Hindi would have a strategic advantage not only in competing for government jobs but when speaking in Parliament or in any dealings with the central government where Hindi-speaking people already have a disproportionate influence.

So the battle goes on. A distinguished elder statesman and leader of the Swatantra (conservative party), Chakravarti Rajagopalachari, tried to address a public meeting at Banaras. 25,000 people kept shouting "Hindi! Hindi!" "C. R." comes from Tamil-speaking Madras. He left the meeting without being allowed to make his speech.

Linguism has now become a divisive political force, unscrupulously used by ambitious politicians for their own ends.

In 1965 English is supposed to be replaced by Hindi as the official language. In anticipation, universities have begun to shift their teaching into regional languages or into Hindi. But since textbooks are lacking, students must continue to know English. The teaching of English has meanwhile deteriorated seriously.

"It's absurd to be throwing the English language out," Dr. Radhakrishnan told me. He believes that both English and Hindi should be continued as official tongues on a national basis, leaving each region free to do as it wishes regarding local languages. "English gives us a window on the world," he said. To maintain its international contacts and influence, India needs English, and needs men and women who are trained in it. "No one is going to use Hindi or Tamil at the UN. We should not drop the bonds that unite us, and English is one of them."

One day we walked up onto the Ridge behind our house—the ridge where a hundred years ago the British had suffered great losses in the mutiny that occurred when a change of rifles had led to the use of grease which their Hindu soldiers thought was extracted from cows; the Muslims, from pigs. (Of course many deeper issues lay behind the mutiny.) Not far from the Victorian Gothic monument to the British dead rises the pillar of Asoka—first erected in the third century before Christ, and more than a thousand years later brought to Delhi. What do hours matter in a country which counts time by millennia? We began to understand why Hindi could use the same word for tomorrow and yesterday.

Things that had puzzled us about Indian etiquette became clearer. Events to which we were invited regularly began an hour or two later than scheduled. Why not? Isn't this politer than starting before the guests have arrived? As for answering an invitation, we discovered that people would accept and then not come, or not reply but show up anyway. The letters RSVP, though they appear, are regarded as a mere decoration due to some eccentricity of the British.

The rhythm of life in a hot country and one which has floated in oceans of time should obviously be different from that of a cold country with a brief history. But it takes getting used to.

But, if the attitude toward time was different, we found in other respects a Puritanism that seemed familiar enough to New Englanders. Prohibition is in force in several states. While near nakedness is natural in a hot climate, it is not exploited on the stage. Vinoba, in fact, conducted a campaign against movie posters which he found obscene, but which exposed nothing and simply suggested buxomness—which is the way women have been portrayed from the earliest days in Indian art. While prostitution does exist, it is being attacked. The transvestites who appear at rural marriages (we even saw some in Delhi) and dance suggestively or, if not adequately tipped, expose themselves indecently until they are—these are definitely the exception to a rather prim attitude toward sex—one that is supported, as we have seen, by a fear that intercourse causes debility. Young men and women hardly look at one another, and only a few Westernized ones in the big cities can dare to date. While we were taking part in an international student seminar in Poona, it became a scandal that our members were actually walking out together in mixed groups after dark, sitting in a restaurant and having coffee together, and returning home after midnight.

When sex does rear its ugly head, however, the means taken to deal with it are sometimes strange to our way of thinking.

A village girl of low caste was so beautiful that she captivated a Brahman who was ready to abandon his caste in order to marry her. The panchayat decided that as her beauty was the cause, it should be destroyed. They would cut off her nose. This form of symbolic castration is quite common still in India; in Rajasthan alone eighty-two people suffered the loss of noses and ears during a recent two-year period. The girl ran away and jumped into a well, intending to drown herself. But she landed in shallow water; someone ran to tell the police, and she was saved.

Did she marry the Brahman? I don't know.

The Puritan outlook which has so much in common with our traditions does not seem to extend to bribery and graft, however. People openly boast that a prospective son-in-law gets Rs 250 a month salary but 300 in "extras." A policeman who gets Rs 55 a month (about $12), but has ten mouths to feed, accepts bribes to overlook lawbreaking, and of course is shaken down by his superiors. In the villages the minor official usually sits on a rug under which the humble client is expected to shove a note or two to get his business expedited. The principal of a college, when asked why he didn't discharge students who obviously had no business there, said, "Their fathers are men of influence. They could ruin the college's finances." When a senior government official publicly demanded an investigation of corruption in high places and promised to testify, Mr. Nehru said he should keep still and stop rocking the boat; he might disturb public confidence.

Our own scandals are bad enough, and in the era of the expense account it is questionable whether our methods of organized stealing from the stockholders and the government are any better than the regular bribe of the 55-rupee policeman. But the difference seems to be that bribery is taken for granted in the Asian system, whereas we continue to regard it with pain if not with surprise.

I listened to the wry speech of a professor of philosophy who asked why it had happened that in India the words vice and virtue applied only to sex.

"If a man is caught in an illicit sexual union," he said, "a great thing is made of it, but no one makes a fuss if he robs the government of a small fortune. If a man sleeps illegally with a woman, he harms at most three or four people. If he bribes a government officer or takes a bribe, he damages the whole fabric of society.

"When a college principal was found guilty of sexual relations with a student, rioting broke out. But no one makes a peep over such common practices as taking part of a teacher's salary as a bribe for hiring him, and getting a cut every month thereafter.

"When we say a man's character is bad, we mean only one thing —sex. He can cheat, bribe, lack integrity, but no one will ever say his character is bad."

The implication was that people made a big fuss over sex in order to preserve intact the thing they loved more—the pursuit of money.

Yet a friend who was in Calcutta during the wartime famine told of seeing starving people outside a confectionery, watching through the window as other people ate inside. When they came out, dropping the sticky papers on the ground, the hungry fought over them to lick them.

"Why don't you break the window and eat the sweets?" my friend asked. "There are no police near. The proprietor is too fat to run. At least you will have something in your stomachs before you die."

"We have suffered enough in this world," they said. "Do you want us also to suffer in the next?"

The humble dignity of that answer speaks volumes. It says that despite the bribery and corruption there is a solid core of ethics based on a rock-firm faith in karma. What we are is a result of what we were, what we did, in previous lives. What we shall be depends on what we do in this one. The universal law sees to it that in the long run things work out as they should.

So as a driver you have to look out for pedestrians. They cross the street in the calm assurance that if they are to live, they will live; if they are destined to die, they will die. Another life is coming.

Yet no sooner have I written this than I must admit that there is a delight in living, and an ability to be delighted with little, that we might envy. The ideal hero of Indian literature, moreover, is endowed first of all with a concentrated presence of mind, a mental alertness which carries him through all tribulations. Mind and spirit are highly regarded in Indian culture; this is one of India's greatest strengths. The present moment of readjustment to the conditions of independence and technological development naturally creates great strains. But India's human resources are rich and deep. The heritage of spiritual knowledge and practice, the habit of deep and intense self-examination and self-realization, will have social as well as individual results once the old hereditary ties give way to voluntary groupings and service to the wider community.

If Western voluntarism and activism can be yoked to the Hindu self-realization, high regard for intellectual integrity and gift of perceiving the spiritual unity of the whole world, India will again lead mankind to a higher stage of civilization.

NINETEEN

The Four R's

We had gone to India primarily because of the interest aroused in us by the Indian Fulbright students we had come to know over the course of ten years. They were almost invariably brilliant, personable, fluent, lively and responsive. If they were samples of the new India, we felt that we would like to live there.

We should have known that they were the cream of the crop— that no country could turn out a large number of such top performers. But it is a weakness of the human mind to generalize from the particulars it has at hand. So we were not prepared for the crisis we found in education, particularly higher education. In India, we learned, a fourth r goes with the other three—riot.

Before independence the British had developed an educational system which provided them with the clerks and administrators they needed, but nothing like universal education existed. In the few years since independence, India has done a heroic job of building such a system, but of course it has just begun. Fifty-five per cent of the children of primary school age get some schooling, but in the age group from eleven to seventeen only sixteen per cent are in school. Under Gandhi's guidance a plan known as Basic Education was drawn up to coordinate book learning with direct experience of the physical and social environment and to prepare children for useful lives in the villages where most of them would live. There would be an emphasis on crafts, farming and household arts, and on village

223

self-sufficiency, with the school as a community center leading the way towards a fuller life for all. The principles are much the same as progressive education, and the whole primary system is gradually being converted to it. At present about one-fifth of the primary students follow this program.

When Gandhi was ready to announce his idea, he first had six proofs pulled, one of which he sent to our friend Gurdial who criticized it for its failure to include music and the graphic arts. Gandhi argued through an exchange of several letters, but finally gave in and asked Gurdial, then teaching at Tagore's Santiniketan, to set up an arts curriculum.

At the top of the educational ladder, free India was able to build on the colleges and universities established by the British, some of them excellent. Yet we found university students seething with discontent.

Soon after our arrival in India I spent an evening with a group of undergraduates discussing the question "What is a university for?" The talk soon spread way beyond the topic, as talk has a way of doing. They were unhappy not only about their college, but about their country. Indians think only of themselves, they said. A man only wants a secure job; he cares nothing about his duty to society. Corruption and bribery are widespread. You cannot get a government job without pull, and, in business, nepotism is the only road to success. Young men go to college not to learn, but to get the degree which is a prerequisite for a government job. But then, since there are not jobs enough to go around, the degree turns out to be no guarantee at all.

Indian universities are asleep, they complained. They do little for the student intellectually and nothing for him socially. Dull lectures make up the teaching method; there is little stimulating contact with good minds. Since university salaries are low, the best men are not attracted to teaching. There is little research in the universities since separate institutions have been set up for such work. Therefore the university is not being constantly refreshed by a widening of the horizons of knowledge.

Pass students (students are divided into pass and honors, English style) take a smattering of many subjects but never dig deep. Honors students concentrate so much in one field that they lack general knowledge. Students are too easily admitted and the standards are low. And since they have no serious interest in learning, and since the examination system is such that they have little incentive to study regularly, they idle away their time, then cram for year-end examinations. Meanwhile they are ripe for riots, strikes, brick-throwing and other mischief.

There is a complete lack of social life; indeed, though men's and women's colleges adjoin each other, the university frowns on any meeting of the sexes, as it is practically forced to do by Hindu traditions.

"What's the use of educating women, anyway?" one student remarked. "They only come to college to get a degree so they can make a better marriage."

"If you men are taking degrees only to get a better job, the girls certainly have a right to take a degree in order to get a better man," I pointed out. The loud laughter which met this and every joke relating to women, however mild, indicated how pent up their social impulses are.

Loud laughter also greeted the boy who said, "Sure, I'll get my B.A.—and I'll probably end up selling pan on a street corner." But this, in exaggeration, is the fear they face—graduation and no job.

Their disillusionment rather frightened me, and I wondered whether the situation could be as bad as they painted it. I talked to educators, government officials, employers, men in the professions. Said a professor:

"These professional educational people always make three points. They blame Macaulay for the system we have, they blame the British for everything that is going wrong today, and they give lip service to Gandhi's basic education when as a matter of fact they won't send their own children to such a school.

"Gandhi," he added, "wanted India to be one big village. He wanted to solve our problems not by raising production to give people more things, but by teaching them not to want anything."

University people agreed that the students had cause to complain. Most serious, they said, was the low pay (lecturers get as little as $30 a month), long hours (twenty-five teaching hours a week), large classes and outdated textbooks with which the teacher must cope. Since virtually all first-rate students go into the Indian Administrative Service (which they must enter by the age of twenty-four), only the second-rate go on to graduate degrees and teaching.

"If government really wanted to improve education, it could make university service equal to the civil service in pay and tenure," said an anthropology instructor. "But it won't." Consequently the morale among teachers is low.

Once again the language problem arises. Many of the students now crowding the universities come from homes where no English is spoken, yet university instruction is mainly in English. They have had insufficient training in secondary school, so they cannot understand the lectures. I am sure that I myself could not understand the lectures of many instructors, who speak English volubly, rapidly, and incomprehensibly. So there is pressure to convert university instruction to the regional language. But textbooks are lacking, Furthermore, many of the instructors come from other regions and could not teach in the local language. Where a university has converted to the regional language, as in the case of Gujarat, its students compare poorly with others when they enter graduate school.

What do the teachers think of the students?

"They're hopeless," said a young don just out from Cambridge. "Or mostly so. Of course there are some good ones. They can't write, spell or speak English properly. They do very little work outside class, counting on picking up enough from the lectures to get them through the exams. All they want is a secure job in government. But they are not suited for jobs that require any sort of expert ability."

"My graduate students are just so-so," said an American visiting professor. "They don't seem to read much. They fill piles of file cards with notes and outlines, but they never seem to get down to writing."

"We're admitting too many students who have no business here," an administrator in Calcutta confessed. "But what are we to do with them? We're keeping thousands of young people off the streets, so instead of becoming delinquents, they're turning into Communists."

Interviewing candidates for Fulbright fellowships, I was surprised to find how few had read well and wisely in their own fields. Their learning and teaching is clearly syllabus-dominated and unoriginal.

But how about the college girls?

"They mostly come from villages where they have had no cultural background," an instructor in a south Indian college said. "They work hard, but only at rote learning. They walk up and down until they have memorized a passage—and then since it comes from an out-dated textbook, it's likely to be wrong. Rote-learning rather than problem-solving is the rule. And they're so rigidly segregated from boys that they get crushes on each other. They hardly think about anything except movies. They know everything about them."

The nature of the college's attitude is illustrated by this press dispatch:

SE(X) GREGATION IN COLLEGE

KARACHI—The principal of a local college has banned the use of nylon clothes by girl students. The reason given is: these clothes are too revealing and distract men students. The nylon-loving girls have already opened a campaign against this order and they appear to have the full support of their men colleagues.

A few months ago the principal had ordered that boys and girls should not talk to each other within the college premises.

Such social segregation has led to a form of behavior quaintly known as "Eve-teasing." It is not unusual to read in the paper that "Seventy-two men said to be Eve-teasers were rounded up by the police during the past two weeks." I never could discover how serious Eve-teasing was—whether it involved only rude or salacious talk or whether a girl was touched. It did not mean sexual assault.

A newspaperman who had spent weeks looking into what is called "student indiscipline" concluded:

"When seven or eight thousand young people, most of whom are not half-educated, many of whom come from rural areas of utter backwardness, are pitchforked into a city to live in semi-slum conditions with no supervision or amenities, with minimal instruction and pitiful equipment, then indiscipline and gangsterism are likely."

On top of all these tragic and inescapable problems comes the professional politician, often a man of middle age posing as a student and registered for years in the university without ever having taken a course or passed an examination. He gets himself elected to the influential student union, which he can easily do since as few as thirty per cent of the students bother to vote. The union, which is supposed to organize social and cultural activities, often does very little of value. But it does provide a focus for the discontent of idle, hungry, hopeless students. The results can be explosive. There is evidence that students are cynically maneuvered in order to embarrass the state government and the party in power. Since the state government controls the universities through budget, appointment of various executive bodies, and legislation relating to education, politicians often come to dominate the universities—even to dictating the appointment of the Vice Chancellor.

The end result of all these factors is seen in such a fiasco as this:

EXAMINATIONS CLOSED BY RIOTERS

CALCUTTA—In at least 10 centers in the city the B.Sc. examination in Physics of Calcutta University had to be abandoned due to rowdyism indulged in by a section of examinees. About 6,000 candidates have been affected.

This was the third time in a week that the intermediate examination had been disturbed on the plea of stiff questions. But Thursday's student disturbances were on the widest scale so far and marked by the worst type of vandalism.

In some cases teachers and invigilators [proctors] were assaulted and manhandled; in others, they were compelled to leave the hall on threats of dire consequences so that the boys could copy from textbooks. And this copying was done on a mass scale.

In one college the disturbing boys had to be separated from the willing ones and given complete freedom to write answers by any means on the understanding that they would not indulge in violence.

Yet few could go on with their work even with textbooks open as they did not know where the answers were.

Some students, willing to sit but prevented from doing so, sobbed. Some were broken-hearted fearing their career was ruined for no fault of theirs. The rowdies paid no heed. Chairs were hurled and benches thrown about. Some were hurled down below on the University lawn from the second floor.

In 1960 two of the four principal universities of India's most populous state, Uttar Pradesh, had to be closed down. Strikes and disorders, frequently reported in the press, often stemmed from resistance to examinations that were "too difficult." But educators say the examinations are disgracefully easy, and can be passed after cramming for a week or two with the help of readily available "market notes." Some examinations cover the entire three years of college work and lead to the bachelor's degree.

So much for the symptoms; how about the cure?

Any educator could set down on a small piece of paper the reforms he would undertake—better academic salaries, a strict control over the admission of qualified students, cracking down on the farce of letting middle-aged agitators continue to register as students and manipulate the unions, updating the syllabi on which courses are built and replacing the antiquated textbooks that go with them, having frequent examinations and personal counseling in place of the dull lecture system and the final examination on which alone the student's whole record and future career depend, better testing and guidance to match students to careers for which they are fitted, and then providing the various kinds of training to prepare them for specific careers instead of herding them all through an antiseptic "arts" program.

Easily said. But for every obvious improvement there are half a dozen impediments. Better salaries—no money to spare in a country which is now straining at the seams to increase its productivity and is just barely able to cope with its population increase. Admissions—strong political pressures force the colleges to admit the unqualified since a degree is the only gateway to the coveted government job.

Modernized texts and syllabi—too many well-entrenched professors have a stake in the system as it is and are either unwilling or unable to cope with up-to-date scholarship. The examination system—everyone criticizes it, but can see no way to do away with it so long as the universities are overcrowded and the staff overworked. So it comes back to money again.

In 1960 the first Agricultural University was opened in Uttar Pradesh. Patterned on our land grant colleges and dedicated to turning out competent experts in the various fields of agriculture, it will also integrate teaching with research and with actual farm work. Its modern teaching methods will include plenty of homework, contact with teachers, and frequent quizzes and papers instead of judging all by a final exam. Perhaps it will lead the way towards better higher education.

The emphasis on labor is encouraging, but it has to fight a strong social bias which regards any form of handwork as debasing. Even a clerk who operates a typewriter will sit idle for half a day if necessary until a peon comes to move his machine across the room to a new location. The thing that strikes Indian students coming to the United States is that even a professor will carry his own suitcase or mow his own lawn. Of course Gandhiji preached the dignity of labor and did his own share of it, including scavenging, throughout his life. But even he could not destroy the prejudice. The better wages offered by industry and the progress of scientific farming, as well as the establishment of all kinds of training schools, are making slow headway with this problem.

Still other ways of tackling indiscipline have been proposed. One ingenious plan, which will get nowhere, is to put the undergraduates, who enter as young as fifteen, on separate campuses from the graduate students. Another, solemnly sanctioned by a ponderous government committee, was to put everyone through a nine months' course of militarized "national service" before admitting to college. The scheme called for placing these youngsters in villages to help with the work there. What they would do, or who would control and instruct them, or where the leaders would be found, or how to prevent a social explosion when young city folk descended on the villages was not spelled out. The plan was quietly shelved for lack of funds. Another committee, on Religious and Moral Instruction, recommended daily meditation, prayer, religious readings and songs, and organized social service work in the schools and colleges, since the home was not doing an adequate job. It sounds very familiar!

The problems in education, like so much else, are enmeshed in the basic economic situation. When an expanding industry offers more jobs for trained people, standards will rise. But industry's gains are dissipated by too many births, which occur in part at least because of poverty, lack of privacy and ignorance. It is a hard groove to get out of, and its symbol is that blindfolded bullock walking day after day around the oil press.

One of the boners authored by an aspirant to the National Defense Academy read like this: "Hillary and Tenzing mountained the great pick of the Himalaya." The error somehow recapitulates India's plight—to mountain the great pick in every field of action. If great challenge produces great men, India will give us a race of giants.

TWENTY

Agra and All That

No one can visit a country as rich in historic fabrics and ruins, as varied in scenery and climate as India without wanting to see as much of it as possible. On one errand or another, my wife and I reached all its extremities though we had to miss a good deal in between. India has less of scenic beauty than its size would suggest—too much of it is barren or flat, or both. It also has the most magnificent spectacle in the world—the high Himalayas, and cozy hill stations (summer resorts) wherever a reasonable eminence permits.

The Nilgiri Hills of the south, for instance, where the British sat out the hot season at a comfortable seven thousand feet. We rode twenty miles up from the plain on a constantly winding road to visit friends there, and found their cottage poised in the midst of tea plantations on the edge of a precipice. If you stubbed your toe in the garden, you would fetch up in another county down below. Our hostess pointed in a downward direction to her field, where she was raising vegetables. But we couldn't see it, it lay so nearly at a vertical angle beneath us. Somewhere down there her housemate intended to build an ashram, at the spot where you would bounce if you fell off the garden, but as we had not brought parachutes, we never got down there. The ashram was to teach the methods of sarvodaya, but it seemed to me that anyone who sarved there would also have to stand and wait—with both arms around a tree to keep from sliding the rest of the way to the bottom. Our friend told us she owned three acres, but was unable to say whether it was measured horizontally or as the land lay. If the former, she must have owned a good half of the mountain.

India has one of the world's unique methods of travel. Every night planes set out from the four main cities of Madras, Delhi, Bombay and Calcutta. Around midnight they all meet in Nagpur in the middle of the country. While the mail bags are being exchanged, you drop in at the restaurant for a free meal, and if you have been in India a while you are sure to meet people you know.

If any one of the four planes is delayed, all the rest have to wait since the whole point is to exchange mail and passengers. If the wait is long, movies are run in the lounge. Then the call will come, and you walk out into the late, blessedly cool night, and take the plane that has your destination printed on a well-lighted board in front of it. There before you awaits quick transport to any of the four quarters of India. The temptation is great to get on a different plane from the one you are booked for. In any case, you have the momentary feel of freedom to go where you like, and a continent before you. The night fares are cheaper, and often you can get a seat on the night plane when the other overcrowded craft are booked weeks ahead.

No one has seen India, on the other hand, who has not traveled overnight by third-class railway coach. India's trains are unbelievably crowded. At first I could not understand how in a country of limited resources people could afford to be traveling all the time. Then I discovered that they often have no choice, since such religious obligations as carrying the bones of a family member to a sacred river cannot be ignored. But I also noticed that hordes of people seem to be on excursions which, though they may include temple visits, seem to be less than essential. Then I discovered ticketless travel. To buy a ticket for a train ride, it seems, is not sporting. You just get on and ride. About 7,000,000 people are *caught* doing this every year. Since I have ridden long distances without ever showing a ticket, or seeing anyone else show one, it is clear that a good many more of the 1,440,000,000 riders who travel 42,000,000,000 passenger miles in a year are riding free.

You prepare for a train trip as for a safari. You collect blankets and a thin mattress and a small pillow, roll them into a canvas carrier, pack sandwiches, fill a water bottle, and make sure of all the other necessities. Whether you are traveling 150 miles or 1,000, the journey always seems to be overnight. At night the great stations hum and throb with life. Elsewhere there is ease and inertia, but India comes to life in its railroads.

Our trip to the Himalayas is as good an example as any. We were eager to visit a Tibetan refugee camp and an English Quaker who with his Indian wife, a doctor, ran a small hospital. We drove to the big Victorian station of Old Delhi, and immediately were surrounded by redcaps—or red smocks, rather, for they use a coiled rag instead of a cap so that their head loads will ride easily. One man will carry as many as three suitcases piled flat, one upon another, on his head. That leaves his arms free for pushing his way through the thick crowd in the station, milling about like ants whose nest has been trampled. In the midst of it all whole families lie sleeping, their bodies completely swathed in a length of cloth.

Our platform was already crowded, and as the empty train steamed in, something like a tidal wave hit us from behind as the crowd surged toward it. Thanks to our porter we managed to get into a third-class sleeper, though in a somewhat crushed condition, and established our beachhead on the lower of three tiers of hard wooden platforms. The human flood poured in around us, shouting, protesting, laughing, crying, dragging the huge loads that seem to go with railroad travelers so that the aisles become freight depots, crawling over each other to reach the higher bunks, opening windows and taking in more provisions from the hawkers alongside as if fearful of a long siege and slow starvation.

When the noise, the crowding and shoving, the shifting of baggage and climbing up and down over us had reached a climax of nightmare impossibility, the bell on the platform clanged, the train whistle squeaked its shrill warning, and we began to move. This was the signal for new activity—chiefly eating and undressing. We stayed in our bunk, our clothes and our blanket roll and let pandemonium reign around us. It reigned. Ultimately we slept.

But not for long. The first leg of our journey took us only to Bareilly, where we stumbled off onto a dark platform at three in the morning, our heads cotton-fuzzy, our tongues much the same, and our hair full of other people's tobacco smoke. A sign said FIRST CLASS RETIRING ROOM. Hardened criminals by now, we made for it. It is one of India's graces to provide the traveler with a resting place, not only in railroad stations where for a small fee you can get a private room, but throughout the countryside in a network of dak bungalows, circuit houses and state guest houses whose facilities range from Spartan to luxurious.

Dividing our blankets, we stretched out on two comfortable wicker beds and slept to the lullaby of train whistles until around six o'clock. A bearer brought us tea to go with our drying sandwiches, a porter took possession of our bags, and we made for the front of the station where both of us and the bags squeezed into a three-wheel bicycle rickshaw for a bumpy ride to the bus station a mile away.

There confusion repeated itself as, with our meager Hindi, we bought the tickets and located the bus for the next stage—a four-hour ride to Tanakpur. Since the cost was trifling, we treated ourselves to first-class seats, which meant that we sat just behind the driver in reserved places, and did not have to compete for space with the overladen passengers behind us. The trip grew more interesting after we had changed buses for the mountain road. Now one-way, it began to wind upward along steep slopes. We ground along at nine miles an hour, the dust pouring in, the driver stopping at every little tea shop.

It was dark when we reached our night stop at Champawat. All we could see was a row of grubby little tea shops, each with one acetylene lantern hung near the door to light the whole establishment. We were lucky enough to get one tiny room, the size of a closet, for ourselves, equipped with one string bed and a very small kerosene lamp. The sanitary facilities were generous—you could go anywhere you liked outdoors. It was also possible to wash by borrowing a bit of water from a pitcher standing on the floor just outside our door where the dishes were cleaned. We brushed our teeth out the window.

We made up the bed with our own roll and, dog-tired, fell asleep. Moments later we were awakened by things scurrying over us. A quick probe with the flashlight caught a retreating rat. The rest of our sleep was on the light side. We had to get up at five anyway, to continue the journey.

At last about midmorning we had a view of the high Himalayas across slopes more intricately and precariously terraced than anything we had seen in Italy or Japan. As many as fifty tiny terraces climbed steplike up steep slopes bright with green growth. Fruit trees clustered about the squat houses roofed with heavy slate— bright flashes of peach, the near white of plum or apple. At midpoint we met the caravan of trucks and buses headed down, stopped again for tea, and continued our climb through clouds of dust and turns that grew ever sharper.

It was noon when we reached Pithoragarh, the end of the line. As we were the only foreigners anywhere in sight, it was not hard for the bearer of our English friend to spot us, take all our bags, and lead us up the three-mile slope to the small private Himalaya on which the Bakers had perched their private, independent hospital. From their terrace the view was complete—ridge after ridge of mountains stepping off into the distance on every side. But the great mountains to the north were shy. They never exposed themselves all at once, but came and went behind their cloud cover as if they themselves were moving—Nanda Devi and her companions, all of them 25,000 feet and more.

The hospital, worth a chapter in itself for its sensible way of dealing with people who have never met modern medicine before and have no conception of its principles, had a number of Bhotia patients. These are the people who travel each year with long-haired sheep which they use as pack animals, over into Tibet in the summer and back into India to winter, trading each way. But now they could find nothing in Tibet to bring back. The families of those in the hospital sat in the sun, industriously weaving rugs. The hospital has no staff but the Bakers. Each family cares for its own.

Our chief reason for making the trip lay forty miles beyond, still closer to the great mountains and to the borders of Nepal and Tibet. We had long been interested in the Tibetan refugees, and one of their remote camps was in the mountains. With the friendly co-operation of the district collector (chief administrator) we were able to ride a dusty three hours with the police chief in his Jeep to a place called Didihat where a country fair was in progress. Women in little black jackets pulled over colorful tight blouses and with tattoo marks on their chins, big gold rings in their noses and heavy jewelry on their arms and legs, stopped looking at the exhibits to look at us. A stage show started, and we all went to it, but still we interested them more than the performance.

The Tibetan camp lay three miles farther on, stretched along a mountain ridge. Climbing the slope, we found rows of low huts built of roughly split rails from nearby native oak. The rails, driven into the ground, had been topped with a roof of poles and straw. Wide chinks appeared between the gnarled palings—a poor protection from winter storms. Above them cloth pennants flew from strings stretched high in the trees—sure sign of a Tibetan settlement.

As news of our arrival spread, the residents came ducking out of their low doors and down the sloped street to meet us—old men with leathery faces and gaping holes where teeth should be, old women with high cheekbones and calm eyes, the children round-headed with blooming cheeks and button noses and bright eyes. Most of them wore the long Tibetan gowns. The women, decorated with heavy jewelry of silver or brass at their necks and girdles, also wore attractive striped aprons and brightly embroidered boots. But many of them were ragged. They had come 400 miles across precarious mountain passes. Nearly a thousand crowded the makeshift camp.

At the invitation of an intelligent-looking young woman, we stepped inside one of the houses. It was dark; the only light came from the chinks and from the open doorway. A layer of small sharp stones had been placed around the sides, and on top of the stones the bedding was spread. An open fire for cooking glowed in the middle of the floor. On a rough shelf two images of Buddha stood in silver frames, flanked by several small brass pots full of water and an equal number of little oil lamps.

We walked on up the ridge, passing an old man who squatted under a little roof of boughs, swinging his prayer wheel and mumbling a continuous prayer. We stopped to watch a woman weaving with the simplest kind of frame and shuttle.

A large crowd was waiting when we approached the only two-story building in camp. From an upper window an old lama with a benevolent face peered out to see what was happening. A spokesman dressed in a robe and a Panama hat stepped forward, fished something out of an inner pocket, and laid it across my hands. It was a length of surgical gauze. In Tibet the symbol of greeting is a scarf of thin silk, but he had done the best he could. He had once been the business manager of a lamasery and had fled with 150 of his people.

"Why did you leave Tibet?" I asked through our interpreter.

"Because the Chinese were taking our children away. And because they came and told us to do this, do that. They even tortured and killed our lamas."

"What are your plans for the future?"

"We want to go back to our own country when it is restored to us. Meanwhile whatever His Holiness [the Dalai Lama] tells us to do, we will do."

But what? I asked the district collector how many Tibetans might find work and a place to live in his area. "None," he said. "We haven't land enough for our own people, or jobs." Sympathetic, intelligent, and full of good ideas, he was still unable to find a place for them.

The greeting ended, we were invited into the building. We climbed a set of outside stairs and stepped into a room lighted only by the little oil lamps in front of a row of framed images. Above them rested piles of oblong packages tied up in cloth—sacred books, brought all the way from Tibet on the backs of the refugees.

But the big surprise lay in the room beyond, where the old lama with the benign face awaited us. At one end stood a palanquin, brightly painted and ornamented and surrounded with lamps. Toward the top I noticed a small window. From behind us someone caught the daylight with a mirror and sent it to the pane. A face leaped into view—smooth, impassive, like a Japanese No mask.

"It is a holy man," our interpreter whispered. "When he died many years ago, he said he would come to life again. His body is softening now. The time is coming." They had carried him, too, over all those dreary miles and lofty passes.

After a visit to an outdoor school where a ring of charming youngsters piped their multiplication table in Hindi, we returned to the slope—to the Jeep, to Didihat, to Pithoragarh, wondering whatever could be done for the 70,000 refugees driven by Chinese tyranny into Nepal and India.

Our trip back home began at four in the morning with a walk downhill in the rain and the dark, and with slippery mud underfoot. After a while the rain stopped, but the mud stayed. We climbed into the ancient-looking bus as daylight was breaking, the driver earnestly making his pujas before a little lamp on his dashboard to the gods pasted up in his cab. A young married woman who was obviously returning to her husband after a visit home began to howl just behind us while her mother, standing outside, tried to soothe her. The bus filled, the driver came and went on obscure errands, and at last the caravan roared into readiness and we began the descent, careening around unguarded curves at nine miles an hour—fast enough for this road.

At one of the places where a bus had gone over the bank a little shrine had been built. The driver stopped, made his pujas before the shrine, received a tilak mark of red and white on his forehead from the attendant, a marigold which he stuck behind his ear, and two more marigolds which the priest put on the radiator. We all put something into the box and went on. The driver, thus protected, began to talk to his neighbors with both hands, which made the curves that much more interesting.

We returned to the plains with the feeling of having left a world that has its own time, protected from the hurly-burly by difficulty of access and by the great mountains brooding in the sky, constantly saying by their neighborly remoteness, their near inaccessibility, their sharpness of white shroud against blue sky and their aloofness of cloud that man lives too briefly to make such a stir about it. These are the mountains in which the forest sages, learning quietness of mind, made the great spiritual discoveries which initiated or influenced all the world's great religions.

And now a new power, making a religion of irreligion, presses into them and forces out the Tibetans who have the calm of the mountains in their faces, and demands the territory for its leaping millions. Across these mountains 2,500 years ago went the Buddhist wisdom they had nurtured. Now, after this long gestation, the return product is ready for export. The Tibetans have tried to escape it. The Indians on the whole have rejected it. But China is patient and persistent. It lives by centuries too.

Another world awaits in south India. The people are different— darker, their features rounded and soft rather than angular and big nosed; smaller—especially the women, who here go draped in saris (the older ones at least) without the jacket underneath. The children run happily naked, and the men working in the fields wear only the briefest loincloths, their ebony skins shining in the sun.

The south has three beasts of burden—donkeys, oxen and women. Men will push a load, but not carry it. The villages have a Polynesian look with their palm-thatch roofs, no window openings and very low doors. By contrast, the south has the world's most elaborate temple architecture, about which there will be a few pages in a later chapter.

Since it is impossible to cover the vast tourist paradise of India in a chapter or even in a book, since more temple architecture and statuary has fallen into the vast abysm and backward of time than Europe ever produced, while leaving behind a tremendous fragment beyond the capacity of one person to assimilate, I can only name the places which in all of India's magnificence were the most exciting to me. They are Agra, Udaipur, Mahabalipuram, Konarak, Kashmir and the Himalayas.

Agra in the Taj Mahal, the Fort and the nearby beautifully preserved imperial city of Fatehpur Sikri presents in perfection one of the great styles of world architecture. The Taj is everything one expects of it—both cool and aloof in its beauty, yet warmly intimate; both noble and charmingly decorative, both architectural and sculptural. Despite its mathematical symmetry it manages to convey a feeling of intricate variety, of tension with repose—the highest achievement of any architecture.

Pictures of the Taj always concentrate on the central building itself. But the beauty of the Taj depends partly on its noble setting— the big gateway of red sandstone and marble through the arch of which the Taj first comes into view at the end of a long garden unbelievably green in arid India, the rows of fountains gushing up in the long marble pools. Since there is nothing behind it but blue sky, the perfection of its line is undisturbed. The four white minarets thrust at the sky as if to form the poles of a canopy for which the sky itself supplies the fabric. Like the swelling dome, smooth except for the carving at the top, the minarets are phallic in shape—so much so that only their geometric perfection and pure, rich creamy whiteness rob them of shock. Well-separated from the central building, two sizable mosques of red sandstone and marble inlay rise in perfect symmetry beyond the minarets. The ensemble seen from the top of the steps leading down to the long garden is at once breath-taking and as calming as a night prayer or wind-borne music.

In daytime the handsome shapes of the Koranic inscriptions and the graceful tracery of flower and leaf in semiprecious stones of many colors are embellishments in a work which seemed hardly to need them—like the ornaments of baroque music. Once seen, however, their function in the plan is inescapable.

But in moonlight! Then the building sleeps as in a white dream, floating free of earth on the shadow cast by the eastern mosque; its marble not pure white, but full of rich and pulsing shadow; its colored stones catching the moon's light and glowing like stars.

Almost as exciting as Agra is the ride there by car, along a narrow road full of oxcarts, two-wheeled horse carts, bicycles, women carrying great piles of new-cut grain on their heads or graceful water jars piled three high, dogs lying asleep in the very middle, herds of water buffalo, cows, goats and sheep filling the whole highway, monkeys gliding with their long, slinking stride, peacocks strutting, parrots swooping in quick streaks of greenlike festoons, camels woodenly parading with that society matron leer, elephants with a back load, bears on a chain, and in a basket a parcel of snakes which the owner quickly uncovers, blowing his horn to entice us into stopping to witness a battle between a mongoose and a snake.

Only a few miles from Agra stands Fatehpur Sikri, the royal city of Akbar—built 400 years ago, abandoned after fifty years for lack of water, and so much of it still in perfect condition that it has the eerie look of a place from which the dwellers have only gone off on an excursion and may, in their sixteenth-century finery, suddenly return and catch you there as interlopers.

The lovely great entrance gate, the little tomb of Saint Salim Chishti with its exquisite stone lattice work and its mother-of-pearl canopy, the great court of the Panch Mahal—all these gleam in the hot sun with a strange dejection of splendor abandoned. In the Pachisi Court with its big squares of red sandstone Akbar once played chess with slave girls as pieces. Though we missed this by four hundred years, we managed to land in the middle of a film shooting on location. The heroine, as buxom as Indian taste requires —which is considerable—and decorated like a Christmas tree, sat accessibly in the shade where we paraded several times past her magnificence. Suddenly it dawned on us that this was exactly what

Fatehpur looked like—a Hollywood set, too perfect and too splendid to be real.

Mahabalipuram, on the coast below Madras, is a display of the most remarkable stonework—much of it done 1,300 years ago—I have ever seen. Huge boulders and outcroppings of stone dominate the little fishing village. Nearly every stone has challenged a sculptor to do something with it, and the results are as various as they are fascinating. All of them have an antique charm which belongs to the rock as well as the sculptures. It is as if the sculptors, Hindus that they were, saw the unity of life too clearly to want to carry sculpture to the point where stone seems flesh. So their figures have a rather charming stiffness of stone in them—the men more than the animals which manage to seem more limber. Much of the work is primitive—the columns left with the roughness of the stone still dominating their surfaces and often veering from the perpendicular. But there is life in it all that comes from the solidity of the unsubdued stone, and from the visible battle to make the stone yield these still lithic results.

We wandered for hours into little shrines and around the haphazard boulders carved into significance, past rock faces (such as the one portraying the birth of Ganges) crawling with a life made eternal because half emerging, half remaining prisoned in the stone. An elephant freed entirely from his stone prison stands among little temples carved from solid rock, not far from a sacred bull who ruminates on his big stone pedestal. Sculpture in a museum always seems a thing wrenched and plundered; at Mahabalipuram it is at home.

By the sea stands a graceful temple, the salt spray breaking on the nearby rocks and wetting the carved spires until they glisten in the sun. An eager boy with a lantern kept insisting that we enter. The guides are everywhere with their smattering of a tongue they believe to be English, and getting in the way of what would otherwise be an idyllic setting. We entered when we thought we had eluded the boy. I promptly stumbled over the prone statue of Vishnu, which seemed to shock our driver. When even the gods lie down in unexpected places, how can one avoid stumbling? How happy the country where one stumbles over its gods!

At Konarak in Orissa the carving is organized into one huge magnificent conception—the rising of the chariot of the sun. Although much has crumbled into the waste bin of time, enough is there to give a hint of the main work—a temple conceived as a chariot with horses, with twelve outlying temples. Every inch is carved, and nearly every carving is a gem of uninhibited, unblushing erotica—gay, specific to the point of exaggeration, as varied as the fertile mind of man has been able to make the act of intercourse. The figures—often with third parties to assist at some elaborate or novel experiment—smile a dreamy, self-satisfied smile that is more innocent than lecherous.

But why the preoccupation with sex, repeated with equal insistence in the many temples of Khajuraho and present to a lesser degree in all the temples with their lingams and heavy-breasted goddesses? The ultimate in lingams we saw in Kashmir, rising out of a pool with a shower head installed so as to squirt it perpetually clean. Perhaps this provides the answer, since no one has ever really explained Konarak or Khajuraho; sex is a holy thing, the source and center of life, but you can never hope to get it clean!

At Udaipur it is the two little lakes, one with two island palaces on its bosom, and the other with a maharajah's palace of European provenance to stay at. The walls of our room were painted to resemble precise columns and architraves, separated by panels of pink festooned with improbable flowers. The bathroom was gorgeous. Only after the first day the water stopped running. The second morning an old bearer came knocking and grinning at the door with a bucket.

"*Garam pani* [hot water]?" I asked him.

"*Nehi, Sahib. Thanda pani* [cold water]," he said.

I took it in. Five minutes later he was back with three more buckets and an extra grin in the shape of a boy helper.

"*Garam pani?*" I asked again.

"*Nehi.*"

"*Agar nehi garam, nehi chahiye* [if it's not hot, I don't want it]," I told him and gently shut the door. Although the sentence produced no hot water, it was, I learned later, perfect Hindi—probably the first and last of its kind considering my difficulty with a language which is full of perfectly logical laws having perfectly logical exceptions and exceptions to exceptions. Since I always fell short one exception, or anticipated one, I was always wrong.

We looked at all the tourist sights, including the temple of Juggernaut where worship was going on at a high decibel level. Then the bell rang, a sign that his honor within had eaten or was eating and that the waiting beggars could eat the food exposed on an outer altar. The flies hadn't waited for the bell; they had already feasted.

We found a boat that would take us out to view the lakeside stone stairs where men and women in separate places and in varying stages of dress bathed themselves or each other or stoned their laundry to death. The common life is always more interesting than the tourist sights because it is unrehearsed, authentic. So we enjoyed the washing ghats as much as the handsome but decaying island palaces. But our best ventures were our own—a ride around our own lake in a pony cart, a walk of exploration during which we found that the best view of the old city and its lakes was to be had from a ruined fort atop a hill where the government had built a cactus hedge to keep people out.

Here, as everywhere, there is a surplus of old palaces and temples. I wonder if so many are good for a people. It must weigh upon them, perhaps with a sense of guilt that the past was better able to conceive and build, or with weariness to think of all the labor their ancestors had to contribute, or with the feeling that all this effort might have been better spent than on ever more stately mansions for the rulers, or with a sense of the heavy hand the past lays on the present, rigidifying life into old molds from which it can hardly break out—narrow streets, dark alleys, moldering houses, and being pent up in fortified towns when there is no sense to it because death can now reach over and through walls.

We had heard so much about Kashmir and life on a houseboat that we were bound to be disappointed. We were. But only mildly. Kashmir is not as green as legend says—anyway not in October, and not if you come from a green land. And the houseboats—well, when the agent who had captured us led us to his shikara—a sort of gondola—to row us across a canal to the line of sagging wrecks on the opposite shore, we said no, we were going to have a boat in Dal Lake.

"But this is Dal Lake," he said. It still looked like a canal. But we crossed.

Outside, the houseboat looked like something a group of apprentice carpenters had trained on. Inside it reminded me of the mill tenements I had seen in my boyhood, with too much of everything—furniture, curtains, rugs—all miscellaneously collected and dispersed.

The owner, appearing at a door in the side as if he had sprung from the waters, only he was dry, took over the praise of his craft from the assistant who had snared us. In the end, of course, we stayed. Despite the tin bathtub and the floor boards that bent beneath the foot, there were intricate wood ceilings in geometric design, paneled walls, good food, clean napkins, and a rather homey atmosphere.

But the best of Kashmir is the shikara that is always at your command. Equipped with a spring bed which forces you to recline as you go, it will taxi you into the wide part of Dal Lake where the mountains rise in the distance to shut in this watery world. It takes you to the terraced gardens of Shalimar or Nishat Bagh where once the running water the Moguls loved cascaded down a dozen terraces through gardens glowing as these were now with the hard bright colors of autumn flowers. Down these now empty courses the water once purled endlessly, and fountains played, and so did the emperor, presumably, with the ladies of his court, perched on a big slab of stone out over the water where it was coolest.

From Dal Lake the shikara slips with only a whisper into Nagin Lake. This is a world where land and water merge and change status. Floating gardens grow tomatoes and melons where no land is visible. Bowered channels invite this way and that. Here everyone is amphibious. Small children paddle the graceful little working boats and gather water weed for their cattle. The working house-boats glide by, the owner patiently walking up and down stairs arranged in the load of brick he is moving as he poles, the wife nursing a baby, the children running around as if they were on dry land.

Boat life crowds the edges of Dal Gate Canal where tall brick houses with steeply sloping roofs which give them a European look plunge their walls straight down into the water. Down the Jhelum River our shikara weaves its way through a tangle of houseboats where women wash their dishes out the kitchen window, then throw their slops in the same place.

Why does life on the water fascinate? It is probably full of in-conveniences, but its suggestion of movement, of being poised for flight, of being always able to escape is a symbol of release from all that binds us. To glide as a spectator through these lakes and canals, lazily watching the real life nearby, is even more irresponsible and poised and enticing, for it is like living a dream—a dream of living without involvement, entering but also passing by, seeing but not being held. To float, to see, to pass, to have every moment a new scene—borne along on smooth water under hot sun and cool breeze, with the grand mountains closing in on what would other-wise be too liquid and uncontained—this rather than the houseboats is the charm of Srinagar.

One of the great views is to see all this from the top of Shank-aracharya, a forty-five-minute walk from Nehru Park. You go at sunset, when the smoke from the supper fires lies over the city, the sun setting behind high mountains touched with snow, and in the foreground the meandering Jhelum and the rows of houseboats. The scene darkens until all but the water goes a velvet gray, and the Jhelum twists like a shiny serpent. Then a full moon rises over the high eastern mountains, and the water darkens, the shikaras become black silhouettes, and the little lights begin to twinkle and glow.

But Srinagar and its houseboats are only a small part of Kashmir. We wanted to get into the hills. Americans usually hire private cars, but since we always prefer to travel with the people, we went by bus —through Awantipur where the ruins of a ninth-century temple shocked us with trefoil windows under arches and spiraled pillars looking like Norman or Gothic. At Achabal, an old pleasure garden, springs come gushing wildly out of the mountain, to be promptly tamed by the Mogul genius for creating deep clear pools and rows of fountains. Passing through Kokarnag where another mountain divulges another river, we came at last to Pahalgam in a valley 7,000 feet high. We were not too happy over the dusty floors and dirty blankets of our hotel until we decided to call it camping; then it came into focus. In the evening we walked out to see the moon rise and shine down into the valley, making the stone ridge across the valley gleam, and picking out the seams of snow in the mountain wall beyond, so that it looked like the moon's own mountains.

The next morning we got ponies for a twenty-mile (ouch!) trip up the piny mountain gorge of a tumbling glacier-blue stream to Chandanwari, where an ice bridge spans the river. All along the way piles of hay had been placed high in the trees—stern warning of the winter ahead. Beyond the bridge rose Shishnag, the highest of the mountains in this area.

A month would not be enough to see and do all that Kashmir offers—treks into the mountains, the fascinating hand industries of Srinagar where you can see a whole family at work weaving a rug that may take a year in the making, or watch the cabinetmakers at their elaborate carving in walnut.

The face of poverty is everywhere in Kashmir, but more clearly in the country where the lack of wheel or cart to ease the burden on human backs, the almost universally dirty clothing and the mud houses are in strong contrast to the tourist hotel in Srinagar and the opulent piles of merchandise available in such emporia as "Subhana the Worst."

Everyone has something to sell in Srinagar. A little boy, when he sees you coming, will quickly pluck a few flowers from the nearest garden and thrust them into your hand. Yet poverty persists, and Kashmiris tend to blame the Indians for it. They blame the Indians for many things—for the loss of trade and the fact that there are now only 300 houseboats where in British times there were 800, for a failure to keep promises, for talking big and doing nothing. Kashmiris simply do not identify themselves with India. Muslims, they feel drawn toward Pakistan, though they know very well that they would fare worse under Pakistani rule. "After all, they are our people," they say. Signs reading QUIT KASHMIR appear overnight on fences.

Yet India has made great efforts to win the Kashmiris and to raise their economic status. A ceiling of twenty-three acres has been imposed on land holdings to give small farmers a better chance. Kashmir gets financial help on a par with other states; an all-weather tunnel has brought an end to its winter isolation, and better roads have been built. Industrial estates have arisen at Jammu, Srinagar and Anantnag to encourage small or medium industries. Drug farming (belladonna, pyrethrum) has been expanded, fertilizer and improved seeds distributed, and local Kashmiri breeds of cattle are being improved. Cooperatives for farmers and crafts have been formed. In the Third Plan, Kashmir's potential for hydroelectric power, industries, mineral resources and food production will be further exploited. In short, Kashmir is integrated into the Indian economy.

But the underlying dispute still goes on, and the United Nations Mission still guards the cease-fire line between India and Pakistan. There is an occasional incident as farmers raid from one side or the other. Then the mission investigates.

"It's hard to get the truth," said an officer. "They tell more than the truth to be sure they will win. If they are right, they lie to be more right."

How can the Kashmir issue be solved? I asked. By plebiscite, as India and Pakistan had once agreed at the United Nations?

"A plebiscite is impossible—the people wouldn't understand. Many or most of the seventy-five per cent who are Muslims would vote for Pakistan, but the others would resist, and there would be bloodshed."

Kashmiris are suspicious of all outsiders, said one of them, a woman educated overseas who had come back to operate her family farm.

Nobody thinks the present situation ought to continue, but what is the solution? There can be no change in the status of Kashmir without a change in the Indian constitution. China's invasion of Ladakh makes India even more reluctant to give way in Kashmir. Could some form of semi-independence be arranged? That, too, is dangerous, for Mr. Nehru knows that the minute he appears to soften on the Kashmir issue there will be demands in half a dozen quarters within India for more linguistic states. Already he has had to accede to a separate state for the Nagas. It is an irony of history that Mr. Nehru, who is so sincerely and deeply committed to finding solutions to world problems, cannot permit himself to apply to Kashmir the principles of self-rule he calls for elsewhere. Nor, while he asks Khrushchev and Kennedy to come to terms, can he come to terms with Ayub Khan.

Yet progress has been made, thanks to the World Bank's good offices, in settling the dispute over the river waters the two countries share. Progress has also been made in settling the division of assets and in the signing of a trade treaty. In time a customs union might follow, and this in turn might open the way for some sort of joint administration of Kashmir. Its neighbors Bhutan, Sikkim and Nepal are all independent mountain nations, tied in one way or another to India. Perhaps a formula can be found for Kashmir, too. If Pakistan and India could look at Kashmir as part of a wider region including, in addition to the mountain nations, Burma and Ceylon, and if areas of economic agreement could be stressed rather than political disagreements, a settlement might in time be found.

Meanwhile Kashmir remains one of the "unspoiled" tourist meccas, the watery beauties of Srinagar and the clean forests and bright skies of Pahalgam or Gulmarg opening up a world far more distant than the flight from Delhi over the bare, sharp-angled hills of the Pir Panjal seems to make it. In the summer months it provides an escape from Delhi's heat, which has to be felt to be appreciated.

Returning to Delhi by plane in the summer, a hot blast of air hits you so hard that you involuntarily step back to escape it. You can imagine the smell of smoke and feel your hair getting singed. Delhi heat is not wet; it is burned dry. It sucks your breath away. It teaches you what a piece of cooked meat must feel like. The big ceiling fans turn endlessly, but what they throw at you is hot air.

If all the temples and palaces were to disappear overnight, India would still be a traveler's mecca because of the infinite variety in the people themselves. And not only in their ethnic variety, but in the clothing. The sari has been praised frequently enough, but who ever speaks of what the men wear? Here is one country where they enjoy a wider variety than the women.

There is the long upper garment like a nightshirt which flares as it descends, until it ends bell-like below the knees where it joins forces either with a dhoti or a pair of loose pajama trousers. Then there is the tight-fitting coat, black or white, buttoned close around the neck and coming almost to the knees, with tight-fitting pants that overhang the heels and have as many wrinkles as an elephant.

The dhoti is infinite in variety. The long type looks like a length of cheesecloth into which the victim has somehow stumbled, grabbing it as he totters along, and from which he has not been able to extricate himself. In desperation he has tucked it about his waist and pretended he always intended to go around in a length of cheesecloth, anyhow. He always has a remedy, for in India he can limit himself to a brief loincloth without being noticed.

Perhaps, then, the perfect travel book on India would be called, not India on a Shoestring, but India in a Loincloth. Far better than seeing it like a pucca sahib.

TWENTY-ONE

The Arts

No living civilization can equal India in the variety and
richness of its artistic output. In temple and palace
architecture, sculpture, dance and music, India's contribution to
human culture is almost beyond assessing. Not only the world-
renowned gems of the Taj, the caves of Ellora and Ajanta and
Elephanta, the temple complexes of Bhubaneswar and Khajuraho,
but the more recently discovered marvel of Mohenjo-Daro, and the
incredible perfection of Fatehpur Sikri are still with us to attest the
fertile and variously rich quality of the Indian imagination expressed
in stone or paint. What we have today is but a fragment of what was,
and it is so vast that a lifetime could not comprehend it. So within
a few pages one can only hope to catch its essence, not its par-
ticularities.

After looking at widely scattered examples of pre-Mogul Hindu
sculpture, several underlying principles become clear.

Creation—the creative act itself—is both what the work is and
what it celebrates. Is not this why lovers twine and couple so
copiously on the temple walls, with phallus and hip and breast so
generously exaggerated, and with the smile that may portray a bliss
both heavenly and earthly? The sexual act is sacred—it is a particular
instance of the divine act of creation. So in rich profusion it fills all
the niches and covers the outer walls of the temple. Inside the god
rests—he may even be shown reclining. But outside and around him
is the beauty and joy and fun which expresses man's closest link

252

with the divine. The amazing lavishness of this sculpture, so prodigal that even seeing, one can hardly believe it, is another aspect of the worship of creation. Anyone accustomed to the severe restraint of Japanese art will at first find this excess, this burst of expressiveness almost repulsive.

Growing out of this celebration of the creative is the realization that religious and secular, spiritual and material, are inseparable, are different aspects of the one. The perception of unity is one of the special qualities of India's spiritual insight, and the sculpture illustrates it. This produces in the figures an anonymity, a generalization which goes in the opposite direction from the West's tendency to portraiture and particularization. The women are intensely female with their heavy round breasts and hips, but the breasts are geometric orbs, not flesh, and the legs are stolid, heavy and shapeless, as if the artist had never seen one or had used a tree trunk for a model. Yet he is capable of close observation and intricate detail. The sculptural ideal is obviously not that of the genre, but of the abstract. The poses, the embraces, the features are so frequently repeated that they wear down the power of observation. The portrayal of gods and mortals is hardly differentiated, for they are all of one creation. In bewildering numbers they cover the walls as if to force the stone into life.

Art illustrates belief; it *is* belief, for it is the act which not only illustrates the divine but partakes of it. Art and ritual are one in India as in all ancient cultures. As the Upanishads sprang from the lips of holy men who were expressing religious truth instead of consciously creating literature, so one feels that these temple artists were uttering their faith in the oneness of things, but in stone instead of words.

The humanity of the gods and the godliness of man—this noble theme animates dance and song and literature as well as sculpture. Ram and Sita, Krishna and the milkmaids all inhabit an idealized pastoral world which, however, is subject to invasion by the most horrible demons. Yet how pure and graspable is this world of Ram where the demons in their startling costumes dance so nimbly and behave like such perfect demons that you know they are only halfhearted in their evil and will melt before the goodness of Ram. So there is even goodness in the very embodiment of evil, since it is susceptible of being overcome by good. Good and evil are but aspects of the one universal truth towards which Indian art and thought is always striving.

Both the sacred fact of creativity and the conviction of oneness account for the reiteration in Indian art—the row after row of statues, the incident after incident in the epics, the inclusion of every color in the costumes, the music whose central principle is one of repetition. The divine frenzy, the excess of creative energy demands of the artist that he somehow embrace all experience, get it all in. They are like John Donne with his sins:

> When I have done, I have not done,
> For I have more.

So the sculptor carves the temple all the way to the roof, where he either puts an umbrella on it as at Bhubaneswar, or crowds a few more statues on it as at Konarak. So the singer adds verse upon verse to his song, or the musician still another variation on his theme, or the storyteller another incident to his narrative, or the worshipper another round of prayers as the beads slip under his thumb, or the yogi still more hours of meditation or exercise. Sometimes the repetitiousness seems to have a childlike quality, as the child for pure joy of discovery repeats a word or a skill over and over, until the first fresh creation hardens into ritual. So in the child world we can see ritual being born anew. What, after all, is ritual, except a repetition done with care in the hope that the original miracle of the creative act may be revived with all the joy and freshness of the child's first grasp, first step, first word?

In this sense all art is childlike, including India's.

Another aspect of Indian art is its way of combining energy with grace. The West thinks of India as full of calm and repose, but India's art is one of movement. The figures on the temples are busy doing things—primping, fighting, marching in procession, copulating, riding elephants, dispensing judgment. Dance and music, since they are time arts, must of course move. Yet India's dance, compared with Japan's, is full of vigorous movement.

The Bharata Natyam, for instance. Its handsome costumes are so designed and draped as to accentuate the exaggerated posturing and facial expressions which act out the story of the song. Much is made of the eyes which, artificially elongated and painted, move expressively back and forth. Expressions change quickly, mercurially, from invitation to displeasure so as to fit the words of the song, and the frequent, vigorous squats seem intended, when reinforced by the costume and its drapery, to draw attention to the sexual area. Bharata Natyam originated in the temples—it is a revival and modification of the celebrated nautch dance once performed by girls who might also be prostitutes. Both symbolic and explicit, it is "art accentuated toward divinity." Erotic and divine, it again asserts the oneness of life and of love.

Kathak, the dance of north India, emphasizes incredibly agile, rhythmic footwork which imitates contrapuntally the voice of the accompanying drum. To demonstrate his skill, the drummer can speak a phrase, then imitate it on his drums with amazing fidelity. He can make the phrase more and more complicated, quick and varied, and still imitate it. The dancer can do the same with her feet. Having seen this demonstrated, one is reminded again of the basic importance of the oral tradition. In the beginning was the word. Even the sculptured temple figures are frequently embodiments in stone of persons who have their origin in the word of epics and ancient stories.

So between dancer and drummer a kind of counterpoint is evoked. Kathak, with its sophisticated foot rhythms, its graceful, stylized eye and neck movements, its rich expression and symbolic gesture, its combination of grace with speed, its rising tempo and gradual involvement of the whole body in the climax, reiterates India's genius for combining the pure with the earthy, the disembodied with the bodily, the abstract concept of movement and form with the particular body and skill of the dancer.

Kathakali, the dance form of Kerala, specializes in enacting epic dramas with a full panoply of male dancers, costumes and music.

While elaborate make-up and costumes help to symbolize the moods and feelings, the gestures with their stylized vitality again provide the arch between human and divine.

Manipuri, the fourth of India's principal dance styles, comes from the northeast where Mongolian overlaps Aryan. The movements of this dance are light and lyric, dealing with the two great themes of war and love which in turn perhaps are symbols of striving and harmony, contrast and union, action and reaction, death and life. A sense of the great systole and diastole of all life pulses in these arts, and India's genius is in sensing that life and death are the reciprocal functions of one great beating heart.

The emphasis on rhythm carries over into music. Even when the musician separates himself from the dance, it is as if the swaying body and the tap of feet dominate him, just as the carved figures on the temples are often caught in poised moments from the dance. Shiva is usually shown in a dancing posture, for dance is the embodiment of movement and thus of life.

The Carnatic music of the south, which has enjoyed a revival along with all the other native arts that a newly independent country has discovered with delighted pride, is very different from the Hindustani music of the north. Though it has a growing audience, it is not as popular as the *bhajans*—songs of a rather emotional religious nature in which all can join.

It is fascinating to watch an accomplished sitar (stringed instrument) player and drummer work together, for here the essence of all Indian music comes clear. The sitarist announces a simple little melody, the drummer a simple rhythm. Then they go to work on it, varying its rhythm, its structure in every imaginable way except harmonically, since Indian music works in unison or in simple following phrases but not through harmony. The complications increase, the artistry is exquisite, and those in the know smile and nod and snap their fingers in sheer joy.

Similarly, a singer will repeat the same melody over and over, but with variations and ornaments to fit the words. The special art of the Hindustani singer is a skill in bunching ornaments around a single note in an intricate manner, emphasized by raising his hand with the fingers pointing skyward, and always with the drum to accent and elaborate the rhythm.

One type of singing I could never understand. Every morning when I tuned in the radio to get the time signal I collided with a gentleman who had apparently been hired to gargle for the public benefit. True, there was a musical accompaniment, if the twanging on a piece of agitated gut could be called that. Still, he gargled. He gargled up and down the rough approximation of a musical scale. It struck me that he would do better either to gargle or to sing, but not to attempt both at once, and in any case not on the radio. I thought of petitioning the station to have him try another mouthwash. But then I discovered that listening to him made my grapefruit taste less sour.

Whether over the radio, or at festivals or fairs or public meetings, in city or in village, music and dance are never very far away. These time arts, since they rise free of the material world and disappear moment by moment even as they come into being, lie close to the heart and closer to spirit. Dance is pure movement in space, music pure movement in sound, and their purity satisfies that deep thirst for the pure which animates habits of eating and cohabitation, erects ashrams, propels saints into politics, and places the saintly tradition above all else.

I was sitting beside an African student one evening at a concert. After we had listened for some while to the complicated-looking string instruments with their big bowl-like sound boxes and their elaborate system of strings running up to fifteen, we began to wonder why an instrument which made such a small noise had to be so big. We wondered, too, about the intricate rhythms and simple melodies varied this way and that but always the same.

"I have lived here three years," he said, "and now I think I am beginning to understand why this music is the way it is. The complications suggest to me the complications of the Indian mind. Only one thing I do not know. Why do they have to be so complicated?"

Most Indian temples are too vast, too crowded, too miscellaneous to assimilate; they are too complicated. But there is one perfect gem, off the road between Mysore and Bangalore, which has managed to retain the complication while reducing it to one unified creation. Somnathpur squats so low behind its protecting stone wall that you hardly see it at all until you step inside. Even here the first glance is disappointing because of the black hand time has laid upon the stone. The building is star-shaped—its three temples and entrance porch make a perfect figure. Around the whole building from ground to roof run rows of perfectly carved figures. The lowest rank is of elephants who manage to look lively, energetic and varied. Then comes an animated row of horses and riders in battle, then a calm and graceful rank of stylized leaves, above which runs a series of elaborate scenes illustrating stories from the sacred books. Above that another animal row, then one of birds. Above all this come the main figures —hundreds of almost life-sized females with domed breasts, guarded above by demon faces. So the sculpture runs on up the towers, live as flame, its intricacies continuing beyond the power to focus on them.

Whether you go to Khajuraho in the north, to the rich area around Madras and Madurai, to Mysore or to Orissa in the southeast, the same lavishness confronts you, until you are exhausted with beauty and cannot see it any longer. And you can never photograph it. If you stand far enough away to get the whole item—tower or cave or temple—you lose the detail. If you come close enough to catch the detail, you lose the whole.

Why did the builders build this way? Was it to overwhelm with a sense of the variety and fertility of life? Does the usually pyramidal tower say that all this overwhelming variety points up in the end to one universal substance? It fits with Hindu philosophy to imagine that as all these particulars dissolve into one shape, so the many are in fact one. As Dr. Radhakrishnan has said, "God is not in the world; the world is in God."

But the total effect is less than the particulars; it is the detail which impresses. The sculptor loved what he pictured too much to subvert it to a vague Allness. Indian art, like the Indian mind, is fascinated by variety. It sees the One in the Many, but it loves to dwell upon the manifold. It longs after unity, but loves plurality. It yearns toward the life of the saint, but delights in bright colors, lively movement, hot spices, fleshy women, vast crowds, railway journeys (with or without ticket), fairs and festivals and processions. So a wedding becomes a whole complex of parties, festivals and parades. Is India seduced by all this rich variety? Or does it thirst so greatly after the One that it must eat, drink, bathe and inhale every aspect of life in order to know the One through all that composes it?

Mogul art was different. In the complex of buildings within the Red Fort at Delhi or at the Agra Fort, at Fatehpur Sikri, in the great tombs like that of Humayun or Safdarjang, and best of all in the Taj there is a repose, a calm perfection and balance, a contentment with the adequacy of geometric forms in space to express man's needs and moods which the Hindus never achieved. Yet this too is Indian. It takes a wide genius to embrace both.

Delhi itself is a lesson in changing architectural styles and in the conquest of Hindu by Muslim. Near the beautiful tower, Kutb Minar, stand the ruins of a mosque which was built with the stones from an ancient Hindu temple. Since a mosque can have no images, whether of man or beast, the lovely Hindu carvings were smashed with a hammer before reincorporating them, but here and there a form still remains.

There are said to be seven cities of Delhi, but there are really more. The archaeology of the area has never been completed. From the heavy rough stone battlements of Tughlakabad towards the south to the perfect little marble mosque within the Red Fort in Old Delhi there is an architecture for every taste. Even the big sandstone buildings of New Delhi—the secretariat and the vast presidential palace—have a certain dignity and charm though it is fashionable just now to sneer at them. The British built them in the twenties when they expected to stay in India forever. Now a President inhabits the viceroy's palace, and the vastness of it and its gardens seems too much of a contrast with the crowded slums and their straw and mud hovels only a few minutes away.

In Bombay the British hand lies even heavier. Bombay has a style of its own; call it Bombay Gothic. Heavy, dignified and a bit pompous, it is strangely attractive, combining Indian domes and minarets and scrollwork with incongruously Victorian ornament. Here Romanesque and Gothic arches surmount doorways borrowed from the Taj. These buildings have the heaviness and solidity of a colonialism which thought it was going to endure, yet disappeared within a generation. Perhaps in time its monuments will come to be as important as Kutb Minar, Khajuraho, or the Taj.

Confronted by all these wonders of the past, one is puzzled by modern India's taste. The old temples and sculptures show a love of the elaborate, the ornate, the voluptuous, but they are good art. The average home, with exceptions, shows little of this aesthetic sense. Cheap color prints of the gods adorn the walls; festivals bring out the most meretricious ornaments. Clutter, dirt, spilled ghee and confusion mark the temples. Homes often fail to be clean or tidy, and even the grand public buildings are often poorly maintained. Offices are cluttered; shops drab, dark and unattractive. Yet in the carefully arranged heaps of fruit in the market, and in the exceptional government handicrafts emporium, good taste does preside. When the present age builds a temple, it produces a ferroconcrete monstrosity like the Lakshmi Narayan in Delhi. Only the Ramakrishna Mission, in its buildings at Calcutta and New Delhi, seems to have found a way of combining the old and the new in an acceptable compromise.

India, like the rest of the world, is undergoing a change from esoteric to popular art. The classical culture flourished under the patronage of princes. That sort of critical, knowing audience no longer exists, although the revival of classical arts is gaining strength and audiences. But to see the trend in modern taste one has to look at the popular films, which still draw upon the old mythological and religious themes.

We went to see the most publicized of them all, a three-and-a-half hour spectacular on the life of the Emperor Akbar, *Mughal-e-Azam*. The life of Akbar appears to have consisted entirely of a hassle with his son over a dancing girl. It came to a climax in an all-out battle of two armies instead of being settled inside the family without a slaughter of innocents. Aside from the battle and some dance scenes at the court in which the décor was too opulent, too dripping with mirrors and jewels even for Akbar, the film concentrated mostly on close-ups of the principals spilling buckets of tears over each other. I had to go out several times during the performance to wring out my shirt, and why the fight between the armies didn't turn into a naval engagement from the flood of tears released thereabouts I still don't know.

At one point I went out to keep an appointment at the External Affairs Ministry, and when I came back ninety minutes later the old man was still frowning and strutting, the young man was still frowning and strutting, the old lady was still grimacing and spouting, and the young woman was still rolling her well-watered eyes around in big circles to see if she could scare up a stray tear. Then came a hot love scene in which the young couple moved up from their usual shouting distance to an Indian clinch that left them yards apart but actively eyeing each other. He kept inching in with the grace and speed of a caterpillar, and she kept ogling him, and when they got close enough so they didn't have to shout, she swooned from the effect and he moved back into his corner as if the bell had rung, and then they started sparring for another round.

When the director got tired of this, and I don't blame him a bit, he consigned her to a dungeon where she was bricked up to die. The bricklayer must have started from the top, a most interesting way of laying bricks, because the last two just happened to be halfway down the wall where her face was, so that you could see her tears flowing busily. If she had had sense enough to take a boat along, she could have floated right out of harm's way, for it turned out that the old man hadn't really immured her, anyhow; her prison opened out into miles of subterranean caves. He didn't really execute his son, either, because a mad sculptor came to the execution spot and started singing a song which had so many verses that even Akbar couldn't stand it and came running out of the palace to dispatch him personally with an arrow.

"For Pete's sake," Akbar shouted, or the Hindi equivalent, "cut out the caterwauling and let the boy go." So they released him. At least I think this is what happened. It was all in Hindi and therefore a bit vague. Great film. Great sets. Great photography. Great flood.

A recent study concludes that love and sex dominate Indian films, which shows that men are really just the same everywhere. In the religious films, gods and goddesses behave like young lovers, which is pretty much the way they behave in the ancient stories, too. And every film is loaded with song and dance.

It is the film heroine who reveals the social pattern. Says an Indian critic: "No film director will ever permit a heroine to be happy. She is perpetually being married off to the wrong man, being locked up in dungeons by stern fathers, being persecuted by cruel mothers-in-law, being made to wash endless stacks of clothes. . . . When she has almost made the last reel, a truck is sure to come round the corner and crush her to pulp.

"If there is one moral to be derived from Indian films, it is that virtue does not pay. The only women who get their due respect are those who are dead. From goddess to kitchen maid, every heroine fights a losing battle against impossible odds, and does it with dignity, sweetness and strength of mind.

"Filmgoers like their heroines plump. . . . Every effort seems to be concentrated on making her look as much like a Christmas tree as possible. Her make-up is laid on with a trowel. . . . She is always innocent, beautiful and good, but never achieves happiness."

Psychologists and sociologists, take over.

As Mr. Nehru points out in *The Discovery of India*, the culture of his country was so richly developed that it exerted a strong influence on all its neighbors and traveled many thousands of miles. The Arabs picked up their numerals—they still call them Indian—and the mathematical concepts of zero, fractions, squares and roots which they passed on to Europe. Buddhism made a peaceful conquest of most of Asia, only to disappear from its home country. The names of Cambodia and Java and Malaya are all Indian. Bali, one of the most fascinating places in the world today, built its whole culture upon Hindu religion and art and still lives them. The Indian influence is clear in Borobudur and Angkor, even in the Buddhas of Japan. No artistic heritage has been deeper or richer, or enriched so many lives.

The art of Japan comes to focus in restraint and understatement, in suggestion rather than amplification. The art of Europe, whether you look at chiaroscuro or the rendering of perspective, at impressionism or cubism or the latest fad, has been preoccupied with technique as the European mind has been with science and analysis. American art at least until yesterday had the pragmatic qualities of our culture—it portrayed our leaders and interpreted our daily life. But Indian art is focused on the quest for the one in the many, the repose in motion, the holiness in sex, the unity in intricacy. It is the art of arts. It takes us back to religion, where art began.

TWENTY-TWO

The Governing of Men

My wife and I arrived early at the impressive big sand-stone secretariat building for our talk with Mr. Nehru, and while we waited in the outer office, I asked his secretary, Mr. Kanna, what was on the Prime Minister's schedule for the day.

"In addition to his regular work, he has thirteen visitors coming in to see him," he said. "He has to do much of his real work in the evening when he is uninterrupted."

When I remarked that he must keep his secretary pretty busy, too, Mr. Kanna said, "He keeps a whole staff of us busy. When he calls one in, another goes in fifteen minutes, because we know the first one by then will have had all he can handle."

Promptly at eleven o'clock Mr. Kanna opened the door to the big corner office. Mr. Nehru, looking as handsome and fit as ever, rose from a large boomerang-shaped desk and came forward to greet us, the inevitable red rose at the breast of his beautifully handwoven, cream-colored achkan coat.

Because we knew how precious his time was, I plunged too quickly into the subject I wanted to hear him talk about. I knew he was being pressed all the time to discuss current problems. My hope was to get him to talk about the essential India. So I asked him what he regarded as the basic elements of India's culture.

"Do you expect me to answer that question in two minutes?" he said, looking even more handsome as his face clouded. "I wrote a book about that."

264

"I've read your book," I said, "and profited from it. To an outsider it seems that the Indian sense of nationality is modified by the strong sense of belonging to a language group. What is it that holds India together?"

The strength of national feeling, he replied, is measured when a conflict arises between two kinds of loyalty, national and linguistic. "When there is real danger to the nation, the national feeling grows stronger. Otherwise, when there is no danger people can afford to break each other's heads over these things."

It is hard for foreigners to get at the forces that do bind India together, I said. "Do they derive from Hinduism or from the general culture?"

"Yes, it must be hard. But the cohesiveness has been there in spite of political and other divisions. It's a cultural thing. It's a funny kind—a unity built on diversity."

We discussed the varieties of Hinduism, the unifying effect of the great epic stories and god-heroes.

"For an Indian there's no great difference between God and man," he said. "Man becomes more divine—it isn't that he becomes a god. According to the Hindu idea everybody is a bit of a god."

"Isn't it, then, the common heritage of folklore and epic mythology that binds the people together?" I asked.

"No, the core is further back, in the Upanishads and the Gita. Do you know the meaning of 'Upanishad'? It means 'sitting nearby.' The teacher and pupil sit near together. That is how learning was passed on."

I suggested that illiteracy had perhaps actually helped to strengthen both the power of these ancient books that have been passed down orally and the ability of even simple people to remember them.

"When people become literate, they tend to fill their minds with useless stuff," he said. Remembering our magazine racks at home, I had to agree.

Yet he must have to cope with a heavy reading load himself. I asked if he would care to tell us how he managed to carry his burden of work.

"Every man develops a way of life, especially as he gets older—food and that sort of thing. But it's not a regime." He sleeps six or six-and-a-half hours at night, he said, and tries to get in a forty-five-minute midday rest.

So we and twelve others had our interview with Mr. Nehru that day. I was always running into people from overseas who had just seen or were about to see him. A friend calling on him had suggested that he send a telegram of congratulation to Albert Schweitzer on his eighty-fifth birthday. Mr. Nehru himself asked for the spelling of the address, wrote out the message, and saw that it got off.

He sees everything and sees to everything. The thing that impressed him most in the United States in 1960 was the frightful cost of everything. He felt that he was unbalancing the national budget by paying his New York hotel bill, though he took only two men with him. "If I'd taken my cotton things along," he said, "the laundry bill would have ruined me."

Son of a wealthy Brahman family, he has none of that callous disregard for the lowborn which has marked many upper-class Indians. His mind is Western trained, logical, agile and comprehensive. But his heart is Indian. He is a sincere democrat who can still act like an autocrat, decreeing what shall be worn by government workers, even to the color and decorativeness of a sari. He is a devotee of freedom, having fought for it most of his life and having spent nine years in jail for it, yet he has not been able to let the people of Kashmir choose their own allegiance. He is a man of absolute integrity, yet he has been unable to make his co-workers live up to his standards. Yet it is he, as much as anything, who holds India together. He is not only Prime Minister and head of the Congress Party, but Gandhi's hand-picked successor—a position practically equivalent in the people's eyes to having been chosen by God himself. He is also Nehru, a man who loves to get out among people who walk a whole day just for the joy of seeing him and getting his darshan. "Panditji" (the wise one) or "Chacha" (uncle) they call him. They are used to seeing him turn up anywhere—at a cornerstone laying, a reception or a public meeting, arriving with no protocol, driving through Delhi's streets without fanfare.

The protocol is reserved for the President*—ailing, genial, dignified Dr. Rajendra Prasad. We had a first-hand experience with it when we arranged a small reception for a friend of his who had just arrived from England. First came the acceptance of the invitation. Then a confidential (though printed) letter asking for a list of guests in duplicate, the issuance of invitation cards to all guests, and our cooperation with the police. We were next visited by a deputation of police officers, then a security officer, then the traffic police.

On the day of the reception the invasion of our premises began about two hours ahead of the reception. Suddenly there was a policeman wherever you looked—on the verandas, the roof, the balcony, the offices adjoining the lounge. We glanced at the Ridge behind. Fifty police sprawled on the rocks. The garden was lined with them, almost as solidly as Mali's rows of potted plants. The traffic cops set up a walkie-talkie on the south lawn. A row of police took their stations all along the road out front. Officers kept coming to ask: "Where will the reception be?" In the lounge, we kept telling them.

Plain-clothes men in very plain clothes—no ties, no coats—occupied every corridor. By five o'clock the place was braced for a major attack, protected on all sides by guards both uniformed and ununiformed, armed and unarmed. Traffic had to forsake our road. Even our guests had to enter by the back gate.

Prompt to the second, an advance Jeep drove in, then motorcycles, then the big black car. It rolled up to our veranda, the door opened, and out stepped the cause of all this uproar—a smiling, benevolent old man leaning on a cane. Not a soul in India would harm a hair of his head. To his side jumped a handsome aide in a uniform practically held together with gold rope. From somewhere or other appeared three bearers with brilliant long scarlet coats covered with gold braid and wearing turbans every fold of which was starchly in place. They served him his tea, and no doubt I broke protocol by offering him a plate or two of cakes myself.

* Until 1962.

He entered the room smiling, bowing, and making the gesture of namaste to the small gathering, all of whom were personal friends. When he had got seated they came forward and reached for his feet in that touching Indian gesture of humble greeting. But he would reach for their hands as if to lift them up, so that they usually touched only his knees. Then after a while the all-powerful uniform appeared, and the President of 438,000,000 people meekly arose and departed, warming us all with his gentle, genial smile and the gesture of greeting which came from him like the benediction of a bishop.

When the American Ambassador and his wife, unable to come on time, dropped in later for an unprotocoled, relaxing chat, we reflected upon the various guises democracy can take.

The center of Indian politics is, of course, the Congress Party—which is more than a party. Because it existed before independent India, because it inherits credit for the independence struggle and for the dream of a great free India in which there would be work and food for all, it is a social movement, a symbol of the dream of India revitalized and democratized. It embodies the sense of spirituality that goes with India's self-image, and it carries along Gandhi's teaching of service and sacrifice. So it tries to be all these things while still functioning as a political party. Party workers of the old school still carry with them the idea that they belong to a great, inspired movement which will rebuild India. They are immediately recognizable in their misnamed Gandhi caps (he never wore one), their handwoven dhoti or *churidar* (tight pants) and achkan or bell-shaped sherwani (long shirt).

But, as always, the reality turns out to be different from the dream. The party finds itself unable to produce all the wonders the movement dreamed of.

There is another difficulty. The party controls the government, yet it is government which makes the decisions. Acharya J. B. Kripalani had expected that as head of the party he could influence government. He envisioned the party as determining high policy.

But it didn't turn out that way. More and more it was the men in government offices who made the decisions.

As long as Mr. Nehru remains on the scene, he will dominate both. His only daughter—he has no sons—is president of the party. In states where the chief minister and the party leader are either the same man or are in harmony, all goes well. If they have differences of opinion, things fly apart.

Perhaps this is why Mr. Nehru refuses to indicate or to train a successor. He says, when asked, that he has enough faith in Indian democracy to let the people choose. When the issue of party leadership recently came up again, headquarters issued a strange document, attributed openly to the Prime Minister himself, which said in effect that the party had full faith in the ability of the Prime Minister to manage the party's affairs.

At the state level it is impossible to carry out reforms or programs planned in New Delhi if local support is lacking. So with land reform, since many landowners small and large are party members and workers, it is politically unfeasible to pass laws against their interest in favor of the landless. So land ownership remains a tax haven, since the state legislators are disinclined to vote taxes which would hit themselves.

The Congress Party, like American parties, is a hodgepodge of conflicting groups, aims and interests. It includes the old Gandhians who (like Sriman Narayan of the Planning Commission) think of socialism as decentralized village self-sufficiency. It includes industrialists who will benefit from the build-up of heavy industry, unionists who in the hope of wider employment favor a dispersed industry, advocates of khadi and other home crafts, farmers large and small, scheduled (underprivileged) castes—a motley crowd who agreed originally on only one thing, that the British must go.

So the party has to be all things to all men. It has to talk in a high moral tone, yet indulge in patronage, political intrigue, and in-fighting. It has to be for big industry in order to meet the needs of a rapidly rising population, yet pay lip service and big subsidies to village industries.

Another problem is what to do with the local party worker. The old idea was that he should render social service to the people; Gandhi's two ideals were *swaraj*—self-government—and *sarvodaya* —a nonviolent social order based on service to the people. But what happens if the Congress through its influence in government appoints these people to community development jobs? When the government was being organized, everyone who had suffered in the cause of independence demanded a job commensurate with his suffering. The government was staffed with the ablest people, leaving the less able in control of the party. To determine which is party and which is government is often like saying which hand does the washing.

Within the Congress a Socialist Party was formed, but in 1948 when parties within the Congress were outlawed, it had to get out. In 1952 it united with another group of dissidents from the Congress to form the Praja Socialist Party. Since that time the leaders of the two branches, Jayaprakash Narayan and J. B. Kripalani, have withdrawn from the party, thus strengthening instead of weakening their personal influence, such is the respect for a man who demonstrates moral force and who shows himself to be capable of sacrifice and free of binding obligations.

The strong feeling against politicians is illustrated by this sentence from a feature article in a leading newspaper:

"An overweening pride, irrepressible confidence and optimism, loose talk of the most vulgar and irresponsible kind, scant regard for good manners, insatiable capacity for wire-pulling, manipulations, manoeuvres and counter moves, resort to every expedient, decent or otherwise, distortion and misrepresentation of the most outrageous kind, invention and employment of the filthiest but most ingenious trick, uninhibited defiance of widely accepted norms of loyalty and outdoing Lucifer and Machiavelli in plan and performance, these are some of the hallmarks of the successful politician in India."

That this description fails to fit many dedicated public servants is not as important as the fact that a leading newspaper would print it as a description of the typical politician and that the public apparently accepts the stereotype as true. At about the same time a young man who had traveled to several nearby countries with a "goodwill mission" organized by the Congress Party wrote to the editor about the boorishness, bad manners and arrogance of the politicians who had comprised a group which was ostensibly for youth, in order that they might buy up a lot of goods unavailable in India with its rigid control of foreign exchange. Such incidents only serve to etch the stereotype more deeply. So when men like J. P. and J. B. renounce their party affiliations, they gain stature in the public eye, and for reasons we shall soon look at more deeply.

J. B. Kripalani, who looks like a Roman senator with his lean aristocratic face dominated by a noble nose and with his costume which, with the homespun shawl thrown about the shoulders, often has the look of Roman drapery—J. B. has been the Socratic gadfly in Indian politics. Formerly general secretary and then president of the Congress Party, an educator, writer, Gandhian, and of course a former prisoner of the British, he is one of the elder statesmen of his country, a keen and sometimes bitter critic, a brilliant and often corrosive speaker when as is often the case he rises in Parliament to castigate the government or a proposed bill. He is in his early seventies. His wife Sucheta, twenty years younger, is also a member of Parliament, a minister in the government of Uttar Pradesh, an impressively efficient, vital, well-motivated person who knows how to get things done. She could emerge as the most influential woman in India; a career of distinction still lies ahead of her.

And while we are speaking of leaders, there is Morarji Desai, whose name is mentioned most often as Nehru's successor. Now in his middle sixties, he lives abstemiously on a diet of cow's milk, raw sugar cane, nuts and fruits, curd and jaggery (unrefined sugar), wears simple homespun clothing of Indian cut, and avoids the social whirl of Delhi. He has spent his whole life in government service, with time out for the inevitable jail terms, and after being chief minister of Bombay, moved up to Delhi where he now serves as finance minister.

"I knew nothing of finance until I became minister," he remarked during the course of a long conversation. "I am only finance minister by chance. My real interest is in these other things." It was of religion that we had been talking. "It is out of the religious base that everything else develops. I would rather talk of these things than finance."

And he did talk about them. If you believe in karma, he said, you believe in the indestructibility of soul just as physicists assert the indestructibility of matter. It is this transference of the soul, not heredity and environment, that really counts. Every man contains both good and evil, either of which may predominate according to the choices we make. We must be able to detach ourselves from considering the result to ourselves of what we do, being concerned only with the common good. We must learn to become automatic in our service to humanity.

Government's aim, he said, is to provide a better life for the people —to achieve social justice. Man has both material and spiritual needs. The truly great spiritual leader learns to do without material supports, but this must not be expected of the ordinary man. Gandhi would have approved of the steps now being taken to raise the condition of the villagers, since agricultural development cannot take place without industrialization. India's whole effort is to develop true democracy.

There are never enough men like Morarji Desai, but they demonstrate the presence of dedicated, capable leadership. The trouble is that, as a result of centuries of conquest and foreign rule, Indians still think of government leaders as alien to themselves, the police as something to be fought or avoided, and officials as obstacles to be bypassed, manipulated or bribed.

The Congress Party because it is so intimately connected with government at every level plays a unique role. How about the other parties?

None of them, singly or in combination, has been able to challenge the Congress, nor even provide an opposition at all comparable to that of the opposition party in a two-party system. The Praja Socialist Party, weakened by the withdrawal of J. P. and J. B., still enjoys the leadership of their good friend Asoka Mehta. Since Mr. Nehru never tires of saying that India is a Socialist country, and since the Congress Party has espoused a program which is in part socialistic, the PSP is at the disadvantage of having to say "Me too—only more so."

"Socialists are like Protestants," J. B. said to me. "They always disagree with each other."

As for socialism in India, which always seems to worry Americans, we have a good deal more of it in the United States. We have old age and survivor's insurance, unemployment insurance, workmen's compensation, aid to dependent children and a good many other humanitarian programs which India lacks. We have great public power and irrigation projects which India envies and is copying as rapidly as she can, with great benefits to her parched and power-hungry land and people. We have public systems of water supply and sewage disposal which exist only in the cities of India where but twenty per cent of the population live. For lack of private capital, India has had to build its basic industries with government money, but even heavy industries are not entirely socialized. The Tata steel mills compete with government enterprises. At least eighty per cent of the economy is private.

The Communist Party has worked hard to get a grip on India, but with meager results considering the opportunities that lie before them in a land stricken with poverty and divisive forces of many sorts. Shortly after independence they chose the Telengana area in southern Hyderabad as a base from which to conduct guerrilla warfare with the hope of spreading their control as the Communists were doing in China. They set up parallel village governments and terrorized the area with night riders in the hope of imposing their rule by fear. They were finally crushed in 1951. Since that time thousands of Communists have been lodged in jail—a fact apparently unknown to Americans who regard Nehru as soft on communism.

Since the failure of the Communist government in Kerala, the several about-faces the party has had to make as the result of Russian shifts of policy and the outrageous seizure by the Chinese Communists of fifteen thousand square miles of territory along India's northern borders, Communist influence has been greatly reduced. They now hold only twenty-nine of 500 elected seats in the Lok Sabha (equivalent to our House of Representatives). The twenty-eight months of Communist rule in Kerala were a disillusionment to voters who had thought it would be more honest and efficient than the Congress government.

A more recent development has been the formation of the Swatantra Party by another elder statesman, C. Rajagopalachari, former governor general in India. Its principles strike an American as being about like those of the Republican Party.

"Our present great government is the result of an extraordinary private enterprise on the part of one man, Mahatma Gandhi," says C. R. "Now the problem has arisen whether that achievement can preserve the main characteristic of the Gandhian movement which is that, in spite of government, private men can achieve something great."

Then there are the Hindu communal parties—the Jan Sangh, the Hindu Masahabha, the Ram Rajya Parishad, but they cut very little ice in national politics and seem to be on the wane. Reactionary and anti-progressive, they have nothing to offer.

The most hopeful and most likely development, after Mr. Nehru's retirement from the scene, will be the development of a two-party system through a splitting of the Congress Party into right and left wings which will attract to themselves the elements from other parties most in harmony with them. It could very well happen that the former Congressmen who founded the Socialist movement would then emerge as the nation's leaders.

Meanwhile the decision-making remains in the hands of those who are both government officials and Congress leaders, rather than in Parliament. Members of Parliament are poorly paid, with inadequate or nonexistent staff and office space. Many lack experience and some are poorly educated. Yet the floor of the Lok Sabha is a lively place, especially when a minister is being interrogated, and debates are useful in making India's various needs and people nationally known—when they can be understood. Since there is no language which all the members understand, this is difficult. Yet Parliament gets a lot of laws passed, and no doubt the members carry back to their constituents reports that foster a sense of national aims and problems. All the members I knew were well-informed people and forceful speakers. One, Dr. A. Krishnaswami, was also spending a good deal of his time serving on a United Nations committee, with frequent trips to New York.

But to look at politics as if it were a matter of parties and Parliament is to miss the real drama. Indian politics are a blend of three traditions—the parliamentary, the traditional and the saintly.* The modern idiom of legislatures and government bureaus and planning has been imposed upon a social tradition which knows no India, but rather an intricate arrangement of statuses locally related to caste, race and religion and controlled by those who have the highest rank in this system. The saintly tradition, whose roots reach deep into the Indian soil, begins with the forest sages and the ancient holy books, and with the search for a life based on truth, nonviolence and abstinence. It lives in the oral tradition, the veneration for the guru, or teacher, the custom of retiring to a life of contemplation, and in the institution of the ashram as a place for meditation. It lives in Gandhi and Gandhiism, and in the life and work of such men as Vinoba Bhave and Jayaprakash Narayan.

Traditional attitudes affect elections and are manipulated to gain votes and to bind people to a party allegiance. (The weakness of the Communist Party may arise from its break with the traditional.) Because Gandhi knew the importance of ideals and goals, and because he felt deeply the necessity of a moral philosophy, he based his whole program squarely upon the saintly idiom in *satyagraha* and *sarvodaya*. His principles still provide a mystique which binds

* I am indebted to Professor William Morris-Jones of Durham University, England, for a discussion in which he offered this valuable suggestion.

the Congress Party together. Without this it would long ago have burst apart.

When the tradition-bound village confronts the planners, when land reform confronts the landowners, when linguism confronts nationalism—then the modern and the traditional face each other as opponents. Gandhi, who believed that all life was informed and integrated by spirit, knew how to wield the saintly tradition so as to blend the traditional and the modern. Similarly, Vinoba has kept the eyes of the nation focused on land reform when without him the campaign would have lagged or died. The saintly tradition has also supported democracy and the slow subsidence of caste.

In another direction, the saintly tradition has encouraged corruption by holding up an ideal so impossible of realization that practicing politicians decide they may as well be shot for a wolf as a sheep and therefore do as well as they can for themselves.

But the true leaders of the country have found firm support in that tradition as they try to define goods and goals and expound them to the people. Through the saintly idiom, again, simple people have an instrument to help them through a period of social change with its threat of moral collapse.

More than one observer has felt that Mr. Nehru with all his greatness has, in rejecting the spiritual guidance that was the source of Gandhi's strength, lost hold of the very thing which could inspire his people to exert themselves for the program of social reform he advocates. He cannot help this; a man is what he is. But his rationalism deprives him of that strong staff of the spirit. In following the West with its penchant for analytical separation rather than synthesis, Mr. Nehru has perhaps rejected a quality of the East the West could well copy—its sense of the oneness of life. Only by integrating politics with spiritual goals could he have succeeded in making it meaningful to a society where ethics itself is a code of behavior based upon caste relationships. In such a society, politics is bound to be looked at as a way of preserving one's own status rather than as a means of lifting the whole nation to higher goals.

The Indian villager does not see India as a vast society of farmers, industrial workers and government employees. He sees it as a collection of villages in which, naturally, his own is most important, and in which the various castes and subcastes have their assigned places. To raise his sights beyond this provincialism requires the genius of a Gandhi. Nehru and Vinoba are the two halves of Gandhi sundered. India needs a leader in which they are rejoined.

When an ancient culture adopts the modern idiom in politics and breaks down old patterns of authority and allegiance there is great danger that its emotions, previously well channeled, may be left unattached. This may be one of the reasons for the frequency of rioting in India. Another reason is the continuing power of the relatively small status group a man belongs to. He has not yet come to see himself as a farmer like all other farmers, or a factory worker or a consumer. A saintly leader, dealing in universals, would further the unifying process Gandhi so spectacularly began. J. P. may yet be that man.

But is Hinduism capable of providing this guidance? A friend who has lived for some years in India and who has thoughtfully studied the problem argues that Hinduism of its very nature cannot provide the ideological base for democracy. Its emphasis on life as illusion, its basing of ethic in caste relationships, its feeling that good and evil are relative and reconcilable, its emphasis on subservience to authority from childhood, and its conviction that social betterment must come through individual transformation rather than through the working of laws and institutions, its tendency to lock men within their own caste and give them no sense of an obligation toward the neighbor or the stranger—all these things, he argues, inhibit democracy.

When he presented these ideas before a group of thoughtful Indians, some interesting rebuttals came back. The village panchayat, an ancient form of home rule now being revived, was offered as evidence of an indigenous democracy. Hinduism's noted tolerance for all points of view, said a historian, showed the presence of a democratic attitude—that all should be free to think and worship as they please. A physician asserted that Hinduism did indeed have a definite ethical code, requiring of all true believers nonviolence, giving up property, abstemiousness, telling the truth, tolerance, and surrender to God. The absence of uniformity in Hinduism proved its broadness and willingness to let each seek out his own path.

But what of the inescapable birthright which pins every man to his caste, his religion, his ethnic group, and thus often to occupation, to privileged employment, or to unavoidable servitude? Again comes the point: democracy is really impossible without voluntarism. You cannot have it in a hereditary society. For in a hereditary society a man is not free to choose and to develop according to his individual merits. Moreover, the ethical system specifies only personal loyalties—not the public loyalty to all, the obligation to pay taxes, to give time and money for the benefit of other countrymen you will never see or know.

Even Jayaprakash, says my friend, illustrates the point. He thinks the way to reform politics is to abolish parties; the way to reform society is to abolish institutions. A better life must come from moral rejuvenation, from a change in the heart of the individual. The path to reform is through self-realization rather than through service to others—through fragmenting society into village-size groups rather than building up broad social institutions on an ethical base of involvement in mankind.

My friend admitted, however, that Hinduism does generate tolerance, a pragmatic approach to everyday problems, and a gift for borrowing from other cultures. Gandhi absorbed much of Christian ethics and gave it to India. The Bhagavad-Gita, as Gandhi interpreted it, asserts a positive ethic of disinterested responsibility essential in a democracy. The current drive to build up rural cooperatives, Vinoba's concept of gramdan—the wholly cooperative village—and his larger vision of a peace army and a society converted by love to a "kingdom of kindness" have the power to arouse hopes and to generate action. Jayaprakash meanwhile, having joined the bhoodan movement, is groping his way towards the concept of a society without political parties, where sixty per cent of industry will be decentralized and in the hands of the local districts. He, like many other leaders in Asia, has found representative democracy unsuited to current needs and capabilities. Many parts of the world are in the same boat. If he can produce an alternative rooted in accepted traditions and customs, he will have a product which could be used in Africa and South America as well as in Asia, and which could successfully compete with communism.

Meanwhile *bhoodan-gramdan* and the Community Development program ought to be able to work together. Vinoba and Jayaprakash provide that anchorage in the saintly tradition which can appeal to the tradition-minded while C.D. can bring in the seed, fertilizer and technical aid to raise village living standards.

It is often said that, thanks to the British, India has one of the world's best administrative services. Maybe so. Here is one personal experience with it:

I met at the airport a colleague who, arriving with wife, two children, camera, typewriter, portable radio and other goods to see him through a stay of two years or more, was politely stopped by a customs officer who left him his wife and children but took his camera, typewriter and radio after sealing them with ominous bureaucratic efficiency. We could go to the Customs House around noon and start the procedure for reclaiming them, said the officer.

So we went at noon, and naturally found nearly everyone out to lunch. After getting through the reception clerk, we were stopped at the door to the "Assistant Superintendent Outdoors" by a Sikh who spoke but did not listen in English. He sent us to the receiving office, which turned out to be a Dickensian place full of people shouting at each other across a long table piled with crumbling papers and files. Some sort of contest over status was apparently under way between two clerks. When we were able to command somebody's attention, we were told our papers had just come in; we should go and sit in the reception room until we were sent for. Half an hour later a peon came and led us back to the office, where we were told to go to the godown where the goods were being held. There we were told to go to the assessing section. By this time we had a growing pile of papers which we presented to the assessor, who told us to go back to the godown. There we stood in line for five or ten minutes until we could present our papers.

"The appraisers are out to lunch. Come back in about an hour."

We came back, but the appraisers didn't. Not then. They sauntered in after a while and asked to have the typewriter opened. At this point American efficiency raised its proud head.

"I left the key in the room," said my friend.

I made a quick forty-minute round trip for the key. By the time I got back the appraiser had disappeared. I delivered the key, went off to pick up some air tickets which as usual involved waiting in line and came back half an hour or so later to find my friend still waiting. We begged another appraiser to have a look, but this meant starting the questioning and examining all over again. He wrote lengthy descriptions of the three articles on a tired piece of yellowing paper which disintegrated even as he wrote, and added this to the dossier.

We now returned to the assessing office where duty of Rs 220 ($44) was demanded. We prepared to pay, but under protest, arguing that the typewriter at least should be admitted under the rule which clearly exempted the tools of a man's trade.

"Oh, you don't pay here," said the assessor. "Anyhow, you must go to the public information office and get a form to fill up."

"Don't you have one here?"

The question was too stupid to require an answer. We trudged off through long corridors to the public information office. No one there. We returned and reported.

"You can copy the form from the book if you wish," he said, shoving a thick book across the counter. So we copied it. Meanwhile the assessor got into a long conversation with another official, the end of which we expectantly awaited. Suddenly remembering our existence, he turned us over to a peon, saying, "Perhaps you would like to see the Assistant Superintendent Outdoors now?"

"No, no," we said in chorus. "We just want to pay and get outdoors without superintendence."

"He must approve first."

Back to the office of the exalted Outdoors, intercepted again at the door by the Sikh who said, "He cannot see you now; he is busy." A peon politely led us to the waiting room. We waited. After a dignified interval he returned with our papers, now apparently approved by Outdoors, and sent us off to the cashier where we stood in a long line, paid, and held out our trembling hands for the camera, typewriter and radio.

"You don't get them here. You must return to the godown."

(Go down, Moses, way down in Customs land; tell ol' Pharaoh to let my radio go.)

Another long wait. Finally we begged their kind indulgence to hand out the items lying at their elbows.

Staggering out of the handsome big building, we flung ourselves into the car, tipped the inescapable boy watchman, and drove off. Halfway home my friend, glancing through the pile of papers he had inherited with his recaptured equipment, said, "They forgot to give me back the landing certificate. I can't get my household goods through without it."

Here I draw a merciful curtain.

It is really not fair to present this as the only picture of Indian officialdom, because despite deliberate slowdown and duplication, it does get things done. Yet most Indians, including those in government, criticize it. Said a friend in Parliament:

"Our civil service is based on the British idea that every man can do any job. That was all right when law and order was the thing, but it doesn't meet our needs today, with so many things in the public sector. There are about two hundred ICS [India Civil Service] men left in government, a legacy from British days, and they are the real rulers of India. The nominal rulers—Nehru and the chief ministers—feel dependent on them because they lack their administrative experience. This old guard wants to perpetuate its power. It prevents the formation of a strong managerial leadership such as we need to operate our public sector industries. If an ICS man is in charge of steel mills, he will prevent India from having more mills unless they are put under him, though he knows nothing about steel and can't manage the mills he's got. If Nehru and his top men were firm with these people, they would have to obey."

Another problem is getting people to take responsibility, to seize the initiative. Officers are committed for life to government; they have no other place to go. They dare not take chances for they cannot afford to lose the job and the security that goes with it. Therefore they become paper-passers.

"We are always asking ourselves," said an American whose Foundation has made a big commitment to Indian development, "how to get our Indian friends to implement their beautiful plans."

Since the trouble goes back to the pattern of authority within the family, it cannot easily be eradicated. The method of recruiting university graduates for the India Administrative Service (successor to ICS) makes matters worse. Since most graduates want to work for the government, the brightest young men follow the general course of studies most likely to help them pass the civil service examinations. They are then dumped into jobs where they succeed chiefly by not sticking their necks out. This does not encourage the study of such needed specialties as business administration, science and engineering by the best students.

The need today is for administrators who are oriented toward social and economic progress rather than toward law and order only.

"Government offices," said a successful American architect who plies his trade in India, "are full of people who know nothing about practical work, who produce nothing but piles of useless paper. One bureaucrat who knows nothing about building made a ruling that all the buildings in a big steel center should have glass exteriors for two-thirds of the height and louvers above. It's not only ridiculous— it is terribly expensive and in the case of some structures impossible. Someone in the University Grants Commission promulgated an asinine order defining the size of windows and balconies for university libraries. What windows? What balconies? Maybe we don't need any. Every time I start a job, I spend days battling such orders, usually all the way to the top, before I can really begin to work.

"But worse than that is the death-grip socialism has on production. Yet private enterprise wants it both ways. Capitalists want government to supply them with capital, yet they resent government industries. Indian capitalism is still guilty of nineteenth-century faults and this in turn encourages socialism."

Was this the biased viewpoint of an American businessman?

I talked to an Englishman who had given years of dedicated, unpaid service to India. "India needs a crisis; it can't carry on this way," he said. "Corruption is built in. Everyone has to find a way to cheat or squeeze everyone else. The pan dealer leaves just a suspicion of an ingredient out of each leaf. The sadhu comes along and squeezes him for a piece of heavenly sugar. Even the favors they do are part of the pattern—a way of obligating you when they need your help.

"Vinoba tried to break through all this by arousing the country to a feeling of spiritual responsibility for the underprivileged. But the old apathy has returned before anything was accomplished. I love India, but altruism hardly exists here. Perhaps it is a luxury few can afford."

From this harsh but reluctant judgment I was just recovering when an Indian woman came to talk with us about the corruption she had found in the social welfare department of a state government where she had been working. She discovered that some food shops were being licensed without any inspection, while the papers of others were being held back for months, depending on whether or not they had paid their bribes. Others who had failed through ignorance to register on time were being blackmailed by officials. When she tried to correct these abuses she was transferred on a few hours' warning to another city, given notice to quit, and had her bags broken open by police and important papers removed. The minister acknowledged all this, but was powerless since other ministers supported the corrupt ones in office.

A young man came to ask us to help him to leave India. "Russia is not the only place where there is no freedom," he said. "There is no chance to advance here. I am a clerk in the —— office, so I know what goes on. Let me tell you only one thing: A rug worth forty thousand rupees was sold from the President's house for two hundred because it was damaged. When an auditor questioned this, which was his business, his chief told him to keep still or he would not be sent out on any more audits."

A man just retired from a government job came to us and said, "I'm sick of corruption and cheating. I want to be with people who don't work that way. I went to help a friend who owns a restaurant, and there I found the waiters taking big tips to forget the bill. I can't stand such an atmosphere. We are taught from childhood to get money—money for itself, without regard for any good that can be done with it."

Reports from the states complain of red tape, nepotism, corruption and a lack of firm, well-conceived direction, especially out in the districts.

Yet the achievements of this government in its short span of life are amazing. It began with only fifteen million children in elementary school and now has more than thirty-five. The number in secondary school has trebled and in universities has multiplied four times. Steel production has trebled and is rapidly climbing to five times the figure before independence, though it still remains at about one per cent of the United States output. Food production has increased by about fifty per cent. Six million refugees from Pakistan have been absorbed. Ambitious five-year plans have been enunciated and carried through with good results. Land reform has got under way, cooperatives have been established throughout the country, huge river development projects are being undertaken. In ten years the output of electrical energy has tripled, and is increasing at about twenty per cent each year.

Where a work of such magnitude is going on, it is easy to see the errors and the shortcomings. But India is in the midst of one of the great adventures of all time.

TWENTY-THREE

The Economy

The poverty for which India is known obscures the wealth of her resources—the six great rivers which are being harnessed to supply more power and to water more farm land than has ever before been cultivated; the largest iron reserves in the world, and plentiful supplies of coal, manganese, bauxite and minerals for nuclear energy; the fourth largest railway system in the world (35,081 route miles); 5,000 miles of navigable inland waterways; a national and international airlines system with a top safety record; and a growing industrial plant, most of which—contrary to American opinion—is in the "private sector." Private enterprise contributes 98 per cent of industrial production. The public sector will probably remain, even at its fullest development, short of the 20 per cent of the American economy which is dominated by government. Americans should stop worrying about Indian socialism, and start worrying about how to help India make a success of a noble experiment which is our chief bulwark against a communized world.

The other side of the picture is all too well known. A typical Indian village family has to live on what a single acre of not very good ground will produce. Three million newspapers and 400,000 telephones for the whole country. One motor vehicle (including motorcycles) for each 850 people. Unemployment in the midst of shortages—a surplus of manpower and a shortage of goods. And a need everywhere for the basic things—schools, medical care, sanitation, clean water, more food.

To tackle these problems, huge and complicated beyond imagining, India launched the First Five-Year Plan in 1951, giving first priority to increasing the food output. This involved irrigation works. Fortunately, irrigation systems can also produce the electric power which would be increasingly needed by industry in the Second Plan. But the First Plan allotted only 5 per cent of its outlay to industry.

Its objectives were on the whole achieved. National income (at constant prices) rose more than 18 per cent, the per capita income 11 per cent. Per capita consumption increased by 8 per cent. Food grains were up by one-fourth, or 11,000,000 tons, and 26,000,000 new acres were brought into production. And the groundwork was laid for the Second Plan with its accent on rapid industrialization, especially in heavy industries, an increase in national income, a more even distribution of output, and the provision of 10,000,000 new jobs. Even this target would not solve the problem of unemployment. For the next ten or fifteen years industry will displace as many cottage workers as it hires. But there is no way out of this dilemma. The one per cent of the population employed by industry accounts for 15 per cent of the national income. Clearly, the only way to raise standards is through industrialization.

During the Third Plan (1961–1966) the national income is supposed to reach nearly twice its 1950 figure. It is now realized that too much of the Community Development effort was in non-productive programs, so the emphasis will be concentrated on farm practices that will greatly increase yields. Along with further development of the steel, fuel and power industries will go an increase in small industries. Planners hope to see a healthy relationship growing between the rural and industrial economies.

Government industries are organized as companies, and could sell shares if so directed at any time, thus shifting the ownership, if not the management, into the private sector. Or they might do both, as Japan started enterprises which it later sold to private business. Whether government managers or private owners will come to dominate Indian industry therefore rests on a political decision rather than on economics.

How sound is India's economic development?

"You are making more progress than you realize," a visiting American management group decided. They were impressed with the quality of the management personnel, but critical of marketing techniques. Other visitors have found India on the verge of the "take-off" stage in economic development, having raised to about 11 per cent the proportion of national income devoted to investment. Within the next ten years it should rise to the level needed to assure steady growth. Indian factories, advised one economist, must get used to two and three shifts. In the United States profit generally comes above the level of one-and-a-half shifts daily.

India must have industry in order to absorb and use its available labor. It must try at the same time to keep consumption at a level which will produce savings and reinvestment. Supporting inefficient producers may seem humane at the moment, but in the long run it withholds goods from all. Once heavy industries are well established and secondary industries get into production, the benefits will be felt throughout the population.

The Plans' weakest point seems to be the lack of entrepreneurship —of vigorous management which can create wealth out of the inert resources lying at hand.

"Consider Gandhi," an Indian planner remarked. "He turned the passiveness of India into a positive force. We need that kind of imaginative leadership in industry."

"India," says John Galbraith, "has a kind of post-office socialism which is out of date and which is working far less well than it should and must. . . . Public ownership that contents itself with avoidance of loss or with modest profit which it returns to the treasury will inevitably prove a stagnant form for economic organization."

Centralizing decision in New Delhi has proved inefficient and frustrating to the engineering personnel. Many Indian critics agree that the time has come for a thorough review of the organization and management of public enterprises.

"The predicament we find ourselves in," said one of these, "is the most natural outcome of the policies of statism. It has none of the precision and steam-roller efficiency of Communist planning. Our Socialist policies," he concludes, "are being jacked up by savings from free societies overseas."

The extent of that aid is impressive. To the First Five-Year Plan the United States alone contributed $519,000,000. To the Second Plan it gave a total of $1,861,000,000, and has promised $1,385,-000,000 for the Third. Out of this impressive total of $3,765,000,000 only $428,000,000 is specifically repayable in dollars.

Between 1949 and 1959 India received $3,462,000,000 in aid, half of which came from the United States. International organizations gave $732,000,000, other countries the nearly equivalent amount of $715,000,000, and the Communist bloc $304,000,000. The Communists get double and triple mileage out of their grants by publicizing them at the time of initial negotiation, again at the signing of agreements, and still again when the aid arrives. As a result, many Indians think Russia has given more aid than the United States.

Is all this enough?

Barbara Ward, distinguished British economist, thinks not. The free world ought to aid India in such a way as to insure the success of its fight against poverty, she believes. At present we are merely making sure that the Plans do not entirely fail. The minimum requirement is for one billion dollars a year for the next five years. When compared with the thirteen billions in Marshall aid given to Europe in four years, this is not much, especially considering the fact that India's population is more than double that of Europe.

If all the countries having yearly incomes of $500 per capita would form a fund in which they placed one per cent of their national income, the needs of India and all the other developing economies could be met. This is a very small price to pay for peace when compared with our present military expenditures exceeding 67 billions yearly.*

In India there is unemployment for lack of industrialization, in the United States from an excess of it. We don't know what to do

* See Barbara Ward, *India and the West*, New York, 1961.

with our surpluses—our abundance drowns us, and we pay a million dollars a day just to store the surplus foods we cannot eat. They don't know what to do about their shortages—they are hungry.

Is there not some way to make sense out of this madness?

They need industrial machines; we have so many they are turning out a glut of goods that go begging for buyers who are already oversupplied with things. They need fertilizer plants, farm tools, metal-working plants, more trucks and buses. We are stalled by our surpluses, they by their shortages. Is there no way to stimulate their economy and ours by transference?

What could they send us in return? Some of their fine textiles and the increasing number of attractive handicraft items, perhaps. But that would hardly make much of a dent. What India gives us by making a success of her economic development is, however, of more value than any pile of goods. If India by her success can prove the workability of democratic process, she will stabilize Asia, and establish a peace without which none of our surpluses will either give us pleasure or do us any good.

Nearly six million people live in Calcutta, a city which sprawls along the Hooghly River on its sluggish way to the sea. One-fourth of these people live in slums so crowded and compressed that the imagination draws back from picturing them. Nearly another fourth lack even these verminous, unsanitary homes—they live on the sidewalks. Somewhat fewer than half the families of Calcutta are fortunate enough to have a whole room for themselves. About nine per cent have a latrine of their own. Three-quarters of the population share a latrine with from ten to a hundred families, and twelve per cent have no latrine at all. Thirty-five municipalities which belong to greater Calcutta have no water supply or sewers, while those of the corporation of Calcutta itself remain the same as they were when the city had half the present population.

At the same time Calcutta is a booming industrial and shipping center. Two-fifths of India's exports leave from its docks, but the

Hooghly has become so badly silted that traffic is seriously affected. Into Calcutta come the materials to supply the great industrial and steel-producing area that is developing around Durgapur to the northwest. Calcutta itself is a major textile center and has the country's largest auto plant.

Quite naturally, Calcutta is a city of discontents and of strikes which often take the form of hartal or nearly complete work stoppage.

The strike is announced as a protest against some grievance of which Calcuttans have an adequate supply. Government then announces that the transport buses and trams will not run "for fear of intimidation." Since most of the public transport is state-owned, this means that few people can get to work. Both government and business staffs are told they may come to work "if they can make it," which further accelerates the inclination towards a general holiday. Postal services are suspended; schools close. Trains stop when demonstrators squat on the tracks. Street traffic becomes so sparse that children have a field day in the roads.

"Any political party can announce a hartal and it will be a success," said a resident. A day never goes by without at least one procession or protest meeting. It is only natural, too, that communism has a stronger appeal here than elsewhere in India. Communists control 32 of the 80 City Council seats and 75 of the 256 seats in the state assembly of West Bengal. The central government has been scandalously lax about Calcutta, treating it as if it were a local problem, until at last Mr. Nehru has intervened and the Third Plan has been expanded by about $11,000,000 to take care of this and similar potential disasters.

Dr. B. C. Roy, Chief Minister of West Bengal, with the help of Sudhir Ghosh who as a member of the upper house in New Delhi has been prodding the central government, has put forward a plan to improve the already salty water supply and the sewage and drainage systems, and to build a satellite town at Behala at an estimated cost of $88,000,000. The Ford Foundation is providing the most distinguished panel of city planners ever drawn together on a single project. The United States, long concerned over the political dynamite contained in Calcutta's desperate situation, welcomes the use of P.L. 480 (wheat loan) funds for this project, and additional help, now that a plan is in the making, will no doubt come from the World Bank and other contributors.

Calcutta's plight dramatizes India's central problem—a population expanding faster than it can be accommodated. In New Delhi block after block and area after area of houses built for government employees testify to the country's effort to house its people. Still more impressive are the new cities built around the great steel mills of Bhilai or Durgapur or Rourkela, the city of Faridabad raised up as one means of accommodating the refugees from West Pakistan, or Corbusier's Chandigarh, capital of the Punjab. Much of the government building looks like a scattering of children's building blocks, and one wonders whether a little grace could not have been built in without added expense, but of course India's basic needs are so great that to think of graciousness may almost seem like treason.

Too many people—that is the root of it. Unlike many nations, India has faced this problem and tried to cope with it. The Third Plan includes a large sum for family planning. Both the Ford and Rockefeller Foundations have been supporting programs of research to find out what beliefs and attitudes motivate parents and to provide them with education and the means of control. "The family planning program is the cornerstone of all development plans in India," says Dr. Douglas Ensminger, Ford Foundation head in India.

The Indian family itself is on the threshold of great changes which may ultimately affect the birth rate, but the population problem is too acute to wait for these to take effect. Gradually the family, even the rural family, is becoming a unit of consumption rather than of production, and its basis is shifting from one of status to one of contract, from the rule of custom to the rule of law. The emphasis is slowly changing from consanguinity to conjugality.

The authoritarian family must give way if political democracy, industrial development and social justice are to flourish, according to a study made by India's Christian Institute for the Study of Religion and Society.* In its present form the family produces citizens unable to cope with tasks requiring initiative and responsibility. It is too interwoven with caste discrimination, and it blocks the fulfillment of what Christians regard as a satisfactory marital relationship. Yet anyone familiar with the breakdown of stable and fulfilling family life in the United States and Europe would hope that India can avoid our errors.

Along with this trend toward industrialization, urbanization and social democracy has gone a contrary social change which Professor M. N. Srinivas calls "Sanskritization"—the urge to return to ancient roots. It is seen in the drive to make Hindi a national language, in the demands for linguistic states, in the rediscovery of classical indigenous arts, in the re-aroused interest and pride in the sacred literature and in the whole vast sweep of India's long history and rich culture. It is also seen in the manipulation of caste, religion and other communal differences for political advantage.

The conflict between these two fundamental currents has caught India in a riptide which accounts for the frequent outbursts of violence. The misery in which many of its citizens are forced to live would be enough to cause men to revolt and give way to violence. The obvious presence of great personal wealth in so poor a country might be expected to spark revolution. Instead, ancient animosities between communities remain the source of most of the conflict that gets out of hand. Most Indians feel themselves to belong to groups they were born into rather than to new economic groups such as the labor union, the political party, the community service organization. They therefore express themselves through their hereditary groups, and too often violently. Until labor unions cease being adjuncts of political parties, squabbling among themselves for the allegiance of the workers, and until something like a liberal-conservative alignment of two strong parties takes place, the shift from

* P. D. Devanandan, ed., *The Changing Pattern of Family in India*, Bangalore, 1960.

hereditary to voluntary group alignment which signifies a free society will probably not take place.

India may develop instruments quite different from ours. If Jayaprakash Narayan and the *bhoodan* movement should succeed in demonstrating even in one area the practicability of Vinoba's "kingdom of kindness," if the cooperative village, the partyless council and the peace worker replacing the policeman could prove their effectiveness—then an exciting form of social democracy could be in the making. But these things have yet to be demonstrated.

The changes which have taken place in India since independence was won are truly remarkable. Never in history has all of India been so unified as now. Never have so many children been in school, or so many through public health programs assured of the chance to grow up. Never has India been so respected a voice in world affairs, with an influence which is felt from Korea to the Congo, and in the halls of the United Nations. Taking Goa from Portugal has raised India's standing throughout Asia, Africa and the Middle East, where she appears as the champion of anti-colonialism.

Never has there been so vast a plan for the improvement of agriculture, industry, transport, and the encouragement of a richly varied culture. The love of new projects is one of the many things that makes Indians and Americans recognize each other as kin. Indeed, India has many of the qualities that characterized America in its period of first growth and are not yet lost—enthusiasm for the task of building a great country, despair over the setbacks and frustrations, a drive for equality and betterment, faith in a future that will be better.

India is no less concerned with the material things of life than we are. How could it be, when it needs to increase its supply of everything—except people? Yet India has managed to retain a sense of the presence of the divine spirit working in and through life. We have tended to replace this with moral and social concern on a purely humanistic level. India helps to alert us to the realities of the spirit.

We never failed to be impressed there by the gentleness, the courtesy and the upwelling of laughter in friends and strangers alike.

We felt at home in India as we had in no other Asian country. One reason for this, of course, is the long presence of the English. Yet the English did not fundamentally change India. This is to the credit of both. The reasons go deeper. Perhaps the aspects of Indian thought which Emerson and Thoreau absorbed have entered more deeply into us than we realize. Surely there is much in the Indian perception of the divine that matches Christian thought, particularly in the mystic tradition. But fundamentally there is a similarity of outlook which Indians and Americans share: their large plans often falling short of fulfillment, their idealism and tendency to moralize, their fits of optimism and despair, their pragmatism in worldly affairs combined with a yearning for a better world, their warmth and out-goingness, their childish love of display, their desire to be loved and praised, their ability to laugh at themselves.

"If I didn't love India so much," an American friend said, "I'd have to admit it's a hell of a country."

We can love it; we do. There are many countries of which Americans could not sincerely say that. India illustrates our own faults, our own virtues. So how can we help beginning in exasperation and ending in love?

TWENTY-FOUR

India and the United States

"Why do you have the highest divorce and suicide rate in the world?" asked one of a group of thirty young men who were plying us with questions. Marion and I had been invited to visit a Gandhian work camp near Bangalore, and we were sitting on the ground in the shade of an orchard of mango trees.

"Why do you have so much unemployment?"

"What are you doing to give Negroes equal rights?"

"Why do you give Pakistan more aid than India?"

"Why do you have bases overseas?"

"Why don't you make your aid economic instead of military?"

"Has your high material standard led to a loss of spiritual values?"

I answered these questions as honestly as I could, trying not to soften the truth but to correct errors. Yet it was plain from this frank exchange that the thinking young men of India do not hold a very flattering image of us in their minds. It is stupid to blame this on Communist propaganda, which surely takes advantage of our weaknesses, but does not invent the serious faults in our society. There is only one way to improve the image others have of us, and that is to overcome our faults. As I tried to point out to these young men, ours is a dynamic, self-critical society which has within itself the power and the freedom to change, which unlike traditional societies holds change to be good, and which sets high goals of achievement toward which it is always striving.

But I kept bumping into these not quite hostile, yet rather accusing and sometimes close to bitter appraisals of American life. After I had given a talk to a university audience on the continuing revolution in the United States, some of the faculty members gave me a hard time about our treatment of Negroes.

"Isn't it true that they get less education than the others?" "Why is their living standard so much lower?" "Why don't you permit them to ride on your buses?" "Your federalism is a bad thing, because it allows the Southern states to deny them the vote." And finally, "Why don't you put an end to discrimination by law, the way we have done?"

I find it hard to keep my temper when that one comes up, because India proves perfectly the impossibility of legislating basic social change. The laws against caste have indeed helped, and they are a valiant move in the right direction, but to pretend that they have put an end to caste discrimination is downright dishonest. My Indian questioners were guilty of a universal fault—comparing their own ideal with our reality.

"You make a mockery of your high ideals by your treatment of Negroes," was the final shot. It hurt, because it was true.

We were riding through the wasteland of central India when a man opened the door of our compartment during a station stop and asked if he might ride with us. He turned out to be the secretary to a minister of state in Madhya Pradesh, and his questions about our country were fascinating.

"How much does a clerk or teacher make?" "Do most wives work?" "How about dating? Isn't it dangerous to have fifteen-year-olds in close proximity? How about illegitimacy?"

"India fears that American capitalists want to take over our economy," he said. "That is why we feel uneasy about aid."

We talked about that, and I explained to him that a good many capitalists were quite opposed to aid—the support for it was political and humanitarian.

"We also fear the influence of missionaries."

"How many Indian Christians are there after more than two hundred years of mission work?" I asked him. The question was of course rhetorical—we both knew the number of Christians (eight million) was inconsiderable.

"They meddle with the *adivasi* [aborigines] and stir up trouble. But of course," he went on to say, "Indians like Americans and feel friendly toward them. We need your aid, too, but we think you worry too much about communism. Even if they should come to power here they would not be able to change things very much"—I detected the saddened voice of an experienced administrator here—"and so we need not fear them."

Said a doctor who had lived for seven years in the United States:

"Americans can afford to be good because they are rich; therefore you meet more kindness in the States. Capitalism and communism are coming round to the same thing—to guarantee a materialistic good life—and already the United States is more Socialist than India which regards itself as a Socialist state. When the material achievements become equal, the political differences between democracy and communism will tend to disappear."

"I don't think so," I told him. "That is when our belief in freedom will begin to pay dividends, because at that point the people in Communist countries will begin to demand freedom, too."

For two years we kept meeting the stereotype of the United States as the land of materialism, divorce, racial discrimination and moral disintegration, contrasted with India as a land where the spirit reigned and there was no greed for material things. Rubbish! The Indian family system makes a virtue of nepotism; the caste system, a virtue of discrimination. India simply uses these words differently. If we could clear up this semantic confusion, maybe we would understand each other better.

By spirit, India means a verbal concern for the nonmaterial aspects of life and a discipline of body and mind aimed at attaining a personal, individual enlightenment which from our point of view is self-centered. Our materialism, on the other hand, is based on spiritual assumptions—the right of every man to have access to as much education as he can use, a belief in human worth and dignity and equality. In India the spiritual life means rejecting the world; with us it means sharing the world's goods for the benefit of all. In Socialist India the socially approved goal is individual self-realization and withdrawal from society. In individualistic America the approved goal is contributing to society for the benefit of all.

Most Indians, I am convinced, in spite of the sharp questions they throw at us and the spiritual superiority they feel, are sincerely interested in understanding us. But, like all of us, they fall into the error of the stereotype. Their minds make a caricature instead of a portrait, and a caricature always exaggerates the less lovely aspects of the subject. A stereotype is a mental short cut; it substitutes the easy caricature for the more difficult portrait. It gives the memory an emotional peg. Stereotypes about ourselves are flattering; about others, critical as a rule; for this is how we build up our egos.

One of the world's major problems, which we ignore because of our preoccupation with politics, defense and aid programs, is the building of stereotypes and symbols which will unite and not divide. This is communism's secret—it has found a simple unifying symbol (the classless society) through which to appeal to all men everywhere, and it has erased religion in order to make sure that all emotions and allegiances will be hitched to this one star. We, too, need to announce and cultivate symbols which can overleap the differences and unite mankind.

Our stereotypes of India are as faulty as are theirs of us. The snake charmers and Yoga experts are mere specks on a landscape which is alive with great dams and irrigation projects, steel mills, universities, research institutes, and Five Year Plans which are converting dream to reality. India is in the midst of the noblest social experiment ever undertaken in the free world. It deserves our admiration and support. Has the American press made this clear? Or has it tended to undercut and minimize? Indians are convinced, for example, that *Time* ridicules Mr. Nehru at every opportunity.

Our attitudes are furthermore shaped by a psychopathic fear of communism. In every Indian move we see friendship for Communists.

Why is India soft on communism?—Americans keep asking.

The first answer is that India has not been soft on communism within its own borders, but has jailed thousands, has replaced the Communist government of Kerala with Presidential rule, has thrown all its effort into building an economy which will be strong enough to guarantee freedom and democracy to its people. It is true that India, with its gift for seeing the good in evil and the evil in good, has not worked itself up over the issue as we have. Neither has the rest of the world; we are the ones who seem to be displaying a national paranoia.

India stands now where we stood at the time of Washington's Farewell Address. It is a country of vast potential, but militarily weak. It is still suffering the effects of a war to which it was committed by a foreign power (Britain) without even the courtesy of consultation. In peace, it has a chance of surviving and developing its greatness; in war it would break up in anarchy and chaos. It fears and hates colonialism as a recent thing. It wants no part of a cold war or a hot one. It wants no part of the entangling alliances Washington warned us of. It wants to get on with the realization of its greatness.

This is why India seems to us to be on the fence. But as Americans raised on Washington's warning against entangling alliances, we ought to understand. And we ought to stop worrying about India's socialism, recognizing in it the inspiration of our TVA, our Western dams and irrigation systems, and a noble experiment in which our own welfare is engaged, since India must succeed with this program of economic and social renewal if she is to survive as a free nation. Her commitment to the principles of freedom, democracy, representative government, due process and all the rest is so evident that it should not be necessary to argue the point.

In her ancient heyday one of the most advanced of human cultures, India as long as 4,500 years ago built well-planned cities complete with sewers, grain storehouses, pleasant homes—even brick swimming pools. Later a leader in mathematics, she introduced among other things as we have seen the concept of zero, which in her decline came to express her influence in world affairs. But now the nation is on the threshold of a great revival. The greatness of its past gives us an indication of what it can and will become.

Modern India, however, has external as well as internal problems to cope with. Relationships with Pakistan are still uneasy, and American military aid has made the situation more sensitive. China, having ruthlessly swallowed up Tibet and continued its invasion of Indian-claimed territory in the north despite protests, negotiations and threats, seems to care little either for the vague but noble terms of its Panch Sheel agreement with India or for Indian friendship stoutly revealed over the years at the United Nations. The fact that India has been unable to make China move back unfortunately demonstrates to all Asia that India, the largest nation next to China, lacks the power to protect itself. Goa hardly alters the picture. Meanwhile Ayub Khan warns Nehru that Afghanistan is rapidly falling under Russian control.

Indians living overseas constitute another continuing problem in diplomacy. Ceylon, settled long ago from India, is now concerned over 700,000 stateless Tamil-speaking Indian laborers who have not been granted Ceylon citizenship and who do not want to return to India. Illegal immigration from India still continues, and anti-Tamil feeling is tense. In the Fijis, Indians, once imported by the British as laborers, now make up more than half the population, controlling most of the shopkeeping and much of the farming. In Africa, too, they have advanced from laborers to traders and merchants, and by their industry, frugality, and power to squeeze out any Africans trying to get into merchandising have got themselves hated. This is a factor Mr. Nehru has to face whenever he seeks to act as the spokesman for Afro-Asian solidarity.

Something might be done to plan the development of the countries around India so that their economies would be complementary rather than competing, but as yet little has been accomplished. There are difficulties, of course. Each country wants to build up industries to supply its own market. Dropping tariffs cooperatively would be a good idea, but the income is needed.

Yet India, Pakistan, Burma, Ceylon and Indonesia face common problems which they might solve through cooperation. Since high world prices have limited their foreign purchases, they might provide one another with markets for food, raw materials and manufactures. They could mesh their planning so as to exchange goods instead of trying to make everything themselves. They could combine in such fields as pharmaceuticals, where foreign cartels presently exploit the market. Their dependence on outside powers for shipping, banking and insurance might be tackled mutually.

In 1955 the United States voted $200,000,000 for an Asian development fund intended to stimulate regional trade, but the results were unimpressive. The countries concerned, since most of them have some form of economic planning, could easily collate their plans to see where cooperation could best begin. In the end they will be forced to work together, if for no other reason than that other regions are doing so, and benefiting greatly.

More intensive work in the economic sphere will not only pay off, but will help to solve problems that now appear political. Pakistan and India, suspicious of each other and deadlocked on Kashmir, have still been able to agree on ways of sharing the waters of the Indus, and have signed a trade agreement which could eventually be enlarged into a customs union and a common market.

This would satisfy India's dislike of power politics and her preference for nonmilitary solutions.

Meanwhile the present armed stalemate between the Communist and non-Communist worlds gives India a great opportunity. It permits her to negotiate with the great powers as if she, too, possessed power like theirs. Instead of criticizing India for this, we should welcome it, for ideologically India is firmly on the side of freedom.

Why, then, do Americans gets the impression that India is against us?

As a country recently under colonial rule, India is still sensitive to any sign of colonialism. She has therefore spoken out against the colonialism of our allies and to this extent has found herself aligned with Russia. Furthermore, since she distrusts military alliances as threats to peace, she has resented SEATO. She has been quick to see in our alliances with Chiang Kai-shek and Syngman Rhee and Ngo Dinh Diem a new kind of imperialism, but has been slow to recognize the Communist imperialism of Russia in eastern Europe and of China in Asia. China's continuing incursions into Indian territory are changing this viewpoint, however.

When India's own interests are vitally concerned, she behaves just like other major powers. She took Goa back from Portugal by force of arms. She has demanded strong UN action against South Africa and Israel, but has ignored Security Council decisions as to Kashmir. In 1954 she recognized Tibet as "the Tibet region of China," an ironic point of view for the country which howled about our recognizing Goa as "a province of Portugal." In Nepal her economic, political and military measures resemble our own in areas where we feel threatened.

India fought hard and long for its own independence, yet is forced to deny independence to the Naga tribes, and for good reasons. India handed Tibet to China, yet acted surprised and grieved when China kept coming southward into Indian territory. Her behavior toward Pakistan is in many ways like ours toward Russia.

"While I lay down high principles," said Mr. Nehru at Bonn in 1956, "I recognize that countries cannot, as countries or governments, function purely on the basis of high principles. They have to consider the facts as they are, the difficulties of a situation, the dangers of it." These are honest words. Would that diplomats always spoke this way!

Because of its avowed belief in nonmilitary solutions and the high regard it has for peaceful negotiation, India has played a leading role at the United Nations, while its part in the various nonpolitical UN agencies is perhaps even more important. It has taken part in more international conferences than I have room to list, ranging from

ECAFE—the Economic Commission for Asia and the Far East— with its several subcommittees on international highways, metal engineering and population data, to projects of UNESCO ranging from East-West cultural values to arid-zone research, research on the social implications of industrialization, and an "international symposium on termites"!

A beneficiary of the various technical programs—Food and Agriculture, World Health, the International Children's Emergency Fund and the Special Fund—India is also a steady and useful contributor of funds and manpower. Considering per capita income, she is among the big contributors. At present more than 692 Indian experts are working under the UN Technical Assistance Program in foreign countries. This, of course, is in addition to Indian personnel in all the other UN agencies, such as FAO. In 1961 the World Health Organization held its international Assembly in New Delhi. Its India work involves an expenditure of over a million dollars, but India in return contributes nearly $400,000 to the WHO budget. Under the UN Special Fund, India was getting help in fisheries, investigation of hydroelectric sites, public health engineering, aeronautical research, and industrial training.

No summary can begin to give an adequate idea of the tremendous impact of all these UN projects upon India's growth. This is the great story, repeated throughout the developing nations of the world, which is consistently overlooked while reporters concentrate on the pyrotechnics along the bank of the East River. Unfortunately the technical nature of the work and the very scope of it make presentation difficult. But in time the results will show—are even now showing in such projects as the eradication of malaria, the control of trachoma, the provision of clean milk in cities.

India also does her share in the Colombo Plan, through which she provides aid to Nepal and technical training to people from all parts of South Asia. She is a participant in conferences on every imaginable subject—broadcasting, engineering, railways, and even planned parenthood. And she plays a prominent part in the various Commonwealth conferences and councils.

The point at which America and India meet most intimately, and where both understanding and animosity can generate, is the aid program—or programs.

"American officials act as if they were doing India a favor when they give us surplus grains," said my friend Sudhir Ghosh. "In fact we are doing them a favor to take it; otherwise what would they do with it? We can use it to stimulate village renewal—for instance in the place where I am working in Bengal. All the tanks there are silted up. But they were expertly placed centuries ago so as to supply the whole countryside with water. Let us give this surplus wheat to feed the villagers. Then they can dig out the tanks in their spare time and start irrigating the land again."

"We do not need your American technicians," said a lady politician, "but we want your machines, your foodstuffs, your loans, and so we tolerate you."

"We are prostituting ourselves if we accept favors from the U. S. A.," said a student. To which another quickly replied: "That's not prostitution. We're really prostituting ourselves at present by accepting favors from everybody."

Accepting help, whether on a personal or national basis, makes feelings tender. We are literally helping ourselves when we help India; let us remember that.

"Man has both material and spiritual needs," Morarji Desai, the Finance Minister, said to me. "Both must be met. India has always had deep respect for the spiritual leader."

Is it not possible, I suggested, that current international aid programs, with their assumption of a moral obligation to help raise standards everywhere, provide an instance of material aid directed toward spiritual ends by establishing a tone of international brotherhood?

He agreed that this might be so, but was careful to assert his preference for bilateral programs rather than a unified UN plan. He thinks them more workable and likely to be better conceived—and possibly likely to be a good deal more remunerative as long as our two-world competition continues! To put it in the student's terms, he seems to prefer prostitution to monogamy.

When President Touré visited India, he told Vice President Radhakrishnan that when Guinea opted out of the French Community
he had begged help from the United States since the French carted
away everything—desks, telephones, supplies. We refused, so he had
to go to Poland and Russia. "I'm not a Communist," he told the Vice
President, "but what could I do?"

That India, thoroughly committed to democratic principles, should
accept aid from Russia should not alarm us. It is a good sign that
Russia wants to see a strong India for reasons of its own, one of them
no doubt being fear of a China grown too strong.

"Americans are bitten by a Communist psychosis, Indians by a
colonial psychosis," says Douglas Ensminger, Ford Foundation head
in India, "and this makes it difficult for us to work together. We as
Americans have come here for only one purpose—to see if we can
help India achieve her democratic objectives. Some of us come out
here expecting to see quick results. We must learn to fit our work
into a pattern of development which will take two generations."

In his attitude and in the work of his and other foundations I felt
the American spirit at its best—activated by a genuine and unselfish
desire to help men everywhere achieve their own objectives. It happened that I met, the same evening, some rigidly orthodox missionaries who were full of eagerness to "better" India with their own
brand of evangelism, so crude and rigid and senseless that they could
not possibly have sold it at home. And it struck me that the true mis-
sionary today is a man like Douglas Ensminger, who is willing to
bring help that is asked for and wanted, fitted into a plan made in
India.

One of the ways we have been helping India is our international
student exchange program. It has been an undoubted success, and
has returned hundreds of specialists to the universities, research institutes, industries and government departments. The Fulbright program
wisely insists that each of its appointees must be given leave from
a job to which he can return. But many students get to the States
by private means. They may go too young or stay too long, and when
they return, they cannot adjust to life at home. They return full of
new knowledge and eagerness to put it to use. Too often they find

they must pay for the privilege they have enjoyed. If they advocate change, they are accused of having been brain-washed or Americanized. They are suspected of wanting to lord it over the stay-at-homes, who in turn try to cut them down to size. Jobs are hard to find. I know a brain surgeon with seven years' postgraduate experience who could find nothing but a job patching up cut fingers in a clinic. Sometimes these Western-educated never do find a place for themselves, but return abroad as immigrants and never feel at home anywhere.

All the way from Willingdon Crescent to Palam Airport the road was decorated with bright pennants. Workmen by the hundred brought headloads of red sand which they dumped in a cloud of red dust. Then sweepers spread it smoothly like a carpet on both sides of the highway. Every hole in every road he would pass over was filled, a blessing to us all. A thousand trucks and buses provided by a thoughtful government would take passengers free of charge to greet him. Eisenhower was coming to Delhi.

Traffic got so jammed that Mr. Nehru himself, on his way to the airport, had to get out and direct it. The enthusiasm was so far beyond estimates that Ike's car was mobbed by friendly thousands, and every public appearance became a rout. India respects leaders. It lacks our democratic uneasiness at the inequality leadership implies. So the plain people of India welcomed Ike as a raja, a great one, a man whose personal strength might overcome the forces of evil in the world just as Ram vanquishes the demons every year and sends them up in flames. At the huge public reception, where nothing could be seen on any side but a vast acreage of squatting human figures, Ike said:

"As you prosper, the whole free world will prosper. . . . A spiral of prosperity throughout the free world will lift the living standards of all our people. . . . From now on I shall be quick to speak out on every possible occasion that India is becoming one of the greatest investment opportunities of our time—an investment in the strengthening of freedom, in the prosperity of the world."

If we are to have a world culture—that is, if while retaining our own distinctive traits we are to come to an agreement as to goals and to enjoy the freedom of exchanging goods, ideas, people—we need to encourage exchanges at every level and in many ways. We need not only the visits of dancers and musicians, but of farmers and workers and businessmen. Scientists and engineers speaking their already internationalized language help to bring us a sense of human unity. Our world will see more and more of this in all fields, until we are gradually able to grow beyond the provincialism of nationality and embrace the concept, essentially religious, of a world community. This is a concept not at all alien to India, who in past times has given the world so many of its fundamental ideas, whose instinct for oneness out of many is fundamental, and whose sense of the spiritual unity of mankind is ages deep.

If I have spoken plainly in these pages it is out of love and deep respect, as I would deal with a thing which is my own. I have never been as critical of India as Indians are, for while they do a magnificent job of representing their country abroad, making us all feel a little guilty for failing to abide by our Christian principles, they are outspokenly critical at home. For there is a feeling that all the fine plans have failed to bring results. The grand reform necessary to end poverty, illiteracy and disease has somehow failed to materialize. The West with its industrialism, luxuries, yellow journalism, movies, gadgets and glitter has somehow corrupted a far higher society. Yet industrialism with its city slums, its displacement of rural populations, its erosion of family authority cannot be avoided. India cannot go backward, as some of the Gandhians and Hindu reactionaries wish. It cannot stand still, and to go forward seems to lead into still greater peril.

Where so much needs doing, it is natural that observers should think nothing is being accomplished. Yet foreign observers assert that the gains made in the past ten years are phenomenal. The real question is whether India can get ahead fast enough to protect herself from China. There is a dawn which "comes up like thunder outer China 'crost the bay"—and whether it will stimulate India to outdo herself or whether it will engulf her, no one yet knows. The outcome is as important for us as for India.

Therefore the free world needs India as much as India needs the free world: that is the most important thing I learned there. By this I mean not only that India must be an anchor of freedom under law for all of Asia, but that she offers us a gateway through which we can enter into the aspirations, the attitudes and the way of thinking of a large sector of mankind.

Long ago India made many significant contributions to European culture and helped both with its learning and then with its stimulus to trade to create the remarkable expansion which fostered the modern world. But the benefits came to us, not to her. Now as we enter an era of world culture, India and the United States are partners linked by necessity in an adventure which is inescapably exciting and could be ennobling.

In one of the ancient stories, Vishnu is represented as sleeping half submerged in the cosmic ocean, delighting in slumber. Inside the god sleeps the unborn cosmos. So India, dreaming a world as yet unborn, is wakening into new and vigorous life.

Delhi, India, and
Shaftsbury, Vermont
1959-1962

Index and Glossary